Indonesian Food and Cookery

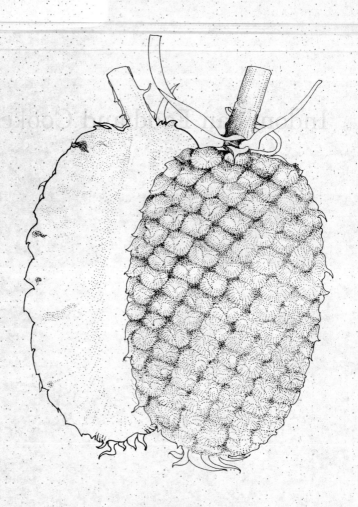

Nenas — Pineapple

Indonesian Food and Cookery

by

Sri Owen

for Roger, Irwan and Daniel

ISBN 0-907 325-00-9

The drawings in the book are by Thao Soun, except for those on page
30 (q.v.) and those on pages 47, 84 and 86, which are the work of
another Laotian artist, Elian Bleton Souvannavong

Published by Prospect Books, 45 Lamont Road, London SW 10 0HU

Indonesian reprint edition 1990
P.T. INDIRA by agreement with the Author.

Design consultant Philip Wills

Set in 11 on 12 point Monotype Baskerville by
Latimer Trend and Company Ltd, Plymouth

Printed by
CV. INDAH GRAFIKA
Jakarta — Indonesia.

Contents

ACKNOWLEDGEMENTS   7

ABOUT THIS BOOK   9
Weights and Measures   10
Pronunciation   11

INTRODUCTION   13
Essential Ingredients   37
Spices, Fruit and Vegetables   45

RECIPES
Rice   91
Fish and Shellfish   106
Beef   126
Lamb   137
Pork   147
Variety Meats   154
Chicken   159
Eggs   176
Duck   180
Vegetables   185
Tahu and Tempe   210
Sambal   221
Side Dishes   227
Sweets   238

BIBLIOGRAPHY   249

INDEX   251

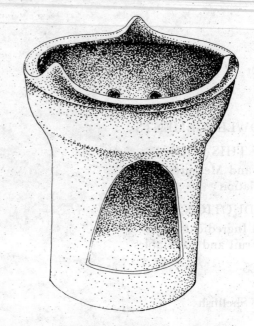

Anglo—Charcoal stove

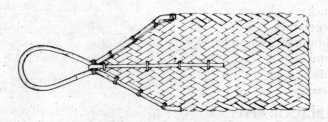

Kipas—Fan

Acknowledgements

One of the rewards of writing a cookery book is that it brings one into touch with so many interesting people. *Indonesian Food and Cookery* owes so much to friends, relatives and colleagues that I must record something of the gratitude I owe them.

This book has grown from *The Home Book of Indonesian Cookery*, published by Faber in 1976. The friend who persuaded me to stop talking about books and get down to writing one was John McLaughlin, and he introduced me to my first publisher. Many people at Faber helped and encouraged me; I must especially mention Rosemary Goad, Eileen Brooksbank and Sue Oudot.

In writing this new edition under its new title, I have collected information and recipes from many Indonesian friends in London and back home, as well as from my own family: from my father, Ahmad Djamil Sutan Indodjati, of Magelang, and my sisters, Dra. Harmini Djamil, Roslina Usman Beka and Nurmalina Anwar, of Bandung, Jakarta and Pontianak; from Abdullah Alamudi, Hasan Asjari Oramahi and his wife Wati, and Iskandar Sukmana of the BBC Indonesian Section; and from two old friends of my student days, Ahmad Wirono and Soeatminah, of Gajah Mada University, Yogyakarta, who have gone far out of their way to send me not only information but also pictures on which a number of the illustrations in this book are based. Back in London, I have been helped in various ways by Dr John Dransfield and Dr Jatmi Dransfield; by Dr Ian Glover and Emily Glover; and by Aboe Hassan of the British Library. Jennifer Davidson and Joy Pemberton Pigott have made the raw manuscript fit to serve up to the type setter, and the book owes much to their judgement and expertise.

Acknowledgements

Finally, I must mention Alan and Jane Davidson, whose hospitality I have so often exploited and whose library of gastronomical reference books I have borrowed from repeatedly. Alan Davidson's books on fish and fish dishes have been to a large extent models for the form and content of my book, though it is scarcely to be compared to them in scholarship. I have to thank him not only for his interest and friendship, but also for undertaking to publish *Indonesian Food and Cookery* on behalf of Prospect Books; and for introducing me to Thao Soun, whose exquisite drawings contribute so much to the book.

In short, with so many helpers and advisers, this ought to be a pretty reliable work. If it is, I thank them for helping to make it so—and reserve to myself the mistakes that may be found among its pages.

Cobham, 31 March 1980   Sri Owen

About this Book

Indonesian Food and Cookery is for the newcomer to Indonesian food as well as for the experienced cook. It will show you how to cook Indonesian food if, like me, you are far away from the islands; if, on the other hand, you are already there, or are planning to go there, either as a tourist or for a longer stay, or if you are planning to emigrate no further than the nearest Indonesian restaurant, then the book will I hope be a useful gastronomic guide.

The long Introduction is for the reader who wants to know something of the general background and something about Indonesian attitudes to food. The botanical notes that follow it should be of practical use to the visitor or resident in Indonesia, and of general interest so far as they deal with vegetables and fruits obtainable in other countries.

The recipes themselves are arranged according to their main ingredients: rice, fish and shellfish, beef, lamb, pork, variety meats, chicken, egg dishes, duck, vegetables, tahu and tempe. Several of these sections were not included in the original *Home Book of Indonesian Cookery*, notably that on pork, since the islands of Java and Sumatra, where most of the recipes in that book came from, are predominantly Moslem. But I could not avoid mentioning pork even then, and now that I am able to include recipes from several other islands as well I feel that pork must have a section to itself.

The three final sections deal with different kinds of *sambal*, side dishes, and cakes and puddings. A sambal is a hot, piquant sauce. The side dishes include some small salty or savoury things to be eaten, with drinks, before a meal.

The list of cakes and puddings is shorter than might be expected, because Indonesian sweet dishes generally appeal less to Western tastes and their ingredients are more difficult to find in Europe. Those that I have selected, however, use accessible ingredients and taste good.

Once it has been cooked, most Indonesian food keeps well, and any left-overs which may have survived your dinner party will taste just as good the next day. In fact, because the spices and sauces have had more time to penetrate, they may taste even better. Many Indonesian dishes are ideal for freezing, and I have added notes about this to recipes where appropriate.

Most of the main-course dishes that are described in this book will be sufficient, with the quantities given, to feed four people; if the quantity is for a larger or smaller number, this is indicated. Of course, any dish which is served as part of a large dinner-party menu, in true Indonesian style, may finish up on the plates of an indefinite number of guests.

Weights and Measures

When you are trying to introduce the cooking of one country to the kitchens of another, misunderstandings can all too easily arise. When these misunderstandings concern the quantities of highly flavoured ingredients, they can lead to unhappy results. I hope this short section may help to prevent confusion. We have three systems to cope with: the British (or 'Imperial'), the American, and the metric.

In the recipes, all quantities are given in metric, with the British equivalent shown in brackets, thus:

> 500 ml (1 pint) santen
> 120 g (4 oz) brown sugar

American readers should remember that the American pint is smaller than the British pint (16 fluid ounces instead of 20), and that 500 ml is therefore more than one American pint. American cups are likewise smaller than British, or at any rate they are smaller than the British cup measure that is marked on many British measuring-jugs. I use a teacup constantly while I am cooking, just because it is so easy and convenient, and it holds one American cupful—eight fluid ounces. In all these recipes, therefore,

one cup = one teacup = 8 fluid ounces = 225 ml.

Likewise, I have used teaspoons (tsp) and tablespoons (tbs) often in the recipes, because they make it easy to measure small amounts quickly. These are all level spoonfuls; if a heaped or rounded spoonful is required, the text says so. Measures such as '$\frac{1}{2}$ tsp' or '$\frac{1}{3}$ tsp' are not intended to be exact to the last grain; the cook will use common sense in interpreting them. And the experienced cook, of course, who has come to know a particular recipe thoroughly, will adjust these amounts to taste.

I have tended, on the whole, to reduce the quantities of chilli to the minimum, for the sake of those with tender tongues and palates. If you like your food really hot, then by all means increase the amount of chilli, at your own risk.

European and Indonesian readers may be puzzled by British abbreviations. 1 lb = one pound weight, and 1 oz = one ounce, which is one-sixteenth of a pound. British readers should beware, in Holland and Indonesia itself, of the *ons*, which is still widely used as a measure. 1 *ons* = 100 g, or about $3\frac{1}{2}$ oz.

Pronunciation

Indonesian pronunciation is straightforward and easy, at any rate if you compare it with what is demanded by some of the world's better-known cuisines.

Vowels are, near enough, like vowels in Italian. A small problem arises with the letter *e*. The *e*'s in *bebek*, for example, are full and open, as in English *pen*. The *e* in sant*en*, on the other hand, is just a short grunt, as in English *open*. A list of words with at least one 'full' *e* (shown as a capital, e.g. bEbEk) is printed on the following page. Note that a final *e* is always a full *e*. Where it seems necessary to remind the reader of this, the final *e* has been given an accent (cabé, peté, etcetera).

About this Book

Consonants present no difficulties, but you need to know that the reformed spelling has been used throughout. This means that *j* really does sound as it does in English *Jack* and not as in yak. Much more important, c is always pronounced as *ch* in English *church*; *kencur* therefore sounds nothing like *concur* and very like *k'ntjoor*. The letter *k*, at the end of a word, is hardly sounded at all, so that a word like *bebek* sounds as if it had been cut off short at the back. *Ng* is like *-ng-* in English *singer*; if you want a hard *g*, as in *finger*, you must write *-ngg-*, as in *panggang*. The letter *r*, even in the middle of a word, is always given its full value, as it is in most kinds of American English.

bEbEk	istimEwa	ondE-ondE
BerEk		osEng-osEng
besengEk	jahE	
bongkrEk		pangEk
	karE	panikE
cabE	karEdok	pEpEs
cengkEh	katEs	pergedEl
cermE	kEcap	petE
cobEk	kedelE	pEyEk
	kelEngkEng	
dEndEng	ketEla	rempEyEk
dEsa	kuE	
durEn		SaridelE
	lEici	satE
Ebi	lEman	SekatEn
Ekor	lodEh	selEdri
EmEs		serEh
Ercis	mEdan	serundEng
Eyang	menggorEng	
	mErah	
GedE	mEtE	tapE
gorEng		taugE
gulE		tEmpE

Introduction

EATING IN INDONESIA

Most Indonesians live in villages or small towns, or at least grew up there before they joined the rush to the big cities. Even if their families have been city-dwellers for generations, the roots and tendrils of the extended family reach far back, often to the countryside of another island which may be hundreds of miles away. However great the distance, the family will try to be together to celebrate Lebaran, the end of the Moslem fasting-month, when gifts are exchanged, mutual forgiveness is begged for the year's shortcomings, and great meals prepared.

Not that all Indonesians are Moslems. The feasts of many religions are celebrated in different parts of the archipelago. But everyone shares a common attitude, which I think I can best describe as a sort of informal piety towards every natural force. Respect is both felt and shown for the earth, the creatures and plants that live on it, the air and water that nourish it and the uncertain terror of the volcano, earthquake or flood. This attachment to the processes of nature is not formalized or fussed over, because it does not need to be: it is taken for granted. There are sound practical reasons for it. A landscape which has been terraced and irrigated for wet rice cultivation represents a prodigious capital investment and a delicate piece of high technology. Unless you want your sons and your sons' sons to do all that digging over again, you had better treat your environment right.

If you do treat it right, the rewards are great: security and enough leisure to develop arts, philosophy, literature and the customs of polite society. Natural piety accounts for the deep-lying animism that so many Western writers have detected in the Indonesian character. At its best, it has produced the art of Bali and Central Java, the woodcarving of Sulawesi, the passionate Islamic mysticism of West Java and Northern Sumatra, the epic poems of many islands. A critic might say that at its worst it grows in on itself and produces the more suffocating conventions of *adat*, or customary law. But it accounts, I think, for a lot that is good in Indonesian food and the way it is eaten.

To begin with, food must be shared, and shared abundantly. At any meal, especially if there are guests present, far more is put on the table than the company can possibly eat. This is not intended as a display of wealth on the host's part, nor will the guests feel bound to try and eat it all. What is not eaten will go back to the kitchen, to helpers and their families, to beggars at the door, or simply to the larder to re-appear at breakfast tomorrow. The point is that everyone must be assured that there is plenty available, they can take what they like. Conversely, guests assume that there always will be food for all, and have an engaging habit of inviting others along with them.

When you eat in an Indonesian household, you will almost certainly find all the dishes placed on the table together, and you will be asked to help yourself. The Dutch took this as the basis of their Rijsttafel. You can sample dishes one at a time if you like, and to take a second or a third or a fourth helping is polite, because it shows you are enjoying the food, or you can mix everything together. You will probably eat with a spoon and fork, which is practical because most food is cut up into mouthful-sized pieces in the kitchen before it is cooked. Rendang sometimes comes in rather large chunks, but they can be split and torn apart with no difficulty. Duck and chicken of course is usually served on the bone, and I imagine that most people, whatever their upbringing, will grab hold of the bone and gnaw it. For the rest, Indonesians like eating with their fingers and will not object if you do the same; I admit I still find food tastes best of all that way. If you go to something like a big village wedding, you may find you have no choice—no cutlery is provided, though finger-bowls always are. Getting rice into your mouth with your fingers can be tricky at first, but all will be well if you remember the golden rule: even if you are left-handed, only your right hand may touch food.

Indonesians eat a lot, when they get the chance, and I dare say the proportion of overweight people is as high there as anywhere else, at least among the better-off. But you rarely see a grossly fat one. To eat with enjoyment is a pleasure and a duty, but to stuff yourself is bad form. No one will mind if you can't finish the food on your plate or the drink in your glass. It is a sign that you really have had enough. The drink may be beer, or more likely fruit juice or squash, clear sweet Java tea or thick black *kopi tubruk*—literally 'collision coffee', and well named since it is made by pouring boiling water straight onto the coffee grounds. Alcohol is more or less unknown in traditional entertaining because, apart from being forbidden to Moslems, it is very expensive. Some non-Moslem areas have brews of their own: the Balinese, for example, produce a rice wine called *brum* which friends tell me can put you under the table pretty fast.

A table, of course, is a Western invention anyway. I spent my first six years in the earthly paradise of a Minangkabau township in Central Sumatra, where my father owned a school and my grandmother managed the family lands; where a matri-archal society preserved, and still preserves, the finely balanced social structures that have been evolved over a thousand years. My parents ate at table, spoke Dutch because they came from different islands, and discussed the affairs of the school. I ate in my grandmother's large kitchen, crosslegged on the square mat-covered platform among relations and helpers, licking my fingers, listening to the buzz of conversation around me, and eating my grandmother's cooking, which even at the age of six I could tell was unusually good. She, my father's mother, is perhaps more than anyone else the guiding spirit of this book.

THE MEALS OF THE DAY

Unless the times are very bad indeed, rice-eaters expect to eat rice three times a day. Rice by itself will do, with a few hot chillis to help it down, or rice porridge (*bubur*), if nothing else is to be had. For the sake of appearances, of course, it must be white rice, even at the cost of losing most of the nutrients and leaving little more than starch. If you think you aren't getting enough vitamins or proteins, and educated Indonesians are acutely conscious of the importance of these, then you may eat unpolished brown or red rice as well, or a health food like *bubur kacang hijau* (green bean porridge), but white rice is to us what white bread is to Europeans—a sign that we're holding our own, respectably above subsistence level.

Rice, then, begins the day, often last night's leftover rice served again as Nasi Goreng (page 100) with a fried or 'ox-eye' egg (*telur mata sapi*) on top of it, or an omelette cut into strips. Or you can cut a fresh papaya from the back garden, chop up the flesh and mix it with rice and *santen* (coconut milk). By slipping out of the house for a minute, you can always find something more enticing on market stalls or in street vendors' baskets. In my student days my girl friends and I, in our little boarding-house on the edge of town, would send a servant out into the streets at sun-up to buy Gudeg (page 168). Earlier, when I lived with my parents and sisters in Ceribon, I was often the one who was sent out to buy the local speciality, little waffles or Scotch pancakes called *serabi*. They were made of rice flour, santen and sugar, and cooked in a miniature wok with a close-fitting lid under which the mixture bubbled up delightfully.

By ten or eleven in the morning, breakfast is a distant memory and the street vendors are busy again, selling Lumpia (Spring rolls), Lemper (page 98), Pisang Goreng (page 239), Kue Bugis (page 244), and a whole range of sticky rice cakes wrapped in banana-leaves. Glasses of sweet, perfumed tea are placed carefully on office desks so that they will not be knocked over, and the lids that keep the tea warm and the flies out are carefully removed and placed where they will not drip on to the boss's signature. Fortified, everyone keeps going till one o'clock, when shops, offices and schools close, most of them for the rest of the day. This means that father and children are back home for a late lunch. The absence of this family meal in the middle of the day in England is something that no Indonesian over here ever quite gets used to. Rice again, with perhaps two or three meat and vegetable dishes; water to drink, or more tea; fresh fruit to follow. Then the stillness of siesta settles over the town. Around three o'clock is perhaps the quietest hour of the whole twenty-four.

In the rainy season, your siesta time is likely to end dramatically: a door slammed by a sudden wind, a thunderclap overhead, and the roar of cool tropical rain hammering on your roof-tiles. In the dry season the afternoon air merely begins to feel a little less heavy after four o'clock. You have a bath anyway, pouring cold water over yourself from the tank, and at half-past four tea is served: rice cakes, fried bananas. Life begins again.

The big meal of the day is supper, which traditionally starts as soon as darkness falls, about 6.30 in the evening. The rice this time will be accompanied by at least four or five cooked dishes and perhaps more. For the first course, you can sit on your terrace and wait for the saté man to come down the street, or the bakmie man, or the soto man. Each has his characteristic cry or sound, a rattle of brass bells or the beating of a Chinese wooden block. The man you summon will squat down by the front gate, fan his charcoal brazier to a glow, and quickly cook what you want. You can eat these people's food with confidence, for they keep their equipment scrupulously clean, and in any case the food is boiled, fried or grilled immediately before you eat it. These street vendors come insistently back to my mind when I recall the pleasures of eating in Java, but I must admit this is because I lived in Java for so long before coming to Europe; in other areas you may find fewer of them or even none at all. In my homeland of Sumatra there were none, and you had to go to the market-place for everything. This, I think, may have been because it was felt to be beneath anyone's dignity to hawk food around the streets. Certainly, in those parts, though you can find plenty of 'helpers' in every household, usually distant impoverished relatives, you will find no paid servants, unless they have been imported from islands where people have a less finicky notion of what makes a respectable job.

PARTIES AND FEASTS

Another generalization: most Indonesians, certainly if they are past thirty, have known hunger at one time or another—not necessarily starvation, but the nagging feeling of being always a bit short on quantity or variety of food. Here in London I see advertisements enticing tourists to attend mediaeval banquets, but the point of a banquet in the Middle Ages was presumably that it might be your last square meal for several months. Today, even the older generation in Britain, who must have known hardship in the 1940s, don't seem to get that uninhibited sensual delight from eating that is the privilege of those who know that hunger, or at least monotony, is never far away.

Putting it another way, a Western observer might say that in a Moslem country food has to do alone what food plus alcohol perform in Europe or America. American friends in Yogyakarta were always amazed at the pitch of noise and jollity a students' party could attain, simply on fizzy lemonade. They overlooked the fact that shy and reserved people are always excited to be brought together in a crowd on a social occasion. However noisy they became, those parties were usually quite formal. The Americans also overlooked the fact that there was masses to eat.

Parties in Indonesia are indeed elaborate affairs, often ritualistic but always lively. I have mentioned the importance of getting the family together for Lebaran, the feast-day that marks the end of Ramadan. Even Ramadan itself can be an occasion for eating a lot, because the fasting rule applies only during the hours of daylight and every year you will hear complaints from orthodox Moslems that certain less spiritual persons are using the fast as an excuse for all-night orgies of gluttony. The Lebaran meal itself is essentially a family affair when we are at home, but for Indonesians abroad it becomes a communal feast, usually held in the Indonesian Embassy or at the home of one of the senior members of the community. In any case, on *Hari Raya*—literally, the Great Day, *Idul Fitri* as we adapt the name from Arabic—there is much toing and froing of neighbours, drinking coffee, exchanging small presents and the proper greeting for the day, '*Harap dima'afkan lahir batin*'—'Forgive me the wrongs I have done you, whether of thought or deed'. The traditional dishes for Lebaran are Ketupat (page 95) and Sambal Goreng Daging (page 126) in Java, Lemang (page 105) and Rendang (page 136) in Minangkabau (Central Sumatra), but these by themselves do not make a feast and many other dishes will appear with them on the table. In Java the centrepiece is usually what it is on any big occasion, a huge plate of garnished yellow rice (Nasi Kuning, page 102). Yellow rice, too, appears at weddings, and if Lebaran is a family feast, a wedding is extremely public. The entire neighbourhood will be invited, everyone from the bride's and groom's places of work, the whole family through to its most distant branches and offshoots, and everybody's friends: a party of at least two hundred, and often many more. The bride's parental home, where the newlyweds are supposed to live for the first seven days of their marriage, is decorated with palm-leaf arches, the marriage-bed is hung with flowers, and the kitchen is occupied around the clock by sisters, aunts and cousins all cooking as if their lives depended on it. The whole affair is terribly expensive, and among my father's people, the Minangkabau in Central Sumatra, a wedding is one of the three emergencies which are held to justify the sale of family land for cash. The other two are a funeral, which also involves a big meal for many people, and the bailing-out of a relative who has got himself jailed. I understand that in feudal Europe almost exactly the same rules applied for the sale of land. I cannot imagine that wedding feasts of the old type can continue in the new suburbs of Jakarta, where neighbourhood social ties are weaker than they were in the villages—the *desa* or *kampung*—and where the bride's father is probably struggling to bring up the rest of his family on a civil servant's salary.

But if the tradition of great feasts dies out in the cities, another tradition I am sure will not, at any rate not for a long while yet. I hope I have made it quite plain that a festive meal is not just a blow-out. It is a ritual as well, and rituals have consequences. Their purpose is not just to fill people up, but to send each guest home a better person, in some way, than he was when he came. The ritual effectiveness of eating together is nowhere stronger than in the *selamatan*, and this tangles too deeply with the roots of Indonesian life for it to be easily abandoned. The word *selamatan* does not translate into English. It is the same word, with the noun suffix -*an*, that you hear in so many conventional greetings: *selamat pagi!* (good morning); *selamat jalan!* (*bon voyage*); *selamat makan!* (*bon appetit*; it is worth noting that the English have to borrow these phrases from the French); or when greeting the newly-married couple at the wedding feast, *selamat bahagia* (may you be happy!). A selamatan is often quite a small gathering. Its name expresses the notions of thanksgiving, blessing, grace. Having given a selamatan, or attended one, you have fed your soul as well as your body. There are a few prayers, a reading from the Qur'an, perhaps some task to perform, such as the cleaning of a gravestone. A foreigner might say that the minds of the participants, as they eat their food, and gossip, are most of the time without any religious preoccupation. This would be true, but it would miss the point. The meal and the conversation are part of the ceremony; the selamatan is an expression of that natural piety that I mentioned at the start. There are clearly stated occasions for holding a selamatan: at intervals of so many days after a birth, a death or a circumcision; on the starting or finishing of a new house; on the completion of the rice harvest, especially if it has been a good one; and so on. Thanksgiving, in North America, originated as a typical selamatan. I know that in my husband's family's farmhouse in Shropshire the harvest-home was celebrated, until the 1920s or 1930s, with a big dinner for everyone who had worked in the fields, and with the plaiting of a corndolly, almost identical in form and meaning with the rice-dollies that are still made in Indonesian villages to honour *Dewi Sri*, goddess of all that is fertile.

It is a long way from these country revels to the high-school or college students' party with which I began this section. There, everyone makes his or her contribution to the table, either in money paid to the organizing committee beforehand, or in kind. 'How do they manage to serve the food hot in that case?' you may ask. They don't. Almost the only fundamental difference that I have found between cooking Indonesian food

Indonesian women pounding rice to make rice flour, after the rice
has been harvested and threshed.

at home and in London is that Europeans, or my family anyway, won't eat cold food if it looks as though it was meant to be
hot. Indonesians do not care one way or the other, except with
a few dishes like Soto (page 128) which become fatty and con-
gealed if they are not warm. So the students' food can all be
put on the table at the beginning of the evening and left there,
and guests will still be helping themselves quite happily at mid-
night. The only guests who do not contribute to the victualling
of the party are those in whose honour the affair is being held,
and they earn their keep another way, for there will be speeches,
many speeches, and above all they will be expected to entertain
their hosts. If you find yourself a guest of honour of the students
at one of these parties, prepare your party piece well. I have
watched performances that ranged all the way from the em-
barrassing, although no one was embarrassed, to the dazzling.
Two, above all, come to my mind: a wild and furious gopak,
danced by a Hungarian couple from UNESCO in full winter
costume and fur-lined boots on a stifling tropical night; and the
farewell of a delightful, rather strait-laced history lecturer from
Calcutta. He had dodged his party obligations for five years,
but now that he was returning to India his students were deter-
mined to get him on the platform. He announced that he would
recite to them a poem by Rabindranath Tagore: 'It lasts for
twenty minutes. It is written altogether in Bengali and you will
understand not one single word.' He beamed at them and
recited for twenty minutes, exquisitely and with gestures. His
audience listened without a murmur, and gave him a standing
ovation at the end.

EATING OUT

The great restaurateurs of Indonesia are, as one might expect,
the Chinese. Some of the most memorable meals I have ever
eaten have been in the district of downtown Jakarta called
Glodok, which is famous for Chinese food. But I have also eaten
well in unassuming little restaurants in small towns, often called
simply *Rumah Makan Canton* ('rumah makan' means literally

'eating house'). As a young student I was rather shy of such places because they served pork and cooked their noodles in pork fat. Contact with the West corrupted me to the extent that I realized pork was actually rather good to eat. I worked as secretary first to one foreign professor, then to another; then I found myself with an English boy-friend. I have pleasant memories of several tiny restaurants in the side-streets of Yogyakarta, where my husband and I spent a lot of our evenings together before we were married. They were rather public places to go courting, but a good deal less so than the local cinemas, where the row behind us was invariably filled by his or my students.

Indonesian regional cooking, however, not Chinese, provides the basis for good restaurants in every town. Western visitors tend not to get to know these so well, perhaps because they feel more at home with a Chinese menu (often glossed in rather doubtful English). But a small-town Indonesian eating-house is likely to serve better food than its flashier Chinese competitor across the street. In particular, as the daughter of a good Minangkabau, I would recommend the *Rumah Makan Padang* that you will find not too far from the centre, whatever town you happen to be in. Padang food is really tasty—but hot, so acclimatize your tongue a little to chillis before you try it. Sometimes a restaurant is owned and run by an exile, a Balinese who has strayed into Medan or a man from Banyumas who woke up and found himself in Pontianak. Just as often, though, it is a local man cooking the specialities of his region, much as you might find in France. Either way, eating in Indonesian restaurants will quickly demonstrate the gulf that separates this cuisine from Chinese.

The Indonesian approach to the restaurant business is entirely pragmatic, as was demonstrated by a deservedly popular eating-house in the main street of a certain Javanese town. During the day, motor-cars were repaired on the premises, but in the evening the tools and grease magically disappeared and were replaced by chairs and tables, spotless tablecloths, and a kitchen from which came a good smell of *bakso*. The kitchen faced straight onto the street, a common practice in small establishments because it let prospective customers watch the chef at work before they committed themselves to eating there. Cooking in Indonesia easily becomes something of a public performance, in which a casual virtuosity is the most admired quality (see the introduction to the recipe for Martabak, page 233). Street vendors dish up hot food as if it were a conjuring trick, or sail through a crowd of shoppers with their stock-in-trade suspended from the horns of great upward-curving yokes of bamboo. Their crying or singing of their wares adds to the operatic effect, and they move like dancers because there is no other way to carry forty or fifty kilos of equipment, including a hot stove, along a crowded street without hitting anybody. Instead of the stove and bottles of *kecap*, the seller's load might consist of two comically-huge, square tins, measuring a metre or more along each edge, looking like some sort of practical joke—similar tins were often tied onto the luggage-racks of bicycles, dwarfing the man at the pedals. They were full of Krupuk Udang or other crisp- or wafer-like snacks; their load was 98 per cent air. I once saw a man who had decided the catering business was not for him, and who carried an ancient clockwork gramophone at one end of his yoke, balanced by a stack of records at the other. He looked unhappy. He had already (this was twenty years ago) been overtaken by the transistor. The whole street-vending economy will no doubt wither away as the country progresses, and we must be glad, because the life was a hard one. No Chinese would ever touch it. But when it goes the pattern of Javanese life will be less rich.

Not every small food-seller walks the streets. The Martabak man, and many others, have too much stuff to be able to carry it around. They set up their stalls in the market or on any patch of waste ground or, best of all for trade, in the big open space that is at the centre of almost every town. This great square may be called a *medan*, like the Medan Merdeka in Jakarta. In central Java it is nearly always known as *alun-alun*, and in the proper arrangement of a Javanese town it fills a key position, astride the main axis that runs from the mountains to the sea, and usually on the landward side of the Sultan's palace or *kraton*. In the alun-alun, on either side of the gate of the kraton, two giant *waringin* trees should grow, for the waringin is the home of spirits who, in the right place and properly looked after, are benevolent. All these ingredients of a well-ordered town are to be found in Yogyakarta, and the alun-alun is a popular place to go and take the evening air, with everyone in their best clothes and more intent on looking and being looked at than on actually getting anywhere. It is a good place to sell food, or batik, or sandalwood fans, or Japanese alarm-clocks, on any evening. Two or three times a year a *pasar malam*, or night fair, would take over the area, and at least once a year workmen would appear with cartload after cartload of bamboo and erect a large theatre in which a nightly audience of a couple of thousand or so would watch *wayang orang*. Wayang is traditional Javanese theatre, with its cycles of heroic stories based on the ancient Hindu epics. Most people have heard of the shadow-plays, but wayang orang is performed by human actors. It is a superb spectacle: but the show lasts for five or six hours non-stop, and few people can be continuously enthralled for that long. So there is a constant coming and going of audience who have decided they must pop out for something to eat, and who often bring it back with them to eat in the theatre. No one objects to this, for the atmosphere is not that of a show on Broadway or in the West End of London and silent concentration is not regarded as the proper way to watch a play. Like so many Javanese occasions, this is an event which you are taking part in, not someone else's production which you are supposed merely to watch.

In Surakarta (or Solo) the pasar malam has become a per-manent fixture, and is called *Sekaten*. It has its own resident wayang company, and some very good restaurants. Really, when the length of the day never varies by more than a few minutes from solstice to equinox, and there is little change in temperature between wet season and dry, it is hard to see why a good evening's entertainment should not run indefinitely.

But not all your eating out is done on special occasions or when you are pursuing pleasure. In introducing my recipe for Gudeg (page 168) I suggested that the Javanese *warung* is the equivalent of the French pavement café—somewhere you can drop in when you need refreshment in the middle of the day's work, where you are likely to find a neighbour or two, and where you can while away cheaply a lot of leisure time, if you have it. The warung plays the roles that in England or America might be filled by the milk-bar or coffee-bar, the hamburger joint, the fish-and-chip shop, the takeaway and the lunch counter. Architecturally, it is extremely simple: a roof, a table-cum-counter and a bench are the essentials. Big-city warungs may develop quite a large covered area with a dozen or so tables, but they remain temporary, unwalled buildings, constantly being patched up or re-invented. The counter is almost hidden under tiers of glass bottles and glass-fronted tins containing cakes, Krupuk, Emping, biscuits, nuts, sweets, Rempeyek, dried fruit, dried fish, dried meat or *dendeng*—anything, in short, that will keep. There are bottles of brightly-coloured *stroop*, or syrupy sweet drinks. Somewhere behind or below this display the cooking goes on, and customers stand, sit on the bench, or squat on the ground nearby. The Javanese squat very low, with the whole foot flat on the ground and the arms extended, resting on the knees, to help the body balance. It is a relaxed position if you are used to it, but it demands great suppleness of the ankles, as you will discover if you try it.

One of my two favourite warungs, all through my student days, was the *warung gado-gado* where my friends and I often had lunch. We used to stop there on our way back, on bicycles, from the decayed nobleman's house that in those days housed the Faculty of Arts and Letters to our lodgings at the other side of town. The warung had a large table with benches on three sides and a nice old lady on the fourth. She chopped and cooked the vegetables, ground the spices for the *bumbu* or sauce, and whisked everything together at tremendous speed so that a dozen of us could all start eating more or less together; again, the virtuosity of cooking, as it were, 'on stage'. My other favourite place was the *warung kopi*, the coffee-shop near the Faculty. There you could get glasses of sweet, heavy *kopi tubruk* and cakes or ready-made savouries like Lemper. When I mentioned the place to my husband recently, I realized he had never been there. He had never suggested taking me, and it would have been improper for me to suggest that I should take him. The only Englishman, I think, who ever got me to the warung kopi was a visiting British Council lecturer who I rather approved of. At that time I was secretary to the Professor of English, and he had asked me that morning to buy him some stamps at the Post Office. I was waylaid and allowed myself to be tempted into drinking coffee instead. The Professor was not pleased when I returned, well over an hour later. I told him that the queue at the Post Office had been—not exceptionally long—but quite as long as usual. It was an explanation he had no difficulty in sympathizing with. If it hadn't been for the queue, he could have bought the stamps himself.

Most of the time, as students, we went around in packs. Our bicycles filled the streets, we flocked to lectures, to speeches and demonstrations, we marched in procession through the town with songs and banners. At weekends we all met up again to cycle off into the countryside for picnics, fifty or a hundred or more of us, everyone with a basket of food, urging our heavy black Dutch bicycles along the dusty roads to the temples at Prambanan, or to a bathing-place among the rice-fields, or to Kota Gede, to see the silversmiths at work and watch the great white turtle in the sacred pool. When I came to read Words-worth in the Faculty of Arts and Letters, I found that his crowd and my crowd had a good deal in common, if you allowed for rather large differences in climate and landscape. His friends, galloping their rented horses through the abbey ruins, and mine, propping their bicycles against the stones of even older temples, were looking for much the same thing. As for the old village lady who kept the tuck-shop where young William spent his long-saved pocket money, she was simply keeping a good old-fashioned warung in that land of lakes and cloudy skies.

And so, further back, to childhood and picnics even more exciting, when we brought in the rice harvest from the *sawah**
of my mother's village, a few kilometres inland from the sea at Ceribon. We were living at that time in her mother's house, a

---

* *Sawah* is a collective term for wet rice fields; *padi* is rice while it is grow-ing, or when it has just been cut. When it has been threshed it becomes *beras*, which is what you buy in the market, and cooked rice is *nasi*.

substantial place, in a village that looked from a distance like an island of coconut palms in a green sea of *padi*.

There was a line of hills behind the house, but in front the north coastal plain was almost level and the fields were large, dropping only a few centimetres from one terrace to the next. As harvest time approached the fields were drained and elaborate arrangements were made with neighbours, for there was no hired labour; everyone worked in everyone else's fields in turn, and you were given a third or a quarter of what you cut. Most of the reaping was done by women, while the men carried the rice-sheaves on poles to the threshing-floor. The work was hard but the atmosphere was distinctly festive as we all set out at first light, out from the tattered roof of palm-fronds to the huge open landscape, a little group of thirty or forty of us, clustered in talkative knots at first as we followed the road into the fields but then strung out in procession along the narrow dykes that separated one field from the next.

The reapers worked in a long line abreast, bent nearly double. Of all the countless millions of rice-stalks that composed this fertile scenery, every one had to be cut with a separate stroke of the knife. No major food-crop anywhere in the world can demand such intense, passionate care as wet rice. The knife we used (and at eight years old I was allowed, as a privilege, to take my place in the line of women reapers) was a tiny razor-sharp blade set in a springy bamboo and called *ani-ani*. On the way to and from the fields, you wore it tucked into your hair, and in use you held it between your second and third fingers, which were slightly crooked, so that you gathered and cut the rice-stalk with a single motion of the hand towards the body. My inexperienced effort hardly collected a single sheaf of rice in this way before the sun was high above us and work stopped for lunch.

We sat on big mats spread out on the ground, seeking whatever shade we could. The men sat in one group, women in another. The food was brought from the village on bamboo trays and in woven bamboo baskets: rice, meat, fish from the pond behind the big house, vegetables, sambal—a complete course of instruction (if I had known or cared) in the regional cooking of west-central Java. There was fresh water in the *kendi*, tall, narrow-shouldered pots that kept cool in the noonday heat. I licked my fingers, tasting garlic and ginger, and stared across the endless fields that were yet to cut. Those harvest lunches, when nothing mattered except work and rest from work—those were perhaps the best eating of all.

THE COOK AND THE KITCHEN

My Sumatran grandmother, who was a wealthy woman and the head of a large household, did most of her cooking in the open air, on wood-fired stoves called *tungku* that consisted of carefully-arranged piles of bricks. There was a big kitchen indoors, but as long as the weather was fine it offered no special advantages that couldn't be had in a shady corner of the big yard behind the house. There was no food storage because everything was bought in the early morning at the *pasar* (market) or taken straight from our own land or from the granary. There was of course no gas or electricity. A heavy Dutch kitchen table with a couple of drawers to hold knives or other small implements was all the essential furniture; I think there were one or two small stools on the tiled floor. Along one wall was an earth platform, faced with brick and tile, where charcoal stoves could stand and the cutting-up of food could be conveniently done. In the room next to the kitchen, where most of the household ate, there was a low mat-covered platform on which we sat, the men cross-legged and the women with their legs tucked demurely together to right or left, while the serving-dishes were placed in the midst of the company and we all helped ourselves.

It sounds attractive, but a little primitive. I would not like to cook in such conditions today; I admit that I would not even go on a fortnight's camping trip without my butane cooker and my polystyrene-insulated cold box. But then I cook more or less alone, whereas my grandmother was at the apex of the complicated social pyramid of the kitchen. She had all the help she could use. There were men to split coconuts and prise out the

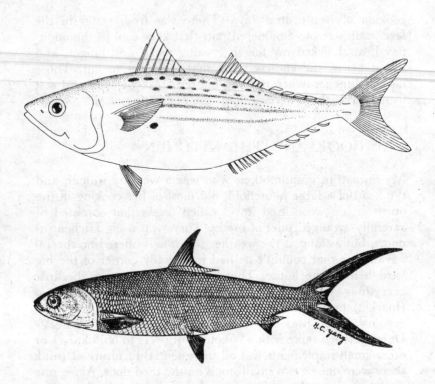

The lower of the two drawings shows the ikan bandeng (*Chanos chanos*, known in English as the milkfish. It is very popular in both Indonesia and the Philippines. Although it is a marine fish, it can be cultured in brackish ponds. It is very bony. The fish in the upper drawing is *Rastrelliger kanagurta*, one of the South-East Asian mackerels. It is known as ikan kembung in Indonesia. It could be used instead of a milkfish for the recipe on page 123; as could the larger Spanish mackerel of the genus *Scomberomorus*.

Both these drawings were reproduced in Alan Davidson's *Seafood of South-East Asia*. The upper one comes from the *Species Identification Sheets* of the United Nations Food and Agriculture Organization. The lower, by the famous ichthyological artist H. C. Yang, was taken by kind permission from *Common Food Fishes of Taiwan*, a **publication** of the Joint Commission on Rural Reconstruction in Taipei.

coconut flesh, women to go and bargain at the market or spend half an hour choosing the perfect cucumber or the slightly un-ripe mango, girls to chop and cut and slice vegetables, old men to give advice, young men to carry sacks of rice down the granary steps and chop more wood for the *tungku*, little boys and girls to get under everyone's feet and fan the charcoal so that it hissed and spat, and then hissed again as the fat dripped from the roasting meat. These people were nearly all relatives in one degree or another, not paid servants, and my grand-mother was not an employer but a matriarch, the chef of a purely feudal cuisine. Years later, in somewhat reduced circum-stances, my sisters and I ran errands and chopped vegetables for my father, who was an enthusiastic and a very good cook, and my elder son seems to have inherited his knack both of making things turn out right and of ordering people around in the kitchen.

The moral of all this is that Indonesians, or at any rate Minangkabau and Javanese of the old school, regard cooking as a craft, to be practised communally if possible but with the observance of a strict hierarchy of roles and jobs; a craft which gives scope for skills and satisfactions of the highest order, and which may, as we have seen, lend itself to public displays of these skills in warungs and small restaurants, but which is never, I think, intended to become an art. There are no great Indonesian chefs, no famous dishes which are regarded as the supreme test of a great cook's genius or about the origins of which the same stories are told and retold until they become myths. Instead we have the idea of the 'masterpiece', in the old sense of the word: the tricky bit of technical expertise which is supposed to prove that you are fit to join the guild or, in the case of cooking, to become a wife. Such a dish is Bandeng Isi, the recipe for which is given on page 123. I confess that in my youth I deliberately did not learn how to make it, thinking that if I did this, it would be taken as a sign that I was looking for a husband. Since marriage dispelled such inhibitions, I have found that the technique can be mastered without too much difficulty. The bandeng—see the preceding page—is quite a large marine fish. The trick is to remove all its flesh, and every

Introduction

single bone, without cutting or marking the skin. The flesh is then spiced and stuffed back into the skin before being steamed, so that it comes to table looking as though it had just hopped out of the water. A mother may well boast of a daughter who can perform this feat; but to my mind the emptying and re-filling of the fish is a matter of mere dexterity; the spicing is the creative operation.

In Indonesia, as elsewhere, cooks range from good to bad. Many are men. But whereas in Europe it is not unusual for a man-cook to become famous and to be regarded as an artist, a similar personality cult would be unthinkable in Indonesian cuisine.

There is no doubt in my mind that Indonesian cooking is a peasant cooking, and none the worse for that. It is very difficult to trace the history or origins of any Indonesian dish; I have made enquiries about many of the recipes in this book, but learnt little. Friends in the academic world, experts in classical Javanese and Balinese, tell me that despite the richness of the literature and the aristocratic, ultra-refined society that produced it, the texts say little or nothing about food. The princes and heroes seem to have been interested in drinking, fighting, making love, gambling, praying, meditating, practising the arts, even in fasting—but eating, it seems, they took for granted. Considering the importance in Java even today of giving food to supernatural beings—little offerings of rice and cooked things, offered on banana-leaf plates to the spirits of almost every crossroads, river or large tree—I find this strange.

Traditional cooking utensils are, as you would expect, simple, though some of them have developed into rather beautiful objects. The Javanese *anglo* is an example. This is a charcoal cooking-stove, about 30 cm high, with a 'basket' on which the charcoal is placed and an air-vent which is designed to be used with a woven bamboo *kipas* or fan. The kipas is ideal for the job because it has enough whip in it to get up plenty of speed on each stroke and move a lot of air through the vent as it is flapped back and forth. See the drawings on page 6.

The three little prongs on the rim of the anglo are to support a saucepan or wok. The Javanese name for this round-bottomed frying pan is *wajan*, but everyone in the West is familiar by now with its Chinese name and I have stuck to wok throughout this book. For rapid stir-frying, and the equal application of heat over the greatest possible area, the wok is unbeatable and I cannot imagine being without at least two. Because of its shape it is also very easy to clean.

My grandmother, as far as I remember, did use a wok, but her regular cooking-pot was a *belanga*—a round-bottomed earthenware vessel, much deeper than a wok and with a definite neck to it. A new belanga would be lined with banana leaves every time it was used, to provide a non-stick surface, but as time went on the rather porous clay absorbed oil and juices from the food and developed a shiny black lining of its own. The clay also preserved the flavour of whatever was cooked in it. I wish I could get something resembling a belanga in Britain, because it is much the best pot for cooking dishes such as Pangek, but the crocks that are available are generally too small or too specialized to have the all-round usefulness of the belanga.

Boiling plain white rice, as I explain on page 92, is an easy task; it helps if you have a steamer, but a thick-bottomed sauce-pan is perfectly adequate. The old-fashioned Javanese steamer has a kind of double-conical outer pan, called a *dandang*, which should be beaten from copper but which nowadays would more likely be of aluminium. The dandang is filled with water to just below the waist, and the conical *kukusan*, with the half-cooked rice in it, sits in the wide mouth with its point just above the surface of the water. The verb 'to steam' is *mengukus*. The kukusan is woven from strips of split bamboo so that the steam can pass through the rice, and a lid—just an ordinary saucepan lid—goes on top. See illustration on page 97.

Other things besides plain rice are steamed; for example, sticky rice cakes, such as Kue Talam or Kue Bugis. Many of the recipes in this book, however, require food to be put in a gas or electric oven, which most Indonesian cooks still do not have. We did have an oven of sorts at home: a big sheet-metal box with trays of hot charcoal to slide into the top and bottom to heat it, but it was a difficult thing to control and a brute to clean, so that we never used it much. Roasting was something we did on a spit, and in Sumatra we thought nothing of roasting half-a-dozen whole sheep in this way for a festivity. Saté, I suppose, is a sort of spitting in miniature, and we used to snatch the saté from the embers of the cooking-fire just as everyone was sitting down ready to tuck in. But the operations of roasting and grilling are considered to be quite distinct, and we have separate words for them: to roast is *memanggang* (as in Ayam Panggang—the *me-* is a verb prefix and converts the *p-* to nasal *-m-*), while to grill is *membakar*. Add *menggoreng* (to fry, as in Nasi Goreng), *menumis* (to sauté, as in Tumis Buncis) and *merebus* (to boil), and you have a good basic vocabulary for the processes of Indonesian cooking. Boiling is particularly important for sauces, or *bumbu*, which are often thickened by boiling the water off them. Another way of giving them extra body is by adding crushed or ground ingredients, and you will find that this is done in many of the dishes described in this book. What no self-respecting Indonesian cook would do, except in a few dishes which mostly show Chinese influence, is to thicken a sauce with flour; the most important exception is Babi Kecap (page 150). Crushed chillis, perhaps, since chilli gives body as well as flavour but not flour.

Some of my happiest memories are of food cooked in what I suppose we would nowadays call disposable containers, many of them made of leaves, some of cut segments of bamboo. I could not resist mentioning Lemang (page 105) as an example of bamboo cookery. This is a Sumatran dish, but there are counterparts in other islands, such as Timbung from Lombok and Ayam Dibuluh (*buluh* is bamboo) from Menado.

I think most Europeans, indeed, would be astonished at the extent to which containers and utensils that must be pre-Iron Age have survived into quite modern Indonesian kitchens. (Of course, a classy Jakarta apartment will be equipped to London or Paris standards.) Half a gourd, or half a coconut shell, attached to a split bamboo handle, makes an excellent ladle; it does not last as long as a metal one, but it can be made without a blast-furnace or a drop-forge, and when you throw it away after a few weeks you create employment for the *tukang* who makes you a new one. Knives must be made of good steel, but wood and stone are what you need to crush and grind raw materials. I don't suppose that anyone reading this book will wish to grind his or her own rice flour, though the exercise of lifting, twisting, and dropping a heavy wooden ram into a stone trough is no doubt healthy. You will, however, need a pestle and mortar (*ulek-ulek* and *cobek* respectively) if you are going to take Indonesian food at all seriously. The western pestle and mortar are excellent, but our corresponding tools are rather different in shape and use. We hold the pestle sideways-on, and rock it rather than thump it into the shallow mortar. I much prefer mine to be made of wood, because the stone ones that you can buy in Indonesia are apt to release tiny particles of grit into

the food; but I have to admit that though my ulek-ulek is genuine my cobek came, years ago, from W. H. Smith in Staines, and was probably meant to be some sort of small fruit bowl.

Making these useful objects could be an excellent woodwork project for someone at school, who could perhaps follow them up by constructing the peculiarly unpleasant instrument known as *parut* in Java and *kukuran* in Sumatra: a wooden board studded with small nails, points outwards, on which to grate coconut, and your finger-ends too if you are not careful. Even more lethal, though I suppose less likely to be misused by accident, is the wooden horse on which you sit to gouge the flesh out of a coconut. This horse, which is also called *kukuran* (coconut carver) has a sharp metal beak. To use it, sit astride the animal and hold a half-coconut with its open end towards you. Anyone who has spent half an hour chiselling fragments of coconut out of the shell with a vegetable knife will realize that the kukuran is a necessity in a country where coconuts actually do grow on trees.

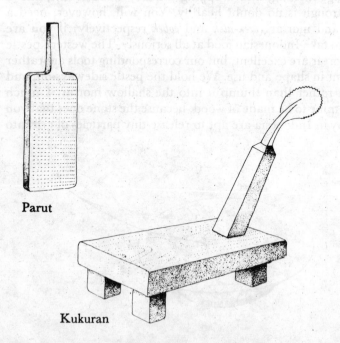

Parut

Kukuran

Essential Ingredients

In this section I have gathered together some notes on ingredients which you are likely to use often—some of them you will need almost every time you prepare Indonesian food. There is nothing difficult or mysterious about the techniques that they call for, and they should all be quite easily obtainable in Chinese or other Asian foodstores in most cities. An Indonesian cook, however, regards a coconut or a bottle of soya sauce rather differently from a cook in Europe or America, so that what this section really deals with is some of the more important differences between the basic processes of Indonesian and western cooking. The section which begins on page 45 is devoted to the general run of spices, fruits and vegetables.

COCONUT, SANTEN, AND COCONUT OIL

Coconuts grow abundantly everywhere in Indonesia, and are used every day in cooking. Broadly speaking, they come to market at three stages of maturity: very young, young, and fairly old. The first two are usually called *kelapa muda*; the last is *kelapa tua*. The coconuts that reach Europe are all kelapa tua, with their smooth green or yellowish-brown outer husks removed, leaving the hard hairy shell.

Kelapa muda may be so young that the flesh can be scraped out with a spoon. The *air kelapa* (coconut water) is deliciously sweet, and is sold with the soft flesh floating in it. Or you can buy a nut by the roadside or on the beach, still fresh from the nearest tree, and have the top expertly sliced off by a man with a heavy-bladed knife. You drink the coconut water from the shell, and he will then split the nut down the middle and slice you off a little round spatula of shell to scrape away and eat the flesh with. A slightly older kelapa muda, sometimes called, logically enough, *kelapa setengah tua* (middle-aged coconut), is firm enough for the flesh to be grated. This can be done across the grain, so that you get small coconut flakes, or along the grain, to give long strands. You can also make coconut strands in a food processor, using the cheese-grating blade; and you can buy coarsely grated young coconut flesh in some Chinese shops in London and elsewhere, deep-frozen in plastic bags.

When the flesh of a mature coconut is prised out of the shell, the tough brown inner skin usually comes away with it. If you are making *santen* (see below), grate this brown skin along with the white flesh; it will produce a thicker, oilier santen, which is just what you need. If you are using kelapa muda in a savoury, the colour of the skin will not be noticed in a sauce which is probably brown anyway, and the skin is not tough enough to affect the texture. In all other cases, however, get rid of the brown skin before you start grating.

SANTEN

In this book, I have translated santen as 'coconut milk', but the Javanese word is shorter and sounds more attractive and is, I think, less likely to be misunderstood. Santen is not the liquid which you pour from a newly-opened nut, but a mixture of water and the oils which can be pressed from grated coconut flesh. It is used all over Indonesia, both to thicken sauces and to add flavour, and generally speaking no other thickening agent is ever used—certainly not wheat flour, which is almost unknown in most areas, nor rice flour. In some recipes, santen forms the basis of a more or less thick sauce; in others, it is absorbed wholly into the meat in the course of cooking, and gives it a delicious nutty flavour which is quite unobtainable in any other way. It is sometimes said that the flavour of santen is an acquired taste, and certainly no one would want their cooking to reek of coconut; but santen, properly used, is indispensable to Indonesian food, and I don't recall meeting anyone who did not acquire the taste within the first mouthful or so.

Santen ought obviously to be made from fresh coconut, but it can be made perfectly satisfactorily from desiccated or creamed coconut as well.

From Fresh Coconut

The flesh of one nut will give about half a litre (one pint) of santen. Grate all the flesh into a bowl, and add one cup of water. Then squeeze handfuls of the grated nut so that the water becomes white and takes up the juices from the flesh. Go on doing this until you are convinced you must have squeezed out every last drop; this is likely to take at least a minute or so, but there is no need to spend an unreasonable amount of time on it. Then strain the liquid through a fine sieve, and squeeze the grated nut good and hard to make sure that all the liquid is out of it. Put the gratings back in the bowl, add another cup of water, and repeat the process; the more water you use, the thinner your santen will obviously be, but you should get a pint of thick santen from a nut. In most of the recipes in this book, that is about the thickness you require; if thicker or thinner santen is to be used, this is indicated.

The dried-up gratings that you are left with at the end are no good for cooking, but in Indonesia, where no one can afford to waste anything, they are not thrown away immediately. They are fed to the family hens; or, if you haven't any hens, you can use them to polish lino or plastic or ceramic tiles to a high gloss.

From Desiccated Coconut

350 g (12 oz) desiccated coconut is the equivalent of one fresh nut. Put it into a pan and pour over it about 150 ml ($\frac{1}{4}$ pint) of water. Heat it gently until the water just starts to bubble (if it actually boils for a short time, this does no harm). Pour this into a liquidizer and add enough cold water to make the amount of santen you require. Run the liquidizer for 20 or 30 seconds, then sieve the resulting mush, forcing it through the sieve with your hand and squeezing the coconut flakes as dry as you can. If the recipe calls for thick santen, the 'first extraction' is sufficient. If you need thin santen, put the coconut back into the liquidizer, add more cold water and repeat the process. If you have no liquidizer, you can still squeeze and sieve the coconut and water, several times over if necessary, until you have the consistency and quantity you require.

Essential Ingredients

From Creamed Coconut

Creamed coconut can be bought from many grocers and super-markets, and also from health food stores. It comes in com-pressed dry white slabs, looking like half a pound of lard. You can use it as a kind of 'instant santen'—but only in those recipes (e.g. Sambal Goreng, page 126) where santen is added at the end, after the main process of cooking is complete. Simply cut off a chunk from the slab and put it in the pan; it will melt, exactly as butter does. If you find, in almost any dish, that your sauce is going to be too thin, this is the easiest and quickest way to thicken it at the last moment.

Storing Santen

Santen does not keep. A 'fresh' coconut that you buy from an English supermarket is, of course, likely to be a few weeks old, at least; but as long as you do not break it open it will be perfect-ly all right for another month or more. Desiccated and creamed coconut will obviously keep for a very long time. Santen, how-ever, must be used within about 24 hours of being made. It can be stored overnight in a refrigerator; it may thicken, like cream, but will melt again when heated. Dishes which are to be refrigerated or frozen must be stored without santen, and the santen added when the dish is heated ready for serving—except in the case of dishes such as Rendang (page 136) or Kelia (page 162), which are cooked in santen from the very beginning and in which the santen is nearly or completely absorbed into the meat. These can be frozen; so, of course, can any dish which uses grated coconut.

In cold conditions, santen may 'separate', with the thick cream coming to the top. This does not matter; just give it a good stir before you use it, or warm it by standing the jug in a saucepan of warm water.

COCONUT OIL

Some people say that Indonesian food must be cooked in coconut oil, and there is perhaps a barely perceptible difference in flavour between this and vegetable oil. However, I certainly do not consider coconut oil by any means essential, and it has one serious drawback; it quickly goes rancid. Oil which is the least bit 'on the turn' will ruin your food. I always use vegetable oil, and vegetable oil is specified in most of the recipes in this book, except for a few cases where olive oil is definitely to be preferred.

TERASI

This is a dark-coloured paste made from shrimps; it looks and smells a little like Marmite, but has the texture of ordinary fish-paste or Gentleman's Relish. You can sometimes buy Indonesian terasi which has been imported from Holland; usually, however, shops in Britain sell terasi from Malaysia, which is called by its Malay name, *balachan*.

Terasi, or balachan, is used in very small amounts as a flavouring in a wide variety of dishes. It is used in two forms: raw, and fried, or, better still, grilled.

'Raw' terasi is always crushed or ground up, with other spices and flavourings, into a thick paste which is sautéed, preferably in a wok with a little oil. The other ingredients of the recipe are then added to this. 'Fried' terasi is used in recipes where the spices are not to be sautéed, but boiled; the terasi is fried or grilled, by itself, before it is made into a paste with the other spices.

If you do a lot of Indonesian cooking, it is worth frying a fairly large amount of terasi—perhaps as much as 50 g or a couple of ounces—and keeping it in a separate jar. In airtight jars, in a cool and dry place, both raw and fried terasi will keep almost for ever, and a normal packet, which contains about 100 g, will last you for a very long time. The airtight jars are for your protection as much as for the protection of their contents; terasi is extremely strong-smelling and strong-tasting, and it is especially pungent when it is being fried by itself.

The exact quantity of terasi that you use in your cooking is up to you, but most Javanese dishes demand at least a little of it. There is an old story about terasi which Javanese mothers tell to their daughters—it is supposed to show how important it is for a wife to obey her husband, but the real moral seems to be more complex. It concerns a marriage which had been arranged between a rich merchant from Sumatra and a sweet young innocent thing from one of the old Javanese cities.

Shortly after the wedding, the husband terrified his new wife by saying: 'And don't forget! No terasi—I can't stand the stuff. The slightest whiff of it, and out you go.' The girl was, of course, devoted to terasi and could not imagine cooking without it. She began adding minute quantities to her husband's food. 'You're an excellent cook, I must say,' her husband told her. 'You see how much better food is without that revolting terasi.' Day by day, the amount of terasi increased, and so did her husband's approval. One evening he tasted a dish so exquisite that his delight turned to a fierce determination to know the secret of its superb flavour. 'Tell me what you put in it!' he commanded his trembling wife, 'or out you go!' She stammered, with becoming modesty, that she had used . . . terasi. 'How much terasi?' roared her husband. 'Oh, only a tiny bit—that much!' She indicated the top joint of her little finger. 'Right!' said her husband. He pulled back the sleeve of his jacket and showed her his right arm, from elbow to finger-tip. 'In future, you use *that* much terasi—or out you go!' But of course she didn't obey him; any cook who used *that* much would deserve to be thrown out.

KECAP OR SOYA SAUCE

This is, in fact, the same word as English 'ketchup'—remember that *c* in Indonesian is pronounced like *ch* in *church*. I suppose retired British colonial servants brought the word back home with them from Malaya, though the *Oxford English Dictionary* says it originated in the Amoy dialect of Chinese. Anyway, the word has got itself so firmly attached in Britain to tomato sauce that the stuff they put on the tables in Chinese restaurants has to be labelled 'soy sauce' instead. At least this has the merit of reminding you that kecap is made from soya beans. Like *tempe* and *tauco*, which are also soya bean products, it is made by fermentation; the process is a long one, and although I have an Indonesian recipe for it I have never tried it and I am sure I never shall.

Kecap is the basis for savoury sauces and marinades for a whole host of dishes. Different kinds of kecap are distinguished by how salty they are. For practical purposes, we need only bother about two types: *kecap asin*, which is very salty indeed, and *kecap manis*, which is less so. Kecap manis is very dark in colour because of all the brown sugar that goes into it; kecap asin is relatively clear or light-coloured.

Original Javanese kecap is still available, even in London, in only a few shops. I sometimes go to the trouble of seeking out a litre of real kecap manis because I was brought up on it and I can taste the difference, but I do most of my cooking with soya sauce bought from Chinese shops and in nearly all cases in this book I have specified soya sauce, either 'dark' (sweet) or 'light' (clear and salty). It is not always easy to tell, from the labels on Chinese tins and bottles, which is dark and which is clear; even holding the bottle up to the light may not give a reliable guide to the taste of the contents. If in doubt, therefore, ask the management for help.

If you cannot get to a Chinese food shop, or only want to buy a small amount of kecap, then use the proprietary brands that you can now find in any English supermarket: Amoy (or similar), which is 'dark', and Kikkoman (or any other Japanese brand), which is 'light' or clear.

All soya sauce should be used in moderation, but clear sauce is especially strong-tasting and must be used very sparingly. Even with dark sauce, additional salt should only be added if the recipe calls for it, and then with caution.

TAUCO

This is yet another product of the versatile soya bean, once again involving fermentation and a good deal of salt. Two types of bean are used, black and yellow. Tauco makes a most mouth-watering strongly aromatic sauce, quite indescribable and not comparable to any taste known in European cooking (see for example the recipe for Ayam Tauco, page 165). The beans should always be crushed to a smooth paste before being mixed with the other ingredients. I prefer the taste of the black beans, but they do make the sauce look rather dark and they leave small black fragments in it. The yellow beans taste very nearly as good and they make a beautiful old-gold coloured sauce which looks more tempting.

In England or the United States you can buy tauco in tins at Chinese food shops, labelled 'salted black beans' and 'salted yellow beans'. You can also buy tinned salted black or yellow bean sauce, but I would recommend the beans themselves if you have the choice. In Indonesia you buy tauco by weight, spooned out from big stoneware jars.

EBI

These are very small dried shrimps, and can be bought either raw or cooked. Most Chinese provision merchants in Britain sell raw ebi, but in Holland you can also buy the cooked ones, which are very tiny indeed; these are usually eaten as a side-dish or a garnish.

VINEGAR

The only kind of vinegar that I recall having seen in Indonesia is clear and colourless, and is called *cuka*. It is very widely used, however. The nearest to it in Britain is distilled malt vinegar. Do not use any kind of vinegar which has been specifically flavoured (e.g. with tarragon).

Spices, Fruits and Vegetables

This section is intended to provide a background of general knowledge about some of the ingredients that are used in Indonesian cooking. I hope that everyone will find something useful and interesting here, but it will perhaps be of special value to Westerners who are going to live or travel in southeast Asia. Anyone who is interested in importing Indonesian produce commercially may also find something helpful in these notes.

For botanical information I have relied heavily on two books: I. H. Burkill's magnificent *Dictionary of the Economic Products of the Malay Peninsula* and G. A. C. Herklots' *Vegetables in South-East Asia*, which is packed with information and also contains many line drawings of plants. I have tried my best to make sure that the facts given here are correct and relate to the plants that are commonly used in Indonesia.

Plants are listed here alphabetically by their Indonesian names. Cross-references are included for English names. In the entries themselves, the scientific names are given and sometimes names from different regions of Indonesia or from neighbouring countries. Here as elsewhere, the final *e* of some Indonesian words (e.g. peté) has been given an accent as a reminder that it should be pronounced.

ADAS, *Foeniculum vulgare* (Malaysia, ADAS PEDAS because of its sharp, minty flavour). This is fennel, which originated in the Mediterranean and the Middle East but must have been taken across Asia many centuries ago. In Indonesia we use the fresh young leaves and flowers (bunga adas) or the newly developed seed (biji adas), but not the bulb or blanched stems that are sold as fennel in an English greengrocer's. Indeed, we do not, as far as I know, earth-up or blanch the plant at all. (See also ADAS CINA and JINTEN MANIS; all these plants, or their seeds, contain either anethol or carvone, which accounts for a certain family resemblance among their different flavours. You would have to get well down into the molecular structure of these substances to appreciate very much difference between any two of them.)

ADAS CINA, *Anethum graveolens* ('Chinese adas'; also ADAS MANIS, 'sweet adas'). This, according to Burkill, is the English dill, but I suspect there is a good deal of confusion in Indonesia between dill and fennel (both called adas), just as there is between cumin and caraway (both called jinten). When you are shopping in the market, you are naturally more concerned with freshness and flavour than with fine botanical distinctions. All these plants are members of the *Umbelliferae* family, and all are 'stomachic and carminative'—that is, they help you to get rid of surplus wind.

ALMONDS see KENARI

ANISE see JINTEN MANIS

ASAM, *Tamarindus indica* (Malaysia, ASAM; also known as ASEM JAWA). This is the tamarind, whose English and botanical names are derived from Arabic *tamr-hindi*, 'Indian date'. Tamarinds and dates do not in fact resemble each other at all when they are growing, but the Arab and Persian traders used to buy the dark brown tamarind pulp from India and it evidently reminded them of the flesh of preserved dates. Fresh tamarind, extracted from the hard pods after they have been cracked open, is brown and sticky and contains large seeds which do no harm in cooking but should be removed before serving. Tamarind is still sold in today's supermarkets in blocks which are probably much like the ones the old Arab traders used to deal in. A block weighs about half a kilogram, and you simply break off as much as you need. However, 'solid' tamarind is normally used only when it has to be grilled or cooked over charcoal before it is added to the dish. If the recipe calls for this, break off a piece weighing about 30 g (1 oz) and either grill it, or heat it in a heavy iron pan, until all its surfaces are just a little charred. In all other cases, use tamarind water. Break off a piece from the block and put it in a little water; then squeeze and press it, so that the water becomes thick and brown.

Strain the water. Repeat this process until you have as much tamarind water as you need. As a guide, 30 g of tamarind (1 oz) makes about 300 ml of tamarind water (½ pint); if the recipe specifies thick tamarind water, use twice as much tamarind.

If you are buying tamarind in the tropics, you may prefer to buy it in the ripe pods, which should be brown and should crack under a good squeeze from your finger and thumb. But you can of course still buy the pulp in blocks, or—in Java at any rate—rolled into little black balls called *asem kawak*.

ASAM GELUGUR, *Garcinia atroviridis*. This is similar to Asam Kandis (q.v.), but the fruit is rather larger. To prepare it for use in cooking, it is thinly sliced and then dried in the sun. In this form, it can be bought in Holland and also in London, where, however, it is sometimes labelled 'Tamarind Slices'. In general, it may be found in Chinese groceries in all parts of the world blessed by their presence.

ASAM KANDIS, *Garcinia globulosa*; *G. nigrolineata*. This is a small, round, thin-skinned fruit, about a centimetre in diameter, which is often used in cooking instead of tamarind. It is easy to find in Indonesia, difficult or impossible in Europe. The pulp is sweet but the skin, which is the part used in cooking, is bitter. When the fruit is picked, it is split down the middle and the half-skins are dried in the sun so that what comes to market is

47

a hard, black, wrinkled fragment. It goes into the pot along with all the other ingredients, but it should, of course, be removed before serving. See also ASAM GELUGUR.

BANANA see PISANG

BEANS, BUTTER or LIMA see KACANG PAGAR

BEANS, FRENCH see KACANG BUNCIS

BEANS, GREEN see KACANG HIJAU

BEANS, SOYA see KACANG KEDELE

BELIMBING MANIS, *Averrhoa carambola.* This fruit has well-marked ridges growing along it from stem to base. 'Manis' means sweet, and some varieties of the fruit are sweet, but others need to be pretty heavily sugared. They are popular dessert fruit. The flesh is soft and juicy and the skin is tender, but the ridges are rather tough and are usually trimmed off with a knife.

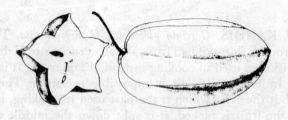

BELIMBING WULUH, *Averrhoa bilimbi*. The fruit is much smaller than belimbing manis, perfectly smooth and without ridges. It is definitely acid and is only used in cooking, rather like asam. Like some other rather bitter fruits, it can be boiled with a lot of sugar to make what we call *manisan*—'something sweet'. The sugar caramelizes and the fruit is then dried in the sun so that it becomes brownish, hard and candied.

BENGKUANG, *Pachyrrhizus erosus*; *P. angulatus* (in Java, also BESUSU). This is a sweetish-tasting tuber, sometimes given the English name of Yam-bean. It originated in Central and South America, and its Indonesian name is probably derived from a Mexican dialect name. It is a quick and easy plant to grow. The tubers are apt to be somewhat starchy but they are perfectly good to eat. The leaves and seeds, on the other hand, are both poisonous in any quantity. The tubers are often used in making Rujak (page 240), where the strong piquant sauce brings out what flavour they have.

BUNCIS see KACANG BUNCIS

CABÉ, *Capsicum annuum* (Malaysia and parts of Sumatra, CHABAI; Java, CABÉ or LOMBOK; see also CABÉ RAWIT on page 51). There is a good deal of confusion of names here, in English and in the Indonesian languages, but what we are talking about is generally clear enough: those long, thin, usually green or red chillis that all Indonesians love and most westerners dread because they are so fiercely hot in the mouth. (Not all westerners, however; I once lost a raw-chilli-eating contest to a Scotsman.) As a rule, the fatter the chilli, the less hot, and even in the hottest kinds most of the really pungent flavour is in the seeds.

For cooking, we need to distinguish between green chillis (*cabé hijau*) and red chillis (*cabé merah*). These can both be bought easily enough in most places. Red chillis, either fresh or dried, are crushed and used to give body to a hot sauce. The crushing (with ulek-ulek and cobek—see page 35) is hard work, and if you have a tender skin or a cut or scratched finger the juice of the chilli can be uncomfortable. You can often, instead, buy ready-pounded red chillis, with a little salt, under the name of Sambal Ulek; or you can, if you develop a taste for it, make your own sambal ulek in larger quantities by stuffing red chillis into a food processor as if you were mincing meat. Take out the seeds and chop the chillis before putting them in, and wash the processor very thoroughly afterwards. Alternatively, make sambal ulek in a liquidizer, adding a little water. Put in a little salt later as a preservative.

Red chillis can also be powdered, and in Britain one can buy tins of chilli powder almost anywhere. Green chillis, however, cannot be powdered, and in this book I have mostly suggested cutting them into very thin slices. In Indonesia, red chillis are also crushed, to release the maximum flavour, and much larger quantities are used than I would dare to suggest here.

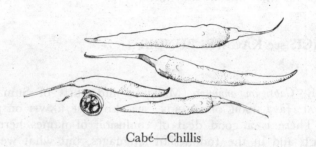

Cabé—Chillis

Cayenne pepper should come from the fruit of *Capsicum annuum* or *C. frutescens* (cabé rawit, below), but the powder that is sold in Britain as Cayenne pepper is nowhere near as hot as I think it should be; it is, as Burkill says, 'very easily adulterated'.

CABÉ RAWIT, *Capsicum frutescens* (Malaysia, CABAI BURONG, 'bird pepper'; Indonesia, CABÉ RAWIT OR LOMBOK RAWIT). These are much smaller than the red and green chillis mentioned on the previous page (see *cabé*) and are consequently much hotter. It seems that the capsicum family was one of Columbus' first worthwhile discoveries in the New World; seeds and cuttings were taken back across the Atlantic at once, and the Portuguese soon transplanted them to their new colonial possessions in India and south-east Asia. The Dutch later pinned onto them one of the Mexican names, *chilli*, so that the East India Company's customers would not confuse this new spice with pepper. A variety of capsicum (*C. baccatum*, or *C. minimum*) often appears in English greengrocers' shops as a neat little ornamental houseplant with bright red or yellow peppers growing profusely on it. Sometimes they are thin cones, sometimes egg-shaped or almost spherical. The thin cones are nearly as hot as cabé rawit and my greengrocer no longer looks startled when I ask him for another ornamental pepper-tree 'because I've eaten all the last lot'.

CANDLENUT see KEMIRI

CAPSICUM see CABÉ and CABÉ RAWIT

CASHEW see JAMBU METE

CASSAVA see UBI KAYU

CAYENNE PEPPER see CABÉ

CENGKEH, *Eugenia aromatica*. Cloves. Originally they grew only on a few islands in the Moluccas, in eastern Indonesia; the Portuguese started to plant the trees more widely, but when the Dutch took over they reversed this policy and it was not until the late eighteenth century that large numbers of seedlings were transplanted to Malaya, Mauritius, Zanzibar and South America. But trade in cloves was well developed centuries before Europeans ever came to the South China Sea. They were in demand, not only as spices, but as medicine and for sweetening the breath. For much of Chinese history, it was highly inadvisable to appear before the Emperor without a clove or two in your mouth. The Javanese mix cloves with tobacco to make *kretek* cigarettes; for anyone who has lived in Java, the smell of burning cloves must be one of the most nostalgic and evocative of all. The word *kretek* (with short, 'grunted' *e*'s instead of the full *e*'s of the cigarettes), is however, quite a common onomatopoeic Javanese word to describe anything that crackles, creaks or splutters, which the fragments of clove embedded in a burning cigarette certainly do.

CERME, *Cicca acida*. This is a small green fruit, hardly as big as a grape, which has an acid taste and can be used for making a kind of jam. Its main use, however, is as a flavouring in cooked dishes, and for this it is generally picked before it is fully ripe.

CHILLI see CABE

CHINESE CABBAGE see SAWI

CINNAMON see KAYU MANIS

CITRUS see JERUK

CLOVES see CENGKEH

CORIANDER see KETUMBAR

CUCUMBER see KETIMUN

CUMIN see JINTEN

DAUN JERUK PURUT see JERUK PURUT

DAUN MANGKOK, *Nothopanax scutellarium* (Sumatra, TAPAK LEMAN*). The Indonesian name means literally 'leaves like cups', and in the old days they were used to hold food as well as being eaten themselves. They are usually cooked with dishes such as Gulai Otak (page 157). In Europe, a good substitute is curly kale.

DAUN PANDAN, *Pandanus odorus*. The Pandanus, or screw-pine, family is a tough-looking collection of plants, with long, broad, fibrous leaves armed with spines, prickles, hooks and other weapons. Their principal use is in making mats, brushes, ropes and so forth. It may seem surprising that such plants should be allowed anywhere near a kitchen, but some species have edible fruits, and Australian aborigines are said to extract

* i.e. 'Solomon's footprint'—though this name is given to other plants also.

and roast the seeds, 'rather laboriously', as Burkill says. In Indonesia, however, it is the young leaves of *P. odorus* which are used by cooks to add a distinctive aromatic flavouring and in some cases a delicate green colour. You buy daun pandan in the market in small square packets, the leaf having been chopped into lengths of about 5 cm; you may get 20 or more pieces in a packet. If you cut a fresh leaf from the garden it should give you at least 10 of these little oblongs. There is no need to trim off the leaf-edges, which are smooth and unarmoured.

DAUN TALAS see TALAS

DAUN SALAM see SALAM

DILL see ADAS CINA

DUKU, *Lansium domesticum*. This is a small, thick-skinned yellowish fruit, which you can easily open and peel with your thumbnail. Inside are a number of whitish segments, the larger of which contain seeds, although the seeds are usually so small and soft that you do not notice them in eating. They are pleasant, quite juicy, rather unexciting fruit. What the Javanese call *langsat* are very similar, but have slightly tougher seeds that need to be spat out.

DURIAN, *Durio zibethinus* (Java, DUREN). No other fruit arouses so much curiosity and even nervousness among westerners in South-East Asia, and I must say that Indonesians, too, have a special regard for durian. It is a big fruit, to start with, not as big as the nangka, which it slightly resembles, but about the shape and size of an over-inflated rugby football, set all over with pyramidal spines that give it, with its khaki-green colouring, the look of something that might go off at any moment. It grows on high trees, anything up to 30 metres tall, and when ripe it lets go and comes crashing to the ground. With luck, the impact of its fall splits the outer casing lengthwise in four places, and you have only to apply firm downward pressure to split the whole fruit wide open. A convenient place to do this is the floor of a car or truck, and you will see drivers using the right foot for the brake and the throttle and the left for opening a durian as they speed along. What makes the durian so famous, or notorious, is the combination of its taste and its smell. Most Europeans say that the smell is nauseating but the taste, if you can nerve yourself, exquisite and indescribable. I think this is too simple. The flavour is indeed difficult to describe in English; this is partly because the flavour of each individual fruit changes rapidly as it matures, and partly because, since almost every tree is grown from seed, every tree has its own characteristic flavour. The durian is indeed exceptionally complex in its make-up of chemical substances, and these interact rapidly in what must be a perfect hell's kitchen in the ripe flesh. The smell of durian I do not find disgusting, and nor do European friends of mine who have become accustomed to it, but it does become a tiresome smell if you have too much of it. You could take a nangka as an inside passenger on a Javanese country bus, and no one would object; if you took a basket of durian, you might be asked to put them on the roof-rack (where, of course, there would be more passengers, but also more fresh air). Smell or no smell, Burkill records that the kings of Burma organized relays of runners to bring durian post-haste to the palace at Ava, which was too far north for the tree to grow. Malay tribesmen, more fortunately placed, set up camp at a respectful distance from any promising-looking tree they chanced upon in the jungle, and waited for the fruit to thud to earth. In my opinion, durian should be eaten when the flesh is still firm but not too hard. Yellowish fruit taste better than the pale white ones. In West Sumatra, we make a most beautiful Sambal Durian from overripe fruit and crushed chillis. Many people would say that durian should be kept, like cheese, until it is beginning to rot. As it matures, this formidable fruit ferments and produces alcohol, so that it is possible to become mildly drunk on it. Really hard cases keep it until it has become maggoty. Burkill says that connoisseurs will not touch it once the flavour of garlic has become pronounced. I have never noticed any hint of garlic in a durian, but it may be in there somewhere. Don't throw the seeds away; they taste nice when they are boiled, or you could even grow your own durian tree.

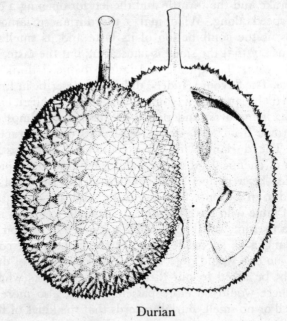

Durian

EGG-PLANT see TERUNG GELATIK

FENNEL see ADAS

GALINGALE see LAOS

GINGER see JAHE

GRAPEFRUIT see JERUK BALI

GROUNDNUTS see KACANG TANAH

GUAVA see JAMBU BATU

JACKFRUIT see NANGKA

JAHE, *Zingiber officinale*. This is good old-fashioned Ginger, whose English and Latin names both derive from the Sanskrit *singabera*. This plant has been cultivated, cooked with and traded in all around the Indian Ocean and the South China Sea for many centuries.

JAMBU. This is a rather confusing general word for several quite different types of fruit. Why they all got lumped together I am not quite sure, but they must have something in common, since it is regarded as perfectly sensible to walk into a shop and say, 'I want to buy some jambu,' though the shopkeeper will then have to ask you which kind you are after. Burkill says that *jambu* is a Sanskritic word, and that among the Malaysians it tends, on the whole, to indicate a cultivated plant (especially of the genus *Eugenia*) rather than a wild one. Here are some of the commoner jambu:

JAMBU AIR, *Eugenia aquea* ('water jambu'; also JAMBU AIR MAWAR, 'rose water jambu'). This tree bears white or pinkish fruits, very juicy and slightly scented.

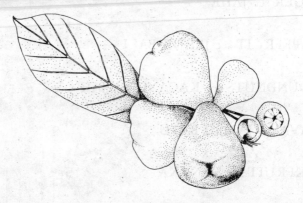

JAMBU BATU, *Psidium guajava* ('stone jambu'; also JAMBU KLUTUK, etcetera). This is the guava, though not all jambu batu are as pink inside as the guavas I have seen imported into England; many are greenish-white. Like many people, I prefer the fruit when it is not quite ripe and is still crisp, like an apple.

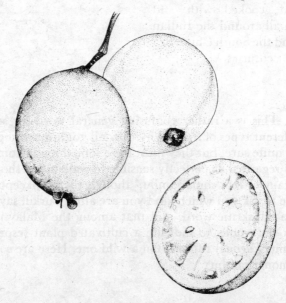

JAMBU MERAH, *Eugenia malaccensis* ('red jambu'; also JAMBU BOL, JAMBU SUSU, etcetera). This is a thick-fleshed, rather sharp-tasting fruit, a common ingredient of Rujak (page 242).

JAMBU METÉ, *Anacardium occidentale* (many regional and dialect names). This is the fruit of a Central American tree whose English name, cashew, comes from the original Tupi Indian word. The cashew nut (kacang meté) grows at the end of, or underneath, the jambu, which is a rather bloated pear-like object. It tastes bitter but is good to eat raw, e.g. in Rujak.

JERUK. This is the general word used in Java and Bali for all citrus fruits. In Sumatra and West Malaysia they are called *limau*, apparently from the Portuguese version of the Arabic word which also gave us our own 'lemon'. Citrus trees seem to have evolved in the warm dry areas of Asia, where they developed the knack of storing water against long periods of drought, but all the varieties we know today are the result of hundreds of generations of selection and breeding. Although the citrus began in semi-desert places, many of its descendants grow well in wet tropical conditions, and in Indonesia we make full use of them. Five of the most important kinds are described below

JERUK BALI, *Citrus maxima, C. decumana*. I have bought these in London under the name of Pomelo, which I assumed was a trade-name invented by Jaffa until I looked it up in the *Oxford English Dictionary*. In fact Pomelo as a species-name is first cited in 1858, but long before that the same fruit was called the shaddock (after a sea-captain who introduced it to the West Indies), the forbidden fruit (a more interesting name, but the *Oxford English Dictionary* gives no reason for it) or the pomple-moose (under this heading, the *OED* offers a fascinating essay in colonial-linguistic history). *Pamplemousse* is, of course, the French for grapefruit, and jeruk bali are indeed the direct ancestors of grapefruit and can be eaten in the same way. Most of them are white-fleshed, but pink-fleshed are also quite common. Regardless of colour, they vary enormously in sweetness. We had two trees in our garden in central Java which looked exactly alike; one produced delicious fruit, the other almost unbearably sour.

JERUK MANIS, *Citrus aurantium, C. nobilis,* or *C. sinensis* (also known simply as JERUK; another Javanese name is JERUK KEPROK). When you are shopping in the pasar you do not worry overmuch about Latin names or fine distinctions between species. *Manis* means 'sweet', and these oranges are very much what a European, brought up on produce from Israel, South Africa, North Africa or Spain, understands by the word 'orange'. Many of them, however, have thin, loose skins and are closer to a tangerine or a clementine.

JERUK NIPIS, *C. aurantifolia.* These are limes, or something very similar. They are perfect little globes, bright green, with a thin hard skin. They are, of course, very sour, but fresh lime juice, with iced water and sugar, is one of the most delicious soft drinks you can imagine in the sticky heat of a Jakarta afternoon. It is called simply *air jeruk* (*air* = 'water'). Lime juice with salt, honey, boiling water and a little root ginger (but no sugar) is excellent for a sore throat or a cough.

JERUK PURUT, *C. hystrix.* The only part of this plant that is usually used in cooking is the leaf, *daun jeruk purut,* one or two of which are put into many of the dishes described in this book. They should be removed before serving. Dried leaves are marketed by Conimex. The English name for this leaf is Kaffir lime leaf. Many Chinese and Indian shops in Britain sell 'curry leaves', which are similar but not the same thing. They, or bay-leaves, can be substituted for Kaffir lime leaves, but bear in mind that bay-leaves have a stronger flavour. Use one bay-leaf instead of, say, two or three Kaffir lime leaves.

The fruit of the Kaffir lime is small and contains more pips than juice, but the juice, if you can get enough of it, is good for soft drinks. It is also very good in a sambal, as is the juice of jeruk nipis.

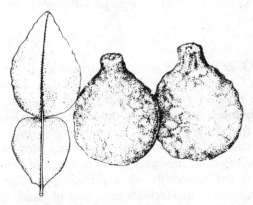

Jeruk purut—Kaffir lime

JERUK SITRUN is a greenish-yellow fruit, a little larger than jeruk nipis, and is more or less what anyone would recognize as a lemon. But it has less flavour than a lemon, and where lemons are mentioned in the recipes in this book you can assume that we would use jeruk nipis in Indonesia. It follows that you can use lime instead of lemon if you wish; but if you do, remember that limes are a good deal more acid.

JINTEN, *Cuminum cyminum* (Malaysia, JINTAN PUTEH, 'white cumin'). The ground-up seeds of cumin have been used all over the Old World for many centuries as a seasoning, although its flavour is not especially pleasant and it should be used very sparingly. Burkill refers to its 'bed-bug-like odour', which is not encouraging. I have heard that in parts of Indonesia the seeds are roasted whole, like coriander, but I doubt if this would be advisable with any of the dishes which are described in this book.

JINTEN MANIS, *Pimpinella anisum* ('sweet jinten'). Anise came to Java before AD 1200, though it is not certain whether it was actually grown there at that time or imported from India. Like other useful *Umbelliferae* that we use in cooking (see JINTEN, ADAS, ADAS CINA), jinten manis provides seeds containing an aromatic oil.

KACANG BOGOR, *Voandzeia subterranea*. These are called Bambara Groundnuts by Herklots, and their home is Africa. *Voandzeia* resembles *Arachis* (*kacang tanah*, peanuts) in that its flowers dip towards the soil and the seeds or nuts develop underground; the pods and nuts themselves also look rather like peanuts, though there is usually only one nut to each pod. *Voandzeia*, however, produces no oil to speak of. These nuts are delicious to eat, especially when still unripe, either roasted or boiled, and eaten, as Herklots says, 'out of hand' or as a side-dish. When I lived in Bogor as a child, I used to buy a screw of banana-leaf with a few cents' worth of nuts in it from one of the vendors who were to be found in any of the main streets. Indeed, you can buy these nuts anywhere in Indonesia, and the name 'Bogor' probably indicates only that the first trees were imported as specimens to the famous botanical gardens behind the Palace.

KACANG BUNCIS, *Phaseolus vulgaris*. This is what any English gardener would immediately recognize as a French bean, and any French gardener as a *haricot vert*, though there are, of course, many varieties and cultivars. Although the generic name, *Phaseolus*, was applied by the Romans to all sorts of beans, *P. vulgaris* was unknown in the Old World until it was brought from the Americas. The word buncis is just an Indonesian spelling of the Dutch *boontjes*—little beans.

KACANG HIJAU, *Phaseolus aureus* (sometimes called by an Indian name, mung beans). These 'green beans' are used more than any other kind for growing bean sprouts, and you can grow your own if you wish; they are ready for eating after 4 to 6 days in a warm room, and need only a well-soaked flannel, thick rag, or even paper towel to grow on. Soak them overnight in cold water, and spread a single layer of beans evenly over the growing surface. The requirements now are moisture, warmth, fresh air, and darkness. A closely woven basket with a cloth over it is excellent, and I put mine in the cupboard under the stairs, which is, of course, the warmest place in any English house because no one ever goes there. Sprinkle a little more water over the seedlings each day or so. After 4 days you will probably be able to take a harvest of the more precocious bean sprouts, leaving the rest another day or two to develop. Whether you grow your own or buy them in the greengrocer's, remove any seed-husks that are clinging to the stems and trim off the little brown root before cooking or serving raw—it won't do you any harm if you leave it on, but the dish looks better without. Trimming bean sprouts takes time and patience, but can be a restful occupation, properly regarded.

There are plenty of ways to eat mature green beans, always after they have been shelled. You can soak them overnight, boil them in salted water for 20–30 minutes, and then deep-fry them (with a little chilli, if you like) to make a savoury snack. You can make Rempeyek Kacang with them, using the recipe on page 227 but with beans instead of peanuts. Green beans also make a very nourishing porridge, which I am told was once used as a staple diet on sea voyages—the equivalent perhaps of ship's biscuits, but softer and a little better-tasting. Soak the beans overnight, then boil for an hour or more (2 volumes of water to one of beans) with a little salt and sugar, until the beans are mushy and there is no more surplus liquid. If you want this a little more de luxe, stir in some very thick santen just before you take the pan off the heat.

KACANG KEDELE, *Glycine maximus*. This is the soy or soya bean, which the world's food experts tell us we are going to have to get used to eating in much larger quantities as other staple foods get dearer. There are over 2000 varieties, but the only two the cook needs to know about are the two leading groups— yellow beans and black beans—and even these two colours have often been lost sight of by the time the processed vegetable reaches the shop or the market. Let us be clear about one thing, however: it is not essential for soya beans to be fermented or otherwise transformed before they can be eaten. Fresh beans, boiled in the pod and then shelled, are a popular and cheap food in countries where they are grown.

However, exported beans are usually dried before they travel. In any case, plain boiled beans do not taste very interesting, and they are somewhat indigestible. Although they are packed with protein, 20 per cent of this goes straight through you unless some way is found to encourage your system to assimilate the stuff. For all these reasons, the future of the soya bean lies in what can be made out of it. The western food manufacturer's answer is to create imitation meat and other familiar-looking things by the use of various additives. The Asian way has always been, generally speaking, to ferment soya beans, using micro-organisms to break down the indigestible substances and at the same time help to impart a variety of characteristic and attractive flavours: see the introduction to the section on Tempe and Tahu (page 210), and the notes on Kecap (page 42) and Tauco (page 44).

In Indonesia we also extract a kind of artificial milk from the yellow beans, which is almost as nutritious as cow's milk (one manufacturer dehydrates it and markets it under the brand name of Saridele). Bean sprouts can also be grown from soya bean seeds, though we usually prefer *kacang hijau* for this.

KACANG METÉ see JAMBU METÉ

KACANG PAGAR, *Phaseolus lunatus* (also KARA in Javanese). These are Lima beans or (in some varieties at any rate) butter beans—the flat, white kind. 'Pagar' means a fence or hedge, and these beans often are grown in the hedges around village gardens. The beans need to be shelled and then well-boiled to get rid of any toxic acid that they may contain, although you would have to eat an awful lot of beans to suffer any ill-effects. We often make them part of a meat-and-vegetable stew, which cooks them very thoroughly. In my experience, however, eating too many kacang pagar can give you a headache—exactly the same dire consequence that Burkill threatens peanut-eaters with.

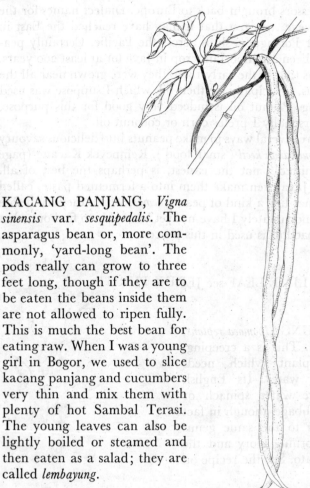

KACANG PANJANG, *Vigna sinensis* var. *sesquipedalis*. The asparagus bean or, more commonly, 'yard-long bean'. The pods really can grow to three feet long, though if they are to be eaten the beans inside them are not allowed to ripen fully. This is much the best bean for eating raw. When I was a young girl in Bogor, we used to slice kacang panjang and cucumbers very thin and mix them with plenty of hot Sambal Terasi. The young leaves can also be lightly boiled or steamed and then eaten as a salad; they are called *lembayung*.

KACANG TANAH, *Arachis hypogaea.* Remember that *kacang* in Indonesian means both bean and nut. The name of this one translates into English quite literally as 'ground-nut', so called, of course, because the flowers of *Arachis* have the remarkable habit of diving back towards the soil and burying their seedpods in it. Like so many other useful plants, the ground-nut or peanut evolved in Central America and the basin of the Parana River; it was one of the first prizes that Columbus' men and their successors brought back to Europe. Dialect names for the plant, however, suggest that it may have reached the East in Spanish or Portuguese ships across the Pacific. Certainly peanuts have been an important crop in Java for at least 200 years. Raffles says that in the early 1800s they were grown near all the large towns, principally for their oil, which I suppose was used for cooking. Peanut oil is indeed very good for this purpose, though personally I prefer corn or coconut oil.

There are several ways to make peanuts into delicious savoury snacks or *makanan kecil* ('small food'). Rempeyek Kacang (page 227), admittedly not the easiest, is perhaps the best of all. People in Java even make them into a fermented paste, called *oncom*, rather like a kind of peanut *tempe*, which they fry before eating. Unfortunately I have not yet been able to find out what strain of bacillus is used in this process.

KAFFIR LIME LEAF see JERUK PURUT

KANGKUNG, *Ipomoea reptans,*
I. aquatica. This is a creeping,
trailing plant which needs
plenty of water. Its English
names are water spinach or
swamp cabbage, though in fact
it belongs to the same genus
as the morning glory and the
sweet potato. See the recipe on
page 203.

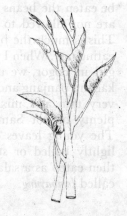

KAYU MANIS, *Cinnamonum zeylanicum.* The Indonesian name for cinnamon means simply 'sweet wood', although it is not the wood but the bark that contains the flavour. The neat little rolls that you find on the supermarket spice-rack are the innermost layer of this bark, which is scraped off, cut up into squares, and allowed to curl up naturally. In cooking, the rolls or quills should be removed before the dish is served.

KECIPIR, *Psophocarpus tetragonolobus* (Malaysia, KACANG BELIM-BING, etcetera). This is a rather unusual bean, which seems to have been brought eastwards by Arab traders out of Africa. Each pod has four wavy-edged wings growing along its length, giving it a distinctly dressy appearance, like a French bean going to a party. The young beans are excellent if you boil or steam them, in the pod, for about 4 minutes, and eat them whole like *mange tout* peas (larger ones can be cut into convenient lengths before cooking). Kecipir make a good substitute for French beans in Urap (page 206).

KEDONDONG, *Spondias cytherea.* This looks a bit like a cross between a plum and a green apple. It is about the size and shape of a hen's egg, and you peel it, like an apple, with a knife. The flesh is firm, and in the centre there is a single, spiny seed. You can cut up a kedondong like an apple to eat it raw, and it has a pleasantly sour flavour. Stewed, it makes a very passable imitation of apple sauce to eat with roast pork.

KELENGKENG, *Nephelium lit-chi.* Spell it how you will, the lychee will never quite live down its reputation as a syrupy but safe dessert in westernized Chinese restaurants. It deserves a better fate, for fresh lychees are delicious. They came originally from South China, and I do not know how they got their Indonesian name of kelengkeng. See also RAMBUTAN.

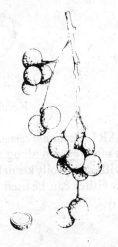

67

KEMIRI, *Aleurites moluccana, Macadamia ternifolia* (also BUAH KERAS). This is a kind of nut, about as big as a walnut, which in English is usually called a candlenut (the name I use) or Macadamia nut (the more official term). It has a very hard shell, and a waxy, white kernel which really can be used to make 'candles'.

The tree which bears the nuts is a native of Australia, where the aborigines have no doubt enjoyed the nuts since long ago. But it was only in the latter part of the nineteenth century that it was 'discovered' and exploited. Many Australian homesteads have such trees, to provide shade, ornament and food. The candlenut tree has also been introduced to South Africa, the West Indies, parts of the southern United States and Hawaii. It is in Hawaii that production of the Macadamia nuts, as they are known there, is most highly developed and on the biggest scale.

In cooking, kemiri are among those troublesome ingredients which are needed only in small quantities, but which are indispensable and irreplaceable. Luckily you can now find them in specialist food shops almost everywhere. They are available in cans or in sealed plastic packs. Kemiri bought in Europe usually come in one of these forms and have always been shelled before shipment, because the shell weighs almost as much as the kernel (perhaps even more, in some varieties) and it would be silly to transport it. Packets often contain broken kernels—not surprising in view of the great force required to crack the shells. In any recipe, '3 kemiri' means 3 whole kernels or the equivalent in fragments.

Kemiri—Candlenuts

KENARI, *Canarium commune*. This is a tall tree that gives shade and is often grown along the sides of country roads. It produces nuts with rather oily kernels that look and taste very like almonds, so that either can be used as a substitute for the other in cooking.

KENCUR, *Kaempferia galanga* (Malaysia and West Java, CIKUR or similar). This is the aromatic root or rhizome of a herb that grows in many tropical countries. Like laos, it is usually dried and cut into small pieces. It must be used very sparingly in cooking because the flavour is extremely strong.

KETIMUN, *Cucumis sativus*. Most Indonesian cucumbers are somewhat shorter than 'ordinary' European ones, but they have a good flavour, only marred from time to time by the bitterness of the *getah*, or juice. To get rid of this, cut off the last inch of cucumber at both ends and rub the cut surfaces vigorously together for a few seconds. This will bring out the whitish getah, which you then wash off.

KETUMBAR, *Coriandrum sativum*. Coriander. The spice used in cooking is the ripened seed, but the leaves are very good to eat raw; they look like *seledri* (continental or flat-leaved parsley), but they taste and smell strongly of coriander.

KLUWEK, *Pangium edule* (Java, PAKEM; West Java, PACUNG, etcetera; Sumatra, KAPAYANG). This is a large tree which produces almost nothing that is of any use to anybody except for its large, handsome seeds. These can be processed to give a good cooking-oil, they can be eaten by themselves if they are carefully prepared, and they are among the ingredients of several fine dishes (e.g. Rawon, page 131), to which they give a distinctive flavour and a denser colour. Don't be put off by Burkill's notes on the poisonous nature of these seeds. By the time they reach market, either in the East or in Holland, they have been made completely safe, and I have used them in family cooking here in England many times without the slightest ill-effect. To prevent the poison (which is hydrocyanic acid) from forming, or to break it down after it has formed, we either boil the seeds several times, soaking them in running water in between, or, as my grandmother used to do in Sumatra, bury them for 10 or 15 minutes deep in the embers of a wood cooking-fire, where the

seeds will become very hot but will not actually scorch. Then
we crush and remove the shells and pound the seeds thoroughly
in a large mortar. Note, by the way, that kluwek bought in
Holland have been dried for the journey, and must be soaked
for 30 minutes or boiled until soft before you start trying to
grind them up. The inside of the nut is very dark red, frequently
almost black.

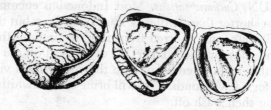

In case, like my husband, you have jumped to the alluring
conclusion that this is the famous Upas-Tree of Java, let me tell
you that it is not. The Upas, or poison-tree, which enjoyed such
an inflated reputation in nineteenth-century Europe, still grows
in the tropics under its Latin name of *Antiaris toxicaria* and
various Malaysian and Indonesian names. See Burkill for a
fascinating study of its properties and public relations history. I
myself have never come across one of these trees, but I believe
that *A. toxicaria* is emphatically not for eating.

KUNYIT, *Curcuma domestica* (Java, KUNIR). Turmeric. Many
of the dialect names for this plant resemble the Indonesian word
'kuning', which means yellow, and certainly yellowness is one
of the most obvious characteristics of turmeric. Yellow is traditionally a sacred colour in the East and India, and Nasi Kuning
(Yellow Rice, page 102) is still thought of as a dish for celebrations. 'Curry,' says Burkill magisterially, 'is impossible without
turmeric,' and it imparts not only its colour but also its pleasing,
pungent flavour to quite a number of Indonesian dishes. The
part you eat is the rhizome, which looks pretty much like ginger,
but in Britain it is, I think, always sold·in dried or powdered
form. If you can get fresh kunyit, cut off a small piece, peel it,
and crush it with the other spices, garlic, etcetera in your cobek.

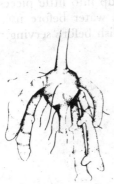

Kunyit—Turmeric

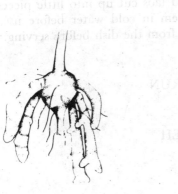

Laos—Galingale

LAOS, *Languas galanga* (in Malaysia and elsewhere, LENGKUAS or variant spellings). This is usually translated into English as galingale, again with many variant spellings. Tennyson made it grow in the land of the Lotos-Eaters, no doubt because he liked the sound of the word. The *Oxford English Dictionary* traces the descent of the name from Chinese via Arabic, and says that galingale is the aromatic root of plants of the genera *Alpinia* and *Kaempferia*, 'formerly much used in medicine and cookery'. 'Formerly' is correct perhaps in English usage, since the Dictionary's earliest citation of 'galingale' dates from about AD 1000 and occurs in a recipe in *Saxon Leechdoms* that used pepper, galingale and ginger.

In the East, however, laos is still commonly used in cooking, though I am not so sure about its medicinal properties. Possibly they belong to a related species. Burkill quotes an old treatise on the care of elephants, which says that laos is good for sick elephants, particularly for one that has gone off its food. He also explains why the name *Alpinia* will not do for the genus; for *Kaempferia galanga*, see KENCUR.

71

Laos can be bought quite easily anywhere where there are oriental grocery stores. The rhizomes of the plant are dried and then powdered. You can sometimes also find, at any rate in London, packets of dried laos cut up into little pieces just right for cooking. Soak them in cold water before use, and remember to remove them from the dish before serving.

LEMON see **JERUK SITRUN**

LEMON GRASS see **SEREH**

LIME see **JERUK NIPIS**

LOMBOK see **CABÉ**

LYCHEE see **KELENGKENG**

MACADAMIA NUT see **KEMIRI**

MANGGA, *Mangifera indica.* Mangoes came originally from India, but have been cultivated all over Indonesia for a long time, wherever the climate is dry enough to give them a chance to fruit. They need no introduction to Western readers, though I cannot say that the imported mangoes I have bought in London have really been worth all that money. There is no substitute for fresh ones, and to my mind the best are from Indramayu or Ceribon in West Java. They need not be ripe; unripe mangoes, apart from making the best chutney, can be cooked like vegetables or simply sliced and served raw in Rujak (page 240).

MANGGIS, *Garcinia mangostana*. The mangosteen: a relation of Asam Kandis, but larger (about as big as an apple) and with a deliciously sweet white flesh inside a thin, hard skin. As with most members of this family, the skin is extremely bitter, and the brownish-yellow fluid that it contains will stain anything it touches irredeemably—so break the fruit open with care.

MANGO see MANGGA

MANGOSTEEN see MANGGIS

MELINJO, *Gnetum gnemon* (also BELINJO). This is a big tree, up to about 20 metres tall, which produces small, round, red or yellow fruit. The soft husks can be cut and peeled off and are occasionally used in cooking, though personally I find them too chewy to be attractive. The nut inside, which looks like an acorn, can in turn be cracked open to reveal a small white kernel, *buah melinjo*, which is added to certain vegetable dishes, particularly Sayur Asam (page 201). Its most important use, however, is in making Emping (page 215), a delicious nutty-flavoured crisp. The kernels are beaten out flat, dried in the sun, and fried. All Europeans love emping; they go well with drinks, or with the meal itself, and are the accustomed garnish for

Gado-Gado (page 196). The young leaves of this tree are also eaten, as the main ingredient of Sayur Asam.

MERICA, *Piper nigrum* (also LADA HITAM, LADA PUTIH). This Indonesian word is pronounced m'*reach*-a, and is straight from Sanskrit. Pepper has been known in the islands at least since the time of the great Hindu empire of Srivijaya, for it was probably one of the commodities of the good life brought by the earliest traders from India, though whether the traders themselves were Indians or Indonesians is something the historians have not yet agreed on.

NANGKA, *Artocarpus integra, A. champeden* (Sumatra, CEMPEDAK). From what Burkill says, the difference between the two species is not reflected in the local names that we give to the fruit. Botanically and linguistically, I am sure he is sound, although I cannot agree with him that the flavour of the jackfruit is 'mawkishly sweet and mousy'. Jackfruit not only smell and taste good, but they look imposing as well: up to 50 kg in weight, irregular in shape, and covered with blunt, flat spines like little pyramids. See the drawing on page 168.

You can eat ripe jackfruit for dessert, but the unripe flesh is also cut up and cooked as a vegetable and is the principal ingredient in Gudeg (page 168). The seeds, boiled and eaten as a snack, are surprisingly filling. If you cut up a jackfruit yourself, beware of the juice (*getah*); it will stick to your hands, and it stains fabrics past hope of cleaning.

Preparing nangka for cooking. Use a small green unripe one, weighing a kilo or so; they are not all giants. Split it open with a sharp knife, cutting it lengthwise into four. It has a fairly hard core down the centre, which should be cut out and thrown away, but the unripe fruit has no seeds. The flesh is somewhat fibrous, with the fibres clustering around what will eventually become the seeds, or would if the fruit was allowed to mature. Cut off the skin in thick chunks, as if you were peeling a pineapple. Then slice the flesh medium-thin, cutting across the long axis of the fruit. Scrape off as much as possible of the gluey *getah* from your hands with a knife before you start washing them. If you are making Gudeg, boil the slices of nangka for 5 minutes with a little salt, then carry on with the recipe as shown on page 168. (A further refinement in the initial boiling is to add a single *daun jati*, or teak leaf, which gives the fruit a fresh, reddish colour.) If you are cooking nangka by itself as a vegetable, see the recipe for Gulai Nangka on page 202. You can, by the way, usually buy nangka already prepared for you in the average market-place: cut into quadrants, peeled, sometimes even sliced and boiled, and all wrapped up in banana leaves to keep everything clean. In the West, canned nangka (the green unripe kind) is fine for cooking with.

NENAS, *Ananas comosus*. Like many good things that grow in South-East Asia, pineapples were cultivated long ago by the Indians of tropical America and were carried by colonizers to anywhere else where they could be made to grow—including European greenhouses, where fresh ones were cosseted into becoming expensive gifts for royalty. Commercial growers in the tropics quickly developed races and varieties with the characteristics they wanted for the market; the first cannery in Singapore was operating by the late 1880s. But even big business cannot spoil the pineapple; it remains a favourite fruit for almost everyone, and succeeds somehow in being both commonplace and exotic at the same time. It is particularly good as a dessert fruit because it contains chemicals that aid digestion. Unripe fruit, indeed, are said to do this to the extent of being violently purgative, but I have known many Javanese eat them as part of a dish of Rujak with no ill-effects. In Java, the best pineapples are those from Bogor.

NUTMEG see PALA

ORANGE see JERUK MANIS

OYONG, *Luffa acutangula*, *L. cylindrica* (Malaysia, Sulawesi, etcetera, PETOLA; West Java, EMES). From the botanist's point of view these are two distinct species, but for the cook they are virtually indistinguishable, because the fruit must be eaten while still very young. As it grows older, *L. acutangula* develops little ribs or ridges along its length, while *L. cylindrica* remains smooth. Both have a fibrous inner structure, which hardens with age, but it is the 'skeleton' of *L. cylindrica* which is easier to separate from the surrounding pulp, so that this species provides, or used to provide, bath-loofahs on a commercial scale. The fruit of both species becomes bitter and strongly purgative when fully grown, and you are not likely to find any on sale which are more than about 20 cm (8 in) long.

The plant is a kind of climbing cucumber. The Arabs call it *luff*, which obviously gives us our botanical and English names, and there is a great confusion of regional and dialect names all over South-East Asia. I think *oyong* was originally a word in the Jakarta dialect, but it seems to be quite generally used in Central and East Java also.

PALA, *Myristica fragrans*. The nutmeg probably originated in eastern Indonesia, but it was carried westward as soon as trade of any sort got going and it had apparently reached Europe by about AD 600. Burkill gives, as he does for many other fruits and spices, a fascinating review of its commercial history, and a pretty bloody story it is. Indonesia has paid heavily, over the centuries, for the richness of her spice islands. Ironically, we do not value nutmegs for cooking as highly as Arabs and Europeans seem to; for us, their medicinal uses are more important. Among other effects, they are alleged to be aphrodisiac, though I suspect this might be said of most foods. We use nutmeg occasionally in cooking, and we also make a very agreeable kind of candied sweetmeat, with a gingery taste, from the flesh that surrounds the nutmeg itself and the red 'cage' of mace. Burkill says that this *manisan pala* used to be exported to Europe; I wish it still was.

PAPAYA, *Carica papaya* (Java, KATES). The Spanish introduced these to the East from Central America, and now they grow everywhere, both wild and cultivated. The flesh, with its orange-pink colour and rather bland sweetness, is certainly very agreeable to eat, though I think one can grow tired of it. The leaves and flowers, however, are more interesting. The male flowers are good for Urap (page 206), and the young leaves are better still; Javanese *urap daun kates* is well worth trying. Burkill says the flowers, fruit and leaves contain papain, which helps to tenderize meat and has many medicinal properties. He doesn't mention, however, that the juice of young leaves can be drunk as a prophylactic against malaria if quinine is unavailable. At any rate, that is what we did during the War, though I daresay it was just the unpleasantly bitter taste of the juice that made us think it must be good for us.

PARSLEY see SELEDRI

PEANUTS see KACANG TANAH

PEPPER, BLACK see MERICA

PERIA, *Momordica charantia* (Java, PARE). If you buy this in tins in London it will probably be labelled 'Bitter Cucumber', though the reference books suggest other names for it such as Balsam Cucumber, Bitter Gourd and Maiden's Blush. Another Indonesian name, *Periok*, recalls a word for a cooking pot and also the name of the seaport of Jakarta, Tanjung Priok. Peria grows on tall vines and is a knobbly, unattractive-looking object which, cooked, is very good to eat, if you like this rather bitter-tasting kind of vegetable. It is not unlike an unpickled gherkin. It is also said, in some quarters, to be good against evil spirits. See illustration on page 204.

PETÉ, *Parkia speciosa* (Sumatra, PETAI). The beans of this plant, with the pod and skin removed, are packed in brine and sold by Conimex under the name Peteh Asin; they look rather like broad beans, shelled. 'Asin' means 'salty', which is not really an accurate description; the flavour is bitter and at the same time nutty—'remotely suggesting garlic', as Burkill puts it. In the tropics you buy fresh peté in pods, up to half a metre long. A favourite way to cook young ones is to top and tail the pod, trim off the stringy edges, and slice the pod very thin with the beans still in it. Crisp-fry the pod, and the beans remain soft in the middle of the slices. Peté is even more delicious mixed with tempe and hot sambal, but I doubt if this would be to the taste of most Europeans. More commonly, fresh peté is taken out of the pod and the skin peeled off each bean with a sharp knife before cooking.

PINEAPPLE see NENAS

PISANG, *Musa* spp. Bananas. Those who have lived in a banana-growing area will know that Europeans and North Americans have scarcely any notion of the variety of size, colour, texture and flavour to be found among bananas, or of the number of different ways there are to cook and eat them. The problem is, of course, that only a few varieties travel well; it is uneconomic to ship fruit that bruises too easily or ripens uncontrollably fast. There are said to be more than 40 different kinds of banana in Indonesia, though many of the best cultivars are members of the same species, *M. sapientum*. For encyclopaedic information on bananas, see N. W. Simmonds' *Bananas* (Longman, 1959). Six of our favourite bananas are described below.

PISANG AMBON. Big, daffodil-yellow fruit, more or less identical to the Gros Michel that Europe imports from the West Indies, and therefore the usual choice of Europeans who have just arrived in the East. In fact, pisang ambon are by no means the most highly regarded dessert banana.

PISANG EMAS. 'Golden bananas'—small, thin-skinned, deep yellow, and I think equivalent to the West Indian Sucrier variety. My grandmother used to tell me a story which all Indonesian children hear so that they may know how the world goes: a bunch of pisang ambon were throwing their weight about on a market stall and being very arrogant towards some less-impressive looking pisang emas. A tall, handsome Dutchman in riding boots walked into the market-place, and picked up the pisang ambon. 'There, you see! Only the finest Ambon bananas are good enough for the *tuan*.' But he bought some of the pisang emas as well, and started eating them on the spot. The pisang ambon were for his horse.

PISANG KELING. 'Tamil banana'—perhaps the variety was brought from South India. The skin is usually spotted, but the flavour and texture are very like pisang emas and this banana has a high place in the league table.

PISANG KEPOK. A flattish, squarish, stubby banana which remains greeny-yellow even when ripe. If you cut one in half, the cross-section is more or less oblong. This is perhaps the best of all cooking bananas, but can be eaten raw as well.

79

PISANG KLUTUK (also PISANG BATU, 'stone banana'). A cooking banana, and always sold unripe for use in (for example) Rujak (page 240). It is chopped up, skin and all (in any case it would be hard to remove the skin from the unripe fruit), along with the many small crunchy seeds inside it. It gives the Rujak an interesting texture and a pleasant, nutty flavour.

PISANG RAJA. 'King bananas'—bigger than pisang emas and slightly reddish in colour. Excellent raw, but often chosen too for frying and for recipes such as Nagasari (page 238).

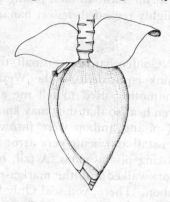

Jantung pisang—Banana heart ('flower')

POMELO see JERUK BALI

RAMBUTAN, *Nephelium lappacium*. The name literally means 'hairy', because the skin of this fruit, which is reddish-pink, has long, soft spines growing from it, though these are too thick and too few to be really like hair. The fruit is about the size of an egg, and the thick rind splits or cuts open easily to reveal a soft-fleshed, white interior. Inside this is a large, rough stone, rather like a plum-stone. The flesh is sweet, juicy, and fragrant, not unlike a lychee (see KELENGKENG), which is indeed a closely related species. The lychee, however, has a smooth skin.

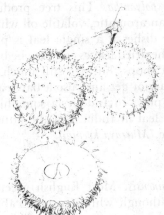

Rambutan

SALAK, *Zalacca edulis*. This is a most attractive pear-shaped fruit that grows on a stemless palm. It has a shiny brown tesselated skin, rather like snakeskin, which peels off easily. The flesh inside is segmented, white, and somewhat dry and waxy, but very good to eat provided you do not get salak which contains too much tannin. Salak from Bali are usually reckoned to be the best and sweetest.

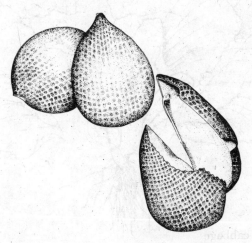

Salak

SALAM, *Eugenia polyantha*. This tree produces leaves, *daun salam*, containing an aromatic, volatile oil which gives a subtle flavour to certain dishes if a single leaf is placed in the pan during cooking. The dried leaves can now be bought in London, at a few specialist shops, but are still much easier to find in Holland. If you cannot get any, use a bay leaf instead.

The salam leaf plays in Indonesia something like the same role as the 'curry' leaf in India. But the latter is the leaf of a quite different tree, *Murraya koenigii*.

SAWI, *Brassica chinensis*. Most English greengrocers call this Chinese cabbage, though white-mustard cabbage is an alternative. Indonesians sometimes adapt its Chinese name and call it pé-tsai. You will find two kinds in most market-places: *sawi hijau* (green) and *sawi putih* (white). Both are cooked. Sawi hijau is sometimes pickled. If your English greengrocer does not know it under any of its names, use cos lettuce instead.

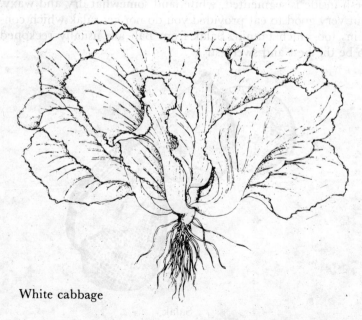

White cabbage

SELEDRI, *Petroselinum vulgare.* This is flat-leafed or 'continental' parsley, which is becoming better-known in Britain and which many people consider has a better flavour than the crinkly-leafed kind. Seledri is sometimes confused with coriander leaves, but the two plants are quite different. In fact, it is Thai cuisine which relies heavily on coriander leaves; Indonesian recipes more often favour parsley.

SEMANGKA AIR, *Citrullus vulgaris.* Water-melon. These are plentiful and cheap in Java, as one would expect on a tropical island with a high rainfall; you often see them for sale at roadside stalls, to refresh the weary traveller. Water-melon seeds, which can be bought at Chinese shops in London and elsewhere, have a pleasant nutty flavour when they are roasted. We call them *kwaci.* Just crack them open with your teeth.

SEREH, *Cymbopogon citratus.* This is called, in English, lemon grass, which gives a very fair idea of it. According to Burkill, Europeans used at one time to grow it in greenhouses and make lemon-grass tea if they found the real thing too strong for them. In cooking, it is used either fresh, dried or powdered. You can grow fresh sereh at home; it makes an attractive house-plant, if you can get a root of it to start you off. Most Indian shops in England sell dried sereh, which you can use as if it were a bay-leaf, putting it into the pan and taking it out again before serving. It is a long, thin leaf—a blade of grass, in fact—so bundle it up a bit and tie a knot in it before putting it in. If you buy sereh powder, which is very good and perfectly adequate for the job of flavouring, use it very, very sparingly.

A drawing of fresh lemon grass is shown on the next page.

SWEET POTATO see UBI JALAR

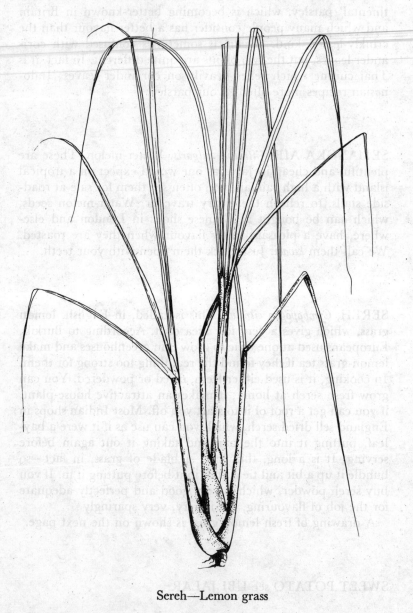

Sereh—Lemon grass

TALAS, *Colocasia antiquorum* var. *esculentia* (Java, TALES; Malaysia and elsewhere, KELADI or BIRAH KELADI). Many English people will recognize this by its Polynesian name of Taro. Herklots and others also call it Dasheen. The *OED* Supplement backs him in saying that this name is derived from French *de Chine*, which makes one wonder whether this is a bit of Louisiana French that got attached to the plant in the southern United States, where I believe it is grown a good deal. It was well known in ancient Egypt and ancient China. If you are living in a tropical or subtropical country, by all means try talas or taro as an alternative to rice, potatoes, sweet potatoes or yams. There are many ways to cook it. I particularly like it boiled, like a floury potato, sliced and eaten with freshly grated *kelapa muda*; or sliced very thin and fried, like potato crisps. Make sure, though, that it is boiled or baked long enough to destroy the calcium oxylate crystals that form in some (not all) varieties. These can taste unpleasantly acrid, or even cause mild inflammation in the mouth and throat.

Daun talas—the huge, waxy leaves, like upside-down spades on playing cards—are often used for wrapping food, but you can also eat them. I include here one of my own very favourite recipes, Buntil (page 192). Children who are playing out of doors and are caught by a tropical shower will break off talas leaves, if there are any nearby, and run down the street waving them over their heads as umbrellas. See illustration on page 194.

TAMARIND, TAMARIND WATER see ASAM

TARO see TALAS

TERUNG GELATIK, *Solanum melongena, S. torvum* (West Java, TAKOKAK). This is a kind, or several kinds, of small aubergine, egg-plant or brinjal. It is about as big as a small plum and comes in a variety of colours—white, purple, green, yellow. The taste is pleasantly bitter; we usually eat it raw.

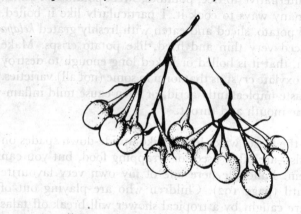

TURMERIC see KUNYIT

UBI. A general name for a rather bewildering variety of edible tubers. To deal with them all, comprehensively and unambiguously, would take many pages. I shall therefore mention the two that are of immediate interest to users of this book.

UBI JALAR, *Ipomoea batatas*, 'rambling ubi'. This is the original potato, as discovered by Columbus and brought back by him to astonish the Old World. Nowadays we call it a sweet potato. Do not confuse it with a yam, most varieties of which have yellow flesh, soft and somewhat watery. Yams (species of

Dioscorea) are not much grown in Indonesia, but they are imported into England, presumably from Africa or the Caribbean, and there is often doubt about which name applies to a particular shapeless tuber on the greengrocer's counter. Yams are not suitable for Getuk Lindri (page 246) or most other sweet-potato dishes; ubi jalar have a reddish skin and a white or pinkish-white interior, with a dry, rather floury texture. The young leaves make an excellent green vegetable when boiled, but I have never seen them for sale in England.

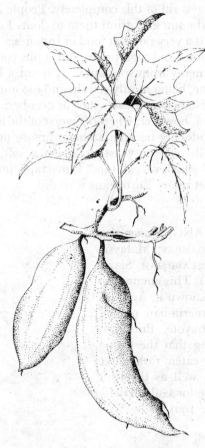

Ubi jalar—Sweet potato

UBI KAYU, *Manihot utilissima*, 'wood ubi' (Java, KETELA or SINGKONG). This is cassava, or the tapioca plant, which has been grown in Java since sometime in the eighteenth century ('ketela' is almost certainly a corruption of 'Castile', which suggests that the Spaniards brought cassava to the East, though other local dialect names pin it on the Indians, the Dutch and the British). It must be well boiled before anything else can be done with it, as the raw tubers, especially if they have been out of the ground for more than a day or two, produce poisonous hydrocyanic acid; boiling gets rid of this completely. People in Java dry out the tubers in the sun and grind them to flour. I cannot say that dried cassava is a very popular food in Indonesia, as we associate it with hard times and high prices, but it fills you up and in the 1940s it kept many from starvation. It is not a healthy food to subsist on alone, being mostly starch, and too much of it reduces the body's resistance to diseases such as beri-beri. I became fond of fresh cassava, however, when the worst of the hard times were over and it suddenly became a cheap luxury again. It can be fermented with *ragi*, or yeast, to make a soft, sweet, mildly alcoholic food which we call tapé. I love tapé, but I must admit I have not met many Europeans who did.

WALUH JIPANG, *Sechium edule* (West Java, GAMBAS; Malaysia and elsewhere, LABU SIAM, 'Siamese pumpkin'). This cucumber-like plant is known in America by its old Amerindian names, Choco or Chayote. Burkill is right in saying that the young shoots can be eaten, rather like asparagus, as well as the fruit (see the recipe for Gulai Pucuk Labu on page 190).

WATER MELON see SEMANGKA AIR

RECIPES

Rice

HOW TO COOK RICE

Nothing could possibly be simpler to cook than plain boiled rice; even a boiled egg requires more finesse. But you can cook rice in Indonesia in as many different ways as potatoes in Ireland, so the matter is worth considering in some detail.

Ideally, rice should be boiled and then steamed. The first process requires an ordinary saucepan, the second demands a steamer with a perforated basket. The traditional Javanese *dandang* is a large copper vessel with a narrow waist; the *kukusan*, a woven bamboo container which holds the rice, is conical in shape and sits on the sloping sides of the dandang, just above the level of the water. See the drawing on page 97.

These elegant pans are still made in Java, and possibly in some other parts of Indonesia, though copper has been largely replaced by tin and aluminium. Many people, however, now use a deep straight-sided pan with a metal basket hung inside it. These can be bought easily enough in Holland, though I have not yet seen one in London. See the drawing on page 93. They are very light and easy to clean, and if not allowed to boil dry too often will last for many years.

If you really eat a lot of rice, you may find it worth while to buy an electric rice cooker. These are imported from Japan and are sold mostly in Chinese and Japanese shops. They are not cheap, and though they are certainly very convenient and efficient I have never felt much need for one.

If on the other hand you cook rice only occasionally, you may not want any special utensils for it at all—and in that case you will find that you can cook rice to perfection in any thick-bottomed saucepan. The only slight disadvantages are that this method requires more care, and a little rice is usually lost.

WHAT RICE TO USE

Buy long-grain rice, often known as Patna rice. Never use 'pudding' rice, which in Britain means all short-grain rice; it is completely unsuitable. The rice that is usually obtainable in Britain comes from the United States and is of very good quality, though not as fine as the best Javanese rice. (There are, of course, many different kinds of rice to be eaten in a rice-growing country, varying enormously in colour, flavour, and texture).

Branded rice in packets is also perfectly good, but it is relatively very expensive. It may be presumed not to need washing, but rice bought loose or in supermarket packs should be washed in three or four changes of cold water.

NASI PUTIH (plain boiled and steamed rice)

People's appetites for rice vary greatly, but I shall assume that four people will get through 2 cupfuls of rice (uncooked measure) at a meal.

Measure and wash 2 cups of rice and put into a saucepan with $2\frac{1}{2}$ cups of cold water. With rice cooked in this way, we never add salt. Bring the rice to the boil, stirring once or twice to keep the grains from sticking to the side of the pan. You can cover the pan if you like, to keep the heat in, but as soon as the rice starts to boil take the lid off. Turn down the heat and keep the water simmering and bubbling gently. The rice grains will absorb the water, swelling up and softening as they do so, until there is no liquid left in the pan. The rice should now be damp, slippery and puffy, but each grain will still have a hard core.

Put 3 or 4 cm of water in the rice steamer and heat this while the rice is still bubbling in the saucepan. Tip the rice into the basket, put the lid on the steamer, and steam the rice for 10 minutes. The rice should now be quite soft and ready to eat; if you rub a grain of it between your finger and thumb, you should find no hard core. The rice will, of course, be slightly moist, but each grain should be quite separate from the others, even though they will tend to cling together.

If the rice is ready before you are, turn off the heat and tilt the lid of the steamer to let steam escape; the rice will not suffer if water drips down into it, but it must come to table hot.

Rice steamer

NASI LIWET (plain boiled rice, without steaming)

Prepare the rice as before, but add only 1 cup of water for 1 cup of rice. Remember that, when cooking rice in this way, we do not use salt. Use the thickest possible saucepan; if you cook on gas and have fairly thin pans, you will have to turn the gas right down low in the last stage of cooking. Bring the rice to the boil and let it bubble, without a lid, until all the water is absorbed. Stir once, and turn the heat low. Cover the pan tightly, if necessary using greaseproof paper or aluminium foil to make the lid as nearly airtight as possible. Leave on this low heat, undisturbed, for 10 minutes. The rice will then be ready.

INTIP (how to use the crust of rice on the pan bottom)

When you turn the rice out of the pan, you will find that a layer about ½ cm thick has stuck to the bottom. One way to get rid of this is just to soak the pan and throw this small quantity away. No Indonesian would throw rice away, however. Instead, put the pan, straight from the stove, on to a wet cloth and let it stand there for 2 minutes. The cooked rice will not lose heat appreciably in this time, and the layer on the bottom —the intip—will not stick; you can take it out like a cake from a cake-tin.

Keep the intip for 24 hours, then put it out of doors in hot sunshine to dry thoroughly. If it is winter or the weather forecast is bad, dry it off in the oven as you would bread before making breadcrumbs. Break up the intip into smaller pieces, and store these in an airtight jar. When you have a good quantity—say, half a kilo or so—deep-fry the pieces until they are golden brown. Sprinkle them with salt (or, when cool, spread them with golden syrup), and you have an unusual and delicious crisp snack. The salty ones will keep in an airtight jar for months; the syrupy ones should be eaten fairly soon, or they will go soft.

NASI UDUK (rice cooked in coconut milk)

This is a rather richer, more aromatic form of Nasi Putih or Nasi Liwet; it can be either boiled and steamed, or just boiled. Instead of water, use santen (coconut milk)—the same quantity —and put in a pinch of salt, a salam leaf or bay-leaf, and a stick of cinnamon. (In Indonesia, we also add a piece of daun pandan for extra flavour.) These solids should be removed before the last stage of cooking; this is easy, as they usually remain on top of the contents of the pan.

LONTONG (compressed boiled rice)

Lontong is always eaten cold, and is traditional Javanese fare at Lebaran—the end of the Moslem fasting month, which is also the beginning of a new Moslem year. It is specially recommended to go with certain dishes, such as saté and gulé, though you can cook rice this way any time. The idea is that the rice is cooked inside a small container, so that as it swells up the grains are pressed into a solid mass which can later be sliced up into chunks the size of a mouthful. In Indonesia, this container is rolled from a square of banana leaf, 15 or 20 cm (about 6") each side. The leaf is softened by heating or in hot water so that it does not crack or split. The cylinder is closed at one end by folding it over and pinning it with a pin made from the spiny rib of a coconut-frond. It is filled one-third full with uncooked rice, and the other end is pinned shut.

In Britain and elsewhere, the banana leaf can conveniently be replaced by using boil-in-the-bag rice. One bag is ample for three people. The cooking method is the same:

Put water in a pan, add a pinch of salt, and bring to the boil. Drop the bags of rice in and simmer for $1\frac{1}{4}$ hours. It does not matter whether the pan is covered or not, but keep an eye on the water level: the rice must remain completely immersed. Pour in more boiling water whenever necessary. At the end of $1\frac{1}{4}$ hours, take out the bags, which will now be plumped out like cushions, and leave them to cool overnight or for at least 6 hours. Then strip off the bag (or leaf) and cut up the lontong, which should be soft but perfectly firm.

KETUPAT (variation of Lontong)

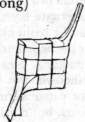

This is made, in Indonesia, in containers of woven coconut-leaf, which look very picturesque when they are hung up, twenty or thirty at a time, to cool under the thatch of a roadside *warung*.

BURAS (a steamed, stuffed rice dish)

This is a kind of stuffed Lontong, but for this you cannot use boil-in-the-bag rice. Make the filling first, using the following ingredients. The quantities given are enough to provide filling for 1 cup of rice, measured raw.

2 shallots	*a pinch of chilli powder (more, if*
1 medium-sized potato	*you want it hot)*
2 carrots	*2 tsp dark soya sauce*
a slice of cold lamb, beef, or	*1 tsp tomato ketchup*
pork (optional)	*1 tbs vegetable oil*

Slice the shallots. Peel and cut the carrots and potato into very small cubes. Cut up the meat, if you are using any. Sauté all these in the oil for about a minute, then add all the other ingredients and mix well; add ½ a cupful of water and cover for 3 minutes. Then take off the lid and continue cooking until there is no more liquid in the pan. Add salt if necessary.

Now prepare the rice as for Nasi Putih (page 92), but to 1 cup of rice add 1 cup of water and 1½ cups santen (coconut milk). Put in also a little salt—about ¼ teaspoonful. Simmer until all the liquid has been absorbed, in the usual way. The rice, of course, will be softer and damper than Nasi Putih would be at this stage.

Next—if you have banana leaf squares—put a dollop of rice on each one, pat it flat, put on a little of the filling, and roll it all up inside the leaf. Fold over the ends of the leaf to seal it up, and put the filled packages into a rice steamer.

If you have no banana leaves, however, simply put a layer of rice on the bottom of a pudding basin and then a layer of filling. Go on with alternate layers of rice and filling, finishing with rice. Either put the basin into the basket of your rice steamer, or tie a cloth over the basin and steam it in a saucepan as you would a Christmas pudding. Steaming time will be 30–40 minutes, whichever method you use. Leave to cool for at least 30 minutes.

Buras can be eaten warm, or may be left until cold. It will keep for 24 hours, but not longer.

NASI KETAN (glutinous or sticky rice)

This is a different kind of rice altogether from that used for Nasi Putih; when raw, the grains do not slide over each other smoothly but in slightly sticky jerks, and when cooked they stick to each other and make a soft mass. Most Chinese foodshops sell glutinous rice. It is cooked in precisely the same way as Nasi Uduk (page 94), but is even richer and heavier. Therefore, only small helpings are taken, and this rice is not served with an elaborate range of side dishes. It goes very well with certain dishes, however, especially the very dry ones, and above all with Rendang (page 136).

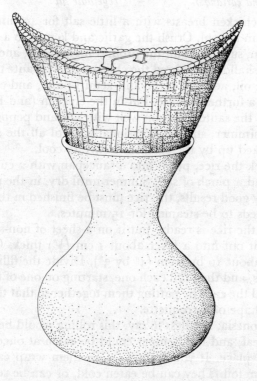

Dandang and kukusan—Indonesian rice steamer

97

LEMPER (stuffed glutinous rice)

This is similar to Buras (page 96) but a little more complicated. It, too, is good for picnics, but in Indonesia it is often served at teatime, instead of cake. With the ingredients shown below, you will need 3 cups (uncooked measure) of glutinous rice. Put the rice to soak in cold water for 1 hour while you make the filling with the following ingredients:

2 chicken breasts	*1 Kaffir lime leaf (optional)*
1¼ cups thick santen (coconut milk)	*¼ tsp cumin*
	¼ tsp brown sugar
4 shallots	*3 kemiri (candlenuts)*
4 cloves garlic	*salt and pepper*
1 tsp ground coriander	*vegetable oil*

Boil the chicken breasts with a little salt for 40 minutes, and allow them to cool. Crush the garlic and kemiri to a paste, add the cumin, sugar and all the ground ingredients, and mix well. Slice the shallots and shred the chicken finely; sauté the shallots in a little oil, add the garlic-and-kemiri paste, and continue to sauté for a further minute. Put in the chicken (and Kaffir lime leaf) and the santen. Season well with salt and pepper. Let the mixture simmer, stirring occasionally, until all the santen has been soaked up by the chicken. Leave to cool.

To cook the rice, put it into a saucepan with 2 cups of thick santen and a pinch of salt. Simmer until dry, in the usual way. For really good results, this rice must be finished in the steamer, and it needs to be steamed for 15 minutes.

When the rice is ready, put it on a sheet of non-stick paper and pat it out into a layer about 1 cm (½″) thick. Cut it into oblongs about 10 by 6 cm (4″ by 3″). Divide the filling among the pieces, and then roll each one, starting on one of the shorter sides. Seal the ends by patting them together so that the Lemper has the shape of a croquette.

In Indonesia, needless to say, this rolling would be done in a banana leaf, and the Lemper could be eaten at once or stored in a cool place. If you want to store them wrap each one in aluminium foil. They can be eaten cold, or can be reheated by steaming them for 5 minutes.

SEMAR MENDEM

Lemper can also be served wrapped in thin plain omelettes.
They are then called Semar Mendem—drunken Semar.

Semar is one of the famous quartet of clowns who appear in
every *wayang* play in the traditional Javanese theatre.* But he
is also a god in disguise; and though he may say outrageous
things I have never seen him anything but sober. How his name
got itself attached to a stuffed omelette, I shall not pretend to
know.

* See Introduction, page 25. Semar is an important person both in
wayang orang, played by human actors, and in *wayang kulit*, where the charac-
ters are intricately pierced shadow puppets, made of leather. Along with
his three sons, he is a licensed Fool, permitted to make rude jokes about
Authority not only in the world of the play but in the real world outside.

NASI RAMES (a miniature rijsttafel)

This is a meal in itself, a plate of ordinary Nasi Putih (page 92)
topped with generous spoonfuls of various side dishes. The
secret is of course to get the right combination of side dishes. A
popular selection in Indonesia is:

Dendeng Ragi (page 135)
Sayur Lodeh (page 200)
Gudeg (page 168) in Java, or, in Sumatra, Rendang (page
136)
Kering Tempe (page 218)
Kelia Ayam (page 162)
Sambal Bajak (page 226)
Krupuk—prawn crackers (page 237)

You can of course make up your own Nasi Rames. And if you
feel hesitant about ordering a variety of dishes in a restaurant,
just say: 'Nasi Rames, please.'

NASI GORENG
Fried rice   to serve four to six

The name Nasi Goreng means simply 'fried rice', and it is really
a collective description of an indefinite number of slightly
differing dishes. You can vary the trimmings and garnishes to
suit your taste; but even the most elaborate Nasi Goreng is
quick to make. It is a particularly good luncheon dish.

To make plain Nasi Goreng for four to six people, you need:

2 cups long-grain rice	*2 tbs vegetable oil* or *clarified*
4 shallots or *1 small onion*	*butter* or *pork fat*
2 red chillis or *¼ tsp chilli*	*salt*
powder and 1 tsp paprika	*1 tsp sweet soya sauce*
	1 tsp tomato ketchup

Boil the rice a good long time before you intend to fry it; you
can fry freshly boiled rice, but the Nasi Goreng will be better
if the boiled rice is allowed to cool. Two hours is a satisfactory
interval. Leaving the rice to cool overnight, however, gives less
good results—the rice has time to go dry and stale. Some hints
about boiling rice are given on pages 91–94, but an important
point to note here is that rice for Nasi Goreng must be cooked
with the least possible quantity of water; this prevents it from
becoming too soft. For 1 cup of rice, use 1 cup of water.

Assuming you have now got your cool, boiled rice, proceed
like this: slice the shallots or onion, seed and slice the chilli
(or pound the shallots and chilli together in a mortar). Heat
the oil in a wok; it makes no difference, by the way, whether
you use oil, fat, or butter. Sauté the shallots and chilli for a
minute or so, and season with salt, soya sauce, and tomato
ketchup. Put in all the rice, and stir it continuously until it is
well heated: this will take 5–8 minutes. Serve in a good large
dish, generously garnished with sliced cucumber, tomatoes,
fried onions, and Krupuk (page 237).

This very plain Nasi Goreng is usually eaten with meat, or
fish, and vegetables. It goes very well with some European
dishes, particularly roast pork, provided there is no sauce or
gravy on the table. I have observed that mankind is divided into

two great classes, the 'wet eaters' and the 'dry eaters'. Nasi Goreng generally pleases both. Europeans in tropical outposts, cut off from anything resembling an English or continental breakfast, can manage fried rice at six a.m. even though plain boiled rice refuses to go down the throat much before midday. But any attempt to moisten Nasi Goreng further simply drowns it; oil and water don't mix.

Nasi Goreng and seafood, however, mix extremely well. For an informal lunch fry a lot of rice and garnish it with Udang Bakar (grilled prawns, page 109), Goreng Teri (page 124), and Goreng Cumi-cumi (fried squid, page 113). At home we would add prawn crackers (page 237), broken up into small pieces and scattered over the rice, and Emping (page 231).

You can also make other kinds of Nasi Goreng, which will stand by themselves as satisfying meals. For example:

NASI GORENG ISTIMEWA

additional ingredients:
2 rashers streaky bacon
a little beef or pork, cut up small

30 g (1 oz) shrimps
1 white cabbage leaf, shredded
1 carrot, cut up small

When you have sautéed the shallots etcetera, but before you put the rice into the wok, add these additional ingredients and sauté for 6 minutes. Then add the rice, and continue as before. When you garnish the dish before serving it, you may add some small slices or strips of ham, and a fried egg (or two) for each person.

NASI GORENG WITH SARDINES AND ONIONS

Chill a can of sardines (about 150 g—4 to 6 oz), open it, remove and skin the sardines. Slice 1 or 2 medium onions and sauté them in a little vegetable oil until slightly coloured. Add a pinch each of chilli powder and salt and a teaspoon of paprika. Stir for about a minute, then put in the sardines—carefully, so as not to break them up more than necessary—and stir gently. Then put the sardines and onion on top of your Nasi Goreng as a garnish; don't—for the reasons given in the next recipe, stir them into it.

NASI GORENG WITH ONIONS, MUSHROOMS, AND SHRIMPS

additional ingredients:
1 or 2 medium-sized onions—or
   more, if you are very fond of
   onions
120 g (4 oz) button mushrooms

60 g (2 oz) shrimps or prawns,
   peeled
2 tsp paprika
1 tsp sweet soya sauce
salt and pepper

You can vary the quantities of these ingredients to suit your taste. Slice the onions and fry them in a little oil until they begin to brown; add the mushrooms and fry for another 2 minutes; then add the shrimps and continue frying for 3 or 4 minutes longer, stirring often. This mixture will need a little more salt than the previous one. Use the onions, mushrooms, and shrimps to garnish the Nasi Goreng just before serving. Don't stir them into the rice, as some people do; this makes the rice unpleasantly oily, and spoils the effect of the garnish.

Indonesians usually prefer to eat with a spoon and fork (or with their fingers) rather than a knife and fork. More than most other dishes, Nasi Goreng requires a spoon, not a knife, for comfortable eating. Eating with the fingers requires practice; it must be done gracefully and tidily, and with the right hand *only*.

NASI KUNING
Yellow rice

In Java, this dish is traditionally served at a *selamatan*. There are many different occasions for such a ceremony, religious and secular, and each must be observed in the appropriate way. What I have in mind here is a family festival to celebrate the birth of a child, the building of a new house, or some other important domestic event. The rooms and garden are decorated with arches of palm fronds, and friends, family, and neighbours fill the house, all enjoying themselves immensely while preserving the gravity and decorum which is proper to Javanese life. Why Nasi Kuning came to be associated with a selamatan I do not know; perhaps it was the bright yellow colour of the rice.

Method 1: with santen (coconut milk)

2 cups long-grain rice
2 cups santen
1 tsp turmeric

a pinch of salt
1 salam leaf or *bay-leaf*
1 clove

Soak the rice in cold water for 1 hour. Wash and drain it, and put it in a saucepan with the 2 cups of santen and all the other ingredients. Boil until all the santen has been soaked up by the rice. Stir this rice, take out the salam leaf and the clove, then steam the rice for 10 minutes. (If you do not use a steamer, cover the pan very tightly after you have stirred the rice and turn the heat down as low as possible; cook on this low heat for another 10 minutes.) Serve hot.

Method 2: without santen (coconut milk)

2 cups long-grain rice
2 cups good stock, or 2 cups
*   water and a chicken cube*
1 tsp turmeric
1 stick cinnamon
1 clove

1 salam leaf or *bay-leaf*
¼ tsp cumin
1 tsp ground coriander
2 tbs vegetable oil or *clarified*
*   butter*

Soak the rice for 1 hour, wash, and drain. Heat the oil or butter in a saucepan and sauté the rice for 2 minutes. Add the turmeric, sauté for another 2 minutes, and then put in the stock and all the other ingredients. Boil until all the stock has been soaked up by the rice; then steam, or continue cooking, exactly as for Method 1.

You can serve Nasi Kuning just as it is, with side dishes of your choice, or you can garnish it. Suitable garnishes include sliced cucumber, seledri (flat-leaved parsley), fried onions, Serundeng (page 232), Goreng Teri (page 124), Dendeng Ragi (page 135), Pergedel Kentang (page 230), or just a plain omelette cut into thin strips. Sambal Bajak (page 226) is a good hot relish.

NASI KEBULI
Savoury rice with crisp-fried chicken

This dish, by itself, or with a dish of vegetables, makes an excellent family meal. It is very good for Sunday lunch, or for a small dinner party. It goes well with other dishes—for example, with any kind of saté—if you are entertaining on a larger scale.

2 cups rice
1 roasting chicken—1½ kg
  (3½ lb) is ample
4 shallots
3 cloves garlic
2 tsp ground coriander
¼ tsp cumin
a pinch of ground laos (galingale)
a pinch of powdered, or a stalk
  of fresh, lemon-grass
a small stick of cinnamon

a pinch of grated nutmeg
2 cloves
salt
vegetable oil (for deep frying)

for the garnish:
a little fried onion
parsley
chives
sliced cucumber

Soak the rice in cold water for 1 hour.

Clean and cut the chicken into serving pieces. Crush the shallots and garlic, and mix these and all the other ingredients together. Put the chicken and all the spices into a saucepan, and add just enough cold water to cover the chicken. Boil until tender (about 40–45 minutes).

About 10 minutes before the chicken is ready, clean the rice and pour the water away. Put 1 tablespoonful of oil in a saucepan and fry the rice for 5 minutes, turning it over constantly. Then strain off the chicken stock and add it to the rice. For 2 cups of rice you will need 2 cups of stock; if you have less than this, add water to make up the difference. Boil the rice in the stock until the stock has been absorbed. Then steam the rice for 10 minutes.

While the rice is cooking, deep fry the chicken in vegetable oil.

Serve on a large oval dish; pile the rice in the middle, arrange the portions of chicken around it, and garnish with fried onions, parsley, chives, and sliced cucumber.

LEMANG
Glutinous rice cooked in bamboo

This is a Sumatran equivalent of Lontong or Ketupat, and like them it is associated with a major feast of the Islamic year—in this case, *Maulud Nabi* or the Prophet's birthday. We eat it then with Rendang (page 136), and neighbours send little packets of Lemang to each other rather as, elsewhere, they might exchange Christmas cards. The Javanese do the same with Ketupat at Lebaran. Throughout the rest of the year, however, Lemang is regarded as a sweet dish and is eaten with kolak, bananas, or durian in season.

It is made from glutinous rice, cooked with thick santen (coconut milk) in segments of bamboo: not just any bamboo, but specifically *Schizostacayum zollengeri*, which we call *telang*. This variety has very thin walls, which let the heat penetrate, and unusually long internodes. The cook may prepare 15 or 20 or more of these bamboo cylinders, 50 cm long and 5 cm across, open at the top and lined with banana leaf. The rice is usually white, but red and black glutinous rice are also used. It is first soaked for several hours, then dried. Each length of bamboo is filled about one-third full of rice, and is topped up with thick, slightly-salted santen. A banana-leaf lid is tied down firmly over the mouth of the tube. A wooden crossbar is rigged over a low fire and the bamboos are placed so that they lean against it, even numbers on one side and odd numbers on the other, like the rafters of a little house. Cooking takes up to 2 hours, with the rice swelling as it absorbs the santen to make a soft, firm mass. When it is cooked, the Lemang is shaken and slid from the tubes, unwrapped from its banana-leaf coverings and sliced into good chunky rounds.

Fish and Shellfish

Indonesia has one of the longest coastlines in the world, and its fishermen bring in large quantities of marine fish—many of them similar to north Atlantic species—and prawns and squid and other seafoods which appear in the following recipes.

However, freshwater fish are more important to many Indonesians. The monsoon rains keep most of the islands not only fertile but well-watered; rivers, lakes, even the flooded rice-fields teem with fish. There are dozens of species which are eaten, both fresh and dried. Few are similar to European species, although some have relations in Australia and in the Gulf States of the U.S.A. In those few recipes which would require, in Indonesia, freshwater fish unfamiliar elsewhere I have recommended substitutes which do very well.

UDANG GORENG
Fried prawns   to serve four

This dish is best made with fresh prawns, if you can get them.

12–16 prawns—the largest you can get, and certainly not less than 5 or 6 cm (3″) long	*¼ tsp ground coriander*
	salt and pepper
	6 tbs breadcrumbs or *plain flour*
1 egg	*vegetable oil*

Beat the egg, add the ground coriander, and season with salt and pepper. Shell and wash the prawns, dry them, and put them into the beaten egg. Heat the oil in a wok or frying-pan. Coat the prawns with breadcrumbs or flour, and fry them 3 or 4 at a time.

As a variation, you can fill the prawns with slices of ham. Hold the prawn upside down and slit it lengthwise, taking care not to cut completely through. Put in a slice of ham, sprinkle it with pepper and salt, close the prawn, and dip it in the beaten egg. Continue as above—coat with breadcrumbs or flour, and fry.

SAMBAL GORENG UDANG
Prawns in rich coconut sauce   to serve four to six

See the introduction to Sambal Goreng Daging (page 126).

750 g (2 lb) large prawns, peeled

100 g (3 or 4 oz) mange-tout or sugar peas

50 g (2 oz) fresh peté beans or peté asin

5 shallots

3 cloves garlic

5 kemiri (candlenuts)

1 slice terasi (page 41)

5 red chillis

1 tsp ground ginger

1 tsp ground coriander

a pinch of powdered lemongrass

a pinch of ground laos (galingale)

2 Kaffir lime leaves or 1 bay-leaf

2 tbs tamarind water

1 tsp brown sugar (optional)

salt

¼ cup thick santen (coconut milk—optional)

vegetable oil

Top and tail the *mange-tout*, and cut the peté beans into two. Peel and slice the shallots and garlic, and pound them together in a cobek or mortar, along with the kemiri, terasi and chillis. Alternatively, put all these ingredients, except the terasi, into a food processor, using the blade for mincing meat. Run the machine until everything becomes a nice smooth paste. Turn this out on to a plate, and with a spoon crush the terasi and mix it well with the paste. Mix in all the other ground ingredients.

Heat the oil in a wok or saucepan. When hot, put in the paste and stir-fry for 2 minutes. Add the prawns and peté and stir. Pour in 1 cup of water, and the tamarind water, add salt and sugar, and let it all cook for 6 minutes. Put in the *mange-tout* and the santen (if you are using it), and continue to simmer until the mixture is almost boiling. Stir continuously for 2 or 3 minutes. Serve hot.

PAIS UDANG
Prawn or shrimp packages   to serve four to six

This is a Sundanese dish which I used to eat often when I went to stay with one of my aunts who lived in Tasikmalaya, a pretty little town in West Java. Most of the households there have their own *balong*, large fish ponds where they farm fish and shrimps for their own use. This Pais is an excellent way to cook small freshwater shrimps. I have also tried making it with frozen 'cocktail' prawns, which are generally easy to get anywhere, and it is not at all bad. It is better still if you make it with large prawns; and best of all if you wrap it in pieces of banana leaf to cook it. But aluminium foil is a good substitute.

1 kg (2¼ lb) shrimps or *prawns*
5 kemiri (candlenuts)
1 small piece of root ginger
1 piece of fresh, or *¼ tsp ground*,
    turmeric
a pinch of ground laos (galingale)
3 red or *green chillis*

a bunch of spring onions or
    chives
a sprig of sweet basil or *mint*
1 small lime or *lemon*
1 salam leaf or *bay-leaf*
salt

Clean and wash the shrimps or prawns. Keep them in a bowl, sprinkled with a little salt.

Pound the kemiri, ginger, turmeric and laos in a cobek or mortar. Next, seed the chillis and slice them finely. Clean the spring onions and cut them into pieces about 1 cm (½″) long. Slice the lime or lemon into thin rounds, discarding the pips. Mix all these ingredients with the shrimps or prawns, add a little more salt, and lay the basil (or mint) and salam (or bay) leaves on top. Wrap in a piece of banana leaf or aluminium foil, made up in an oblong parcel, and steam or bake in a moderate oven (350°F, gas mark 4) for 15 minutes.

In Tasikmalaya we would then grill the Pais Udang in its banana-leaf wrapper on a charcoal stove, turning it several times. When the leaf was pretty thoroughly charred we would unwrap the contents very carefully and serve hot. Using aluminium foil, I find the best method is to grill the 'parcel', or heat it on a heavy cast-iron pan on the stove, for about 10 to 15 minutes. The purpose of this final grilling is to reduce almost to nothing the juices inside the wrapping, without of course making the shrimps or prawns too dry.

Serve at once, hot, after removing the various leaves.

UDANG BAKAR
Marinated and grilled prawns   to serve four

At home we used to use fresh large green prawns (probably *Penaeus semisulcatus*, the species illustrated on page 111) for this dish. Similar prawns are available in Australia, and the jumbo shrimps of North America are equally suitable. Here in England my fishmonger sells me what he calls Mediterranean prawns, and very good they are too. In fact you may use whatever prawns are available. The real variations in the recipe are in the marinade. My own favourite is the real hot one—chopped ripe tomatoes, soya sauce, a little brown sugar, grilled terasi and plenty of lombok rawit, the very small chilli peppers. My husband and two sons, however, prefer something simpler, as follows. With 12 to 16 large prawns you need:

3 tbs clear soya sauce
3 cloves garlic, crushed
a small piece of grilled terasi (page 41—optional)
1 cabé rawit (page 51), crushed, or a pinch of chilli powder

2 tbs tamarind water or lime juice
1 tbs olive oil, or melted butter
1 tsp brown sugar

Mix all these ingredients in a bowl. Clean the prawns and discard the heads. Partly shell them, leaving the tail (i.e. the fan-shaped piece right at the back end) of each and its backplates in place; then turn them over, slice them lengthwise and open them out flat. Marinate them in the spices etcetera for at least 30 minutes, then grill them for 6 to 8 minutes, turning them from time to time and brushing them with the marinade.

Serve hot.

REMPAH REMPAH UDANG
Prawn and beansprout fritters

100 g (4 oz) prawns, shelled	*¼ tsp chilli powder*
225 g (8 oz) beansprouts	*4 spring onions*
50 g (2 oz) rice flour, or	*2 tbs chopped chives*
self-raising flour	*2 tbs coarsely grated coconut*
1 tsp baking-powder	*(optional)*
2 shallots	*3 tbs water*
2 cloves garlic	*salt and pepper*
1 tsp ground coriander	*1 egg*
1 tsp ground ginger	*vegetable oil*

Chop the prawns up finely, or mince them. Slice the shallots, crush the garlic and chop the spring onions into thin rounds. Clean the beansprouts.

Now mix all the ingredients with the baking-powder, grated coconut, flour, and the powdered and ground ingredients. Pour in the water and knead the mixture thoroughly by hand or blend it with a fork. Add salt and pepper to taste, and fold in the egg. Roll the mixture into little balls about as big as walnuts; if you wish, you can flatten these slightly so that they look like miniature beefburgers. Deep fry them until they are golden brown, using very hot oil; this will ensure that the beansprouts cook fast. Serve hot or cold. Rempah Rempah Udang makes an excellent side dish with a rijsttafel, or it can be served as a snack with drinks.

In the original recipe, you will find that Rempah Rempah is made with more coconut. I find that too much coconut makes them too filling. Rempah Rempah were originally intended to be light vegetable fritters, but adding prawns to them makes them better still.

UDANG GORENG BALADA
Fried prawns with a chilli coating   to serve two to four

This is a very hot dish, because of the chillis in the bumbu. If you don't like very hot food, leave out some or all of the chillis and use a little paprika instead.

*500 g (1 lb) prawns—use
    green, uncooked prawns if
    possible*

for the batter:
2 tbs rice flour

1 tbs cornflour
1 tsp ground coriander
1 clove garlic, crushed
¼ cup santen (coconut milk)
salt and pepper

Mix the ingredients of this batter well, and put the prawns into
it. Leave them there for at least 15 minutes. Then heat 1 or
1½ cups of vegetable oil in a wok. Fry the prawns, 6 or 7 at a
time, till they are golden brown and crisp. Keep warm.

for the bumbu:
10 shallots (not onions)
*4 green chillis, or red chilli, but
    not pimiento*

1 tbs brown sugar (optional)
1 tbs sweet soya sauce
salt if necessary
vegetable oil

Seed the chillis and slice them and the shallots finely. Fry them
in a little oil for about 2 minutes; then add the soya sauce and
sugar, and mix well. Just before serving, put in the fried prawns
and stir them around so that they are all well coated with the
bumbu.

Less exotically, cod can be cooked this way if it is cut up into
cubes. Even cauliflower, believe it or not, is delicious if you cut
it into small flowerets and cook it by this method.

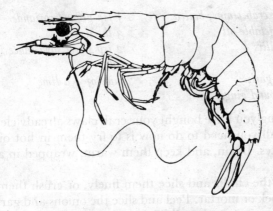

Udang windu—Green tiger prawn

UDANG PINDANG TUMIS
Spiced prawns cooked in
tamarind water
to serve two to four

500 g (1 lb) prawns, frozen or
  fresh
1 slice terasi (page 41)
3 cloves garlic
6 shallots
1 green chilli
vegetable oil

¼ tsp laos (galingale)
¼ tsp powdered, or 1 stalk of
  fresh, lemon grass
salt
¼ cup tamarind water
1 tsp vinegar

Clean and shell the prawns. Pound the terasi and garlic
together. Slice the shallots and chilli, and remove the chilli
seeds. Fry the shallots in about 2 tablespoonfuls of oil until they
are tender; then add the chilli, the terasi and garlic paste, the
laos and lemon grass, and a little salt. Put the prawns in, stir
everything well together in the pan for 2 minutes while frying
continues. Pour in the tamarind water and vinegar. Cover, and
simmer for 15 minutes. Uncover, and continue cooking for a
further 3 or 4 minutes, stirring continuously. Serve at once.

KEPITING PEDAS
Spicy hot crab
to serve four

12 large crab claws, boiled
4 tbs vegetable oil
8 red chillis
2 onions
4 cloves garlic
1 tsp ground ginger

¼ tsp ground coriander
3 tbs water
2 tsp sweet soya sauce (optional)
salt
juice of ¼ a lime

Assuming you have bought your crab claws already cleaned and
boiled, all you need to do now is to fry them in hot oil for 4 to
5 minutes. Drain, and keep them warm, wrapped in absorbent
paper.

Seed the chillis and slice them finely, or crush them roughly
in a cobek or mortar. Peel and slice the onions and garlic finely.
Fry the onions and garlic for 2 minutes, stirring continuously,

in the remainder of the oil in which you fried the crab claws. Add the chilli, ginger and coriander, stir, then add the water, soya sauce and salt. Simmer for a minute or two, and put in the crab claws. Add the lime juice, and stir until the crab claws are well coated with the red chillis, etcetera. Serve hot.

You can also make Kepiting Pedas with a whole crab. Clean it and, for preference, take out the brown meat and use that for something else. Chop the body into four pieces and each claw into two or three; then fry the pieces, and proceed as described above. My father used to buy live crabs from the market and cook them in a kitchen opening on to a little courtyard; on one evening of torrential rain, a big crab jumped out of the basket and made a bolt for it among the puddles of the yard. It was a good try, but he finished up in the pot along with the others.

GORENG CUMI-CUMI
Fried squid   to serve four

This dish needs to be marinated in tamarind water and spices for a good 2 hours before cooking.

750 g (1½ lb) squid	*4 shallots, sliced*
4 tbs tamarind water	*3 cloves of garlic, crushed*
½ tsp turmeric	*½ tsp salt*
1 tsp ginger powder	*1 tsp dark soya sauce (optional)*
pinch of chilli powder	*vegetable oil for deep frying*

Clean the squid and cut off the tentacles and the head. Throw away the head and the ink sac. Slice the body into thin rings, and cut the tentacles into pieces about 2.5 cm (1″) long.

Marinate the squid for at least 2 hours in the tamarind water mixed with all the other ingredients. Then drain off the liquid and throw away it and the solids. Deep fry the squid for 5 to 6 minutes (this is best done in a wok), and serve hot. Fried squid is excellent as a side dish with rice, or by itself as a starter.

SAMBAL GORENG CUMI-CUMI
Squid in red chilli sauce   to serve four to six

People connect the name 'Sambal', quite rightly, with the hot relishes that are so popular in Indonesia. However, many kinds of sambal are in fact main dishes, and this is one of them. It needs to be good and red, so if you think that even seeded red chillis are going to make it too hot, use paprika or red pimientos instead.

1 kg (2 lb) squid	*a pinch of ground cumin*
1 tbs white vinegar	*a pinch of turmeric*
5 kemiri (candlenuts)	*a pinch of lemon grass (powdered)*
6 large red chillis, seeded	*2 tsp cooking oil*
6 shallots, or 1 onion	*3 tbs tamarind water*
1 slice terasi (page 41–	*1 tsp brown sugar*
optional)	*salt*
2 tsp ginger powder	*150 ml (¼ pint) water*

Clean the squid and throw away the ink sac and the head. Chop the tentacles into pieces about 1 cm (½″) long. Then cut up the squid into small squares, and rinse all the pieces in 1 tablespoon of white vinegar diluted with 600 ml (1 pint) of cold water. Strain off the water immediately.

Pound the kemiri, chillis, shallots and terasi until blended into a smooth paste. Add the ginger, cumin, turmeric and lemon grass. Sauté this paste in the oil for 1 minute, add the squid and tamarind water, and sauté for 3 more minutes. Add the sugar, salt and water. Continue cooking for 5 or 6 minutes, stirring frequently. Serve hot.

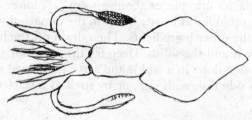

Indo-pacific squid

GORENG IKAN DENGAN UDANG
Fried fish prepared with dried shrimps   to serve four

This is a dish to be made with sea fish. What is needed is a species with reasonably firm white flesh. Those which we would use in Indonesia, or some of them at least, are known in Australia and have relations in the Caribbean region; but there is little point in trying to find a fish in, say, northern Europe which resembles an Indonesian species. The fact is that any fish with white flesh will do; and any search should be for what is abundant, cheap and fresh. From my own experience I know that turbot, haddock and skate are all suitable; and angler-fish and dogfish would also do very well.

You will also need dried raw shrimps, which in Indonesia are called *ebi* (page 44). These are a staple food in South-East Asia and can be found in any large Chinese or Oriental grocery, or in large foodstores with specialty departments.

700 g (1¼ lb) fish, cut up into small cubes
30 g (1 oz) dried shrimps or prawns
10 shallots

2 green chillis, or ½–1 tsp chilli powder
2 tsp sweet soya sauce
3 tsp lemon juice
salt
vegetable oil

for the marinade:
1 tbs thick tamarind water
1 clove garlic
salt and pepper

¼ tsp ground ginger
¼ tsp turmeric
1 tsp ground coriander

Marinate the fish for 2 hours. If you are using dried prawns, soak them in cold water for half an hour; if you are using the tiny dried shrimps, this soaking is not necessary. Slice the shallots and green chillis finely.

Deep-fry the fish cubes until golden, then keep them warm while you prepare the rest of the dish. Heat 2 tablespoonfuls of vegetable oil in a wok, sauté the shallots and chilli until slightly brown, then add the dried shrimps or prawns. Continue stir-frying for 2 minutes before putting in the soya sauce and a little salt. Stir for 1 minute more and add the fried fish; mix well. Just before serving, sprinkle with lemon juice. Serve hot.

IKAN ASAM MANIS
Fish in a sour and sweet sauce   to serve three

For this dish in Indonesia we use *ikan gurami*, of which a drawing appears on page 125. This is a fresh-water fish, quite large, with delicious thick white meat. In the town where I lived, you could go down to an enclosure near the Sultan's palace and see an artificial pond stocked with live gurami; you chose one, and a man would fish it out and truss it up in a sort of wicker basket for you. I have never found a completely satisfactory alternative fish in England, but Dover sole tastes very good when cooked this way. You will need three or four Dover soles, however, to make as big an impression as one gurami would make—served, at a party, on a large plate, as the centrepiece of your table.

3 Dover soles or, *e.g. in north America, flounders*

for the marinade:
2 tbs white malt vinegar	*1 tsp ground coriander*
¼ tsp chilli powder	*¼ tsp ground ginger*
2 cloves garlic, crushed	*salt*

After you have cleaned the fish, marinate them for 1 hour, turning them over once or twice.

for the sauce:
3 shallots	*2 tbs vinegar*
2 cloves garlic	*1 tbs lemon juice*
1 green chilli	*1 tsp dry mustard*
3 kemiri (candlenuts)	*1 cup water*
¼ tsp ground ginger	*salt*
¼ tsp ground turmeric	*2 tbs vegetable oil*
1 tsp brown sugar	*spring onions*

Slice the shallots finely; seed and slice the chilli. Pound the kemiri and garlic into a smooth paste. Then heat the oil in a wok or frying-pan, sauté the shallots and chilli for 1 minute, and add the kemiri paste, ginger and turmeric. Stir continuously for another minute. Put in the vinegar, sugar, mustard, lemon juice and salt. Stir, and add water. Simmer for 15 minutes. You will need about ¾ of a cup of this sauce, so add some more water if the quantity has lessened too much during cooking. But don't forget to taste the seasoning; the sauce should taste sweet and sour. You can reheat the sauce quickly just before serving; this is the time to put in the chopped spring onions.

Now heat about half a cup of oil in a large frying-pan. Fry the fish, one at a time, until both sides are golden brown. Put them on a large dish and pour the hot sauce over them. Serve immediately.

PINDANG IKAN
Fish cooked with tamarind   to serve four

This is good cold or hot, and it can be eaten as a main dish with rice or as a first course by itself.

4 mackerel, cleaned, and with the heads removed	¼ tsp ground laos (galingale)
¼ tsp chilli powder	1 tbs sweet soya sauce
¼ tsp cayenne pepper	salt
about 30 g (1 oz) tamarind	vegetable oil
6 shallots	2 cups water
4 cloves garlic	sliced cucumber
	wedges of lemon

Wash the mackerel with vinegar and rinse in cold water. Steam them for 20 minutes.

Slice the shallots and garlic, and fry in hot oil for 1 minute. Add the chilli, cayenne pepper, laos, soya sauce, tamarind and water. Add a pinch of salt, and taste. Pour this sauce over the fish in a deep saucepan or casserole. With the saucepan, bring the contents to the boil and simmer for about 1 hour. With the casserole, put it in the oven and cook for about 1 hour on gas mark 3 (about 325°F).

When it is cooked, put the fish on a serving-dish, strain the remainder of the sauce over it, and garnish with thin slices of cucumber and wedges of lemon.

PALLU MARA IKAN
A fish dish from South Sulawesi   to serve six to eight

This is a dish from the Bugis region of South Sulawesi. A Bugis friend tells me that Pallu Mara means food that is cooked until all the liquid has evaporated—in this case, a fish poached until dry. The recipe is said to have originated in Ujung Pandang (formerly Macassar), where you can find good tomatoes and where tomatoes are used more lavishly than in other parts of Indonesia. But there are many variations of it, and a friend from Alor, further east, says that Pallu Mara is also an Alor dish. The recipes that my two friends gave me differ slightly. I think on the whole I prefer the one from Bugis. My Bugis friend maintains that it is a dish for a lazy cook, meaning, I think, that you do not have to do any laborious pounding of the spices.

Alan Davidson, in *Seafood of South-East Asia*, says that he used *cakalang* (skipjack) to make Pallu Mara, and my friend confirms that this is indeed the first choice but goes on to say that *tongkol* or *ambu-ambu* (mackerel, tuna or little tunny) will provide a good Pallu Mara.

1 fish or fish steaks weighing	*3 cloves garlic*
2 kg (4¼ lb)	*a piece of root ginger or 1 tsp*
1 tsp turmeric	*ginger powder*
10 red chillis	*1½ cups tamarind water*
8 shallots or 2 onions	*salt*

Clean the fish and rub it with the turmeric and salt. Seed the chillis and cut them lengthwise into two. Slice the shallots (or onions), garlic and ginger. Put the garlic and ginger with half the sliced shallots and five chillis at the bottom of your fish pan. Lay the fish or fish steaks on top of these. Put the remaining chillis, shallots, garlic and ginger on top of the fish, and pour the tamarind water over everything. If you are using ginger powder, dissolve this in the tamarind water first. Add some more salt. Cover the pan and cook slowly for 40 to 50 minutes. Shake the pan gently from time to time and make sure the fish is not burnt. You can add a little more water during cooking if you think the fish is becoming too dry and is in danger of burning.

This fish should be served the next day, cold. Remove the solids that have been cooked with it, put it in a serving-dish and garnish with sliced tomatoes.

KARAMELATI
A special way of grilling fish   to serve four to six

In giving me this recipe, my friend from Alor said that the best fish to use would be *ekor kuning* (which means yellow tail) or *kakap* (the sea perch of South-East Asia and Australia, where it is also known as barramundi). The latter can be substituted by sea bass or the like. The former is one (*Caesio erythrogaster*) of a large tribe of fish known as fusiliers, which are among the few economically important fishes of the coral reefs of South-East Asia. There is nothing very special about them, and one might as well use, if in Australia or America, any other members of the snapper family, to which they belong; or, if in Europe, one of the tribe of sea breams. I find that the cod family is also suited to the recipe—cod itself, haddock and perhaps others too which I have not yet tried.

1 whole fish, or *half a fish*,	*6 shallots*
of 1¼ kg (3¼ lb)	*¼ tsp white pepper*
juice of 1 lime or *small lemon*	*salt*
4 red chillis	*2 tbs vegetable* or *olive oil*

Clean the fish about an hour before you are going to grill it, and rub it well, inside and out, with the lime or lemon juice and a little salt. Seed the chillis, peel the shallots, and slice them all thinly. Then pound them, with a little salt, to a very smooth paste. Mix this paste with the oil.

Rub half of the mixture on to the fish and start grilling it slowly, preferably over a charcoal fire. Turn it every so often. When it is about half cooked, spread the rest of the paste over it with a spoon, covering both sides. Continue grilling, and turning, the fish until it is cooked.

Serve hot.

PEPES IKAN
Marinated fish baked with coconut   to serve four

This is one of those useful recipes which can be used for almost
any fish, whole or in steaks or in fillets. I have used the recipe
for both turbot steaks and whole, cleaned trout, with good results.

1 kg (2¼ lb) fish (see above)

for the marinade:
¼ cup tamarind water
2 cloves garlic, crushed
¼ tsp chilli powder
salt and pepper

and thereafter:
2 cloves garlic
6 shallots
¼ tsp chilli powder

*120 g (4 oz) freshly grated or
desiccated coconut*
1 slice terasi (page 41—optional)
1 tsp brown sugar
juice of half a lemon
salt
olive oil, or clarified butter
*2 sprigs fresh mint—apple mint
if possible (we use a kind
called kemangi in Indonesia)*
chives

If you are using a large section or steak of fish, such as turbot,
cut it into 4 pieces. Mix together the ingredients of the marinade
and pour this over the fish. Cover, and leave for about half an
hour, turning the fish from time to time.

Then lay the fish side by side in a casserole, and pour over
them the marinade plus the clarified butter or olive oil. Bake in
the oven for 25 minutes at gas mark 4 (about 350°F).

While waiting, chop the shallots and garlic finely; and, if you
are using terasi, crush this to a paste with the garlic. Fry in a
little olive oil until slightly browned, and add the chilli powder,
sugar, lemon juice and salt. Mix well, then add the water and
coconut. Taste. Bring the whole lot to the boil and simmer for
2 or 3 minutes; then pour it over the fish in the casserole to
which you have added the sprigs of mint. This mint must be
taken out of the casserole before serving. Continue cooking—
uncovered—in the oven, at the same temperature as before, for
30 minutes. Alternatively, put it under slow grill until the fish
browns on top. Sprinkle with chopped chives just before serving.

This is how I make Pepes Ikan in England. In Indonesia, we
cook it wrapped up in banana leaf and supported on a metal
tray over a charcoal stove. Cooking takes about 50–60 minutes.

KARÉ IKAN
Fish curry   to serve four

Fish curry is the literal translation of Karé Ikan; but I should
explain that Indonesian 'curry' is rather different from Indian
curries. The recipe may be used for almost any fish. In the
former version of this book I suggested salmon steaks, which it
suits well; but these are now rather expensive. It is better to
select a white fish with firm flesh, such as haddock, angler-fish,
swordfish or dogfish. In Australia the various fish known as
whiting would be a good choice. Americans might like to use
snappers.

700 g (1¼ lb, cleaned weight)   *1 salam leaf or bay-leaf*
* fish—see above*   *¼ tsp turmeric*
6 shallots or 1 large onion   *¼ cup tamarind water*
2 cloves garlic   *1 cup of thick santen (coconut*
2 tsp ground coriander   * milk)*
1 tsp ground ginger   *2 tbs vegetable oil*
¼ tsp powdered, or 1 blade   *salt*
* fresh, lemon grass*   *sliced cucumber*
1 tsp chilli powder   *mint*

Whatever fish is used, it can be cut into small cubes or slices
before frying. Heat a little oil in a heavy frying-pan, and
carefully brown the fish in it.

Meanwhile, in another frying-pan, fry the chopped shallots
(or onion) and garlic until tender. Stir in the chilli, ginger,
turmeric, coriander, lemon grass, salam, salt and tamarind
water. Let this mixture simmer for 10 minutes, then put in the
fish. Cover, and simmer for another 10 minutes. Add the santen
and cook for a further 5 minutes.

Serve hot, garnished with very thin slices of cucumber and
chopped mint. (Alternatively, put the cucumber and mint into
the karé itself for the last 2 minutes of cooking.)

Incidentally, the same karé can be made with prawns. There
is no need to fry the prawns separately; but fry them in the
mixture of onion, etcetera for a few minutes *before* you put in
the tamarind water.

PANGEK
Fish cooked in coconut milk with fiddleheads

For the best results, this dish needs to be made in large quantities. It is quite expensive, admittedly; but it will keep for a long time in the refrigerator—as much as a month, perhaps, if it is reheated from time to time. Frequent reheating actually improves the flavour. In West Sumatra, where the recipe is supposed to have originated, we used to make and keep it in massive, deep earthenware jars, burned black on the outside by the wood fires. An enamelled saucepan is perfectly satisfactory for cooking Pangek on the stove.

Pangek is normally made with river fish, so I suggest using 6–9 trout, cleaned and sprinkled with salt. You also need:

500 g (1 lb) fern-shoots (fiddleheads in North America, paku or pakis
  in Indonesia—see the drawing below)—or curly kale
6 kemiri (candlenuts)
4 cloves garlic
2 onions
1 salam leaf or bay-leaf
1 tsp chilli powder
2 tsp ground ginger
¼ tsp ground laos (galingale)
1 tsp ground turmeric
3 cups fairly thick santen, made
  from 1 coconut or 350 g
  (12 oz) desiccated coconut
¼ cup tamarind water
a handful of fresh mint

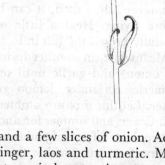

Crush the kemiri and garlic, and a few slices of onion. Add the salam leaf, chilli powder, ginger, laos and turmeric. Mix thoroughly with the santen and tamarind water. Arrange 3 of the trout on the bottom of your saucepan—it should be big enough for them to lie side by side. (To prevent the fish sticking to the bottom of the vessel, cover it with a thin layer of butter, or banana leaf). On top of the trout put a layer of fern-shoots or kale and sliced onions. Then put another layer of fish and another layer of the vegetables—and so on, up to the top. On the very top, put the sprigs of mint. Over the whole lot pour the spiced santen, having made sure that it has enough salt. It should just cover the fish. Cover tightly, and simmer gently on the stove for $2\frac{1}{2}$ hours.

BANDENG ISI
Stuffed milkfish (or other fish)

I learned this recipe (see page 31) from Mrs Kobir Sasradipoera. Fresh milkfish (see page 30) are not available in Europe, but frozen ones are in some Chinese shops. Otherwise use large mackerel or grey mullet. Ingredients are for fish of 700 g ($1\frac{1}{2}$ lb).

Scale the fish and beat it well on both sides with the flat of a large knife. Snap the backbone at the tail end, but leave tail (and head) in place. Withdraw, in turn, through the gill opening, the entrails, backbone and all meat, leaving the skin intact. Discard entrails and all bones and chop the meat thoroughly.

Pound 4 shallots and 3 cloves garlic to a paste, add 1 tsp ground coriander, season with salt and pepper, and fry the paste in oil or butter until it smells savoury. Let it cool, then mix it with the fish meat, adding 2 or 3 tbs very thick santen (1 tbs creamed coconut in 2 tbs hot water); 1 tsp brown sugar; 1 large beaten egg; and 2 Kaffir lime leaves or 1 bay-leaf, crushed. Carefully push the mixture back into the skin and sew it up if necessary. Wrap the fish in banana leaf or foil, and steam for 15 minutes. Unwrap, and prick the skin to prevent bursting. Re-wrap loosely and steam for 10 to 15 minutes more. Just before serving, brush the fish with butter or olive oil and grill it until brown. Serve it hot or cold, cut into thick slices.

GORENG TERI
Fried dried anchovies

Teri are very small fish, young anchovies measuring about 2 cm (nearly 1"), which have been dried and salted. You can buy imported ones in London under their other name, *ikan bilis*. Unsalted teri are obtainable, but I prefer the salted ones; if you find that they have too much salt in them, you can remedy this by rubbing them with absorbent paper (for example, paper towel) before you fry them. The heads of the fish should be discarded.

120 g (4 oz) teri	*½ tsp chilli powder*
4 shallots	*vegetable oil*
1 clove garlic	

The fish are to be deep-fried in a wok (2 or 3 minutes are ample), then put on one side and kept warm.

Slice the shallots, crush the garlic, and fry them both in a little oil. Add the chilli powder and mix it well in. Then put in the teri, and stir them around in the pan so that every fish is well covered with the shallots, chilli, and garlic. Either serve immediately with rice, or leave to cool before storing in an airtight jar. Teri that have been stored can be served cold or reheated in a frying-pan or wok.

Teri can also be fried just as they are, without shallots or chilli; but it would be a shame not to put in at least a little garlic.

GARANG ASAM IKAN
Spiced fish steaks   to serve two

This is a salty, spicy way to cook fish whose meat is rich and compact. It is very well suited to fresh tuna and other fish of the same family. But it can also be used for steaks of turbot or halibut; for angler-fish, the tail of which yields good firm steaks; for swordfish; and even for the humble dogfish. Other options open to Australian cooks would include the sea perch (*Lates calcarifer*, kakap in Indonesia); and Americans could choose red snappers or groupers, such as abound in the Caribbean region.

2 fish steaks (see above)	*2 tbs sweet soya sauce*
1 red chilli	*a little tamarind paste, grilled*
1 small vegetable marrow	*for about 1 minute on each*
1 slice terasi (page 41)	*side*
4 shallots	*1 cup water*
2 cloves garlic	*1 tbs vegetable oil*
¼ tsp ground laos (galingale)	*salt*

Wash and dry the fish. Seed and slice the chilli. Slice the shallots thin, and crush the garlic and terasi. Peel and cut the marrow into small cubes.

Fry the shallots and chilli in a tablespoonful of vegetable oil. Add the terasi and garlic paste, a cup of water, the soya sauce, the tamarind and laos. Stir well and let the mixture boil for 1 minute, then put in the fish and the marrow. Cover the pan and cook on a low flame until the fish has soaked up almost all the sauce: this will take 40–50 minutes. Add salt to taste. Stir carefully, remove the tamarind, and serve hot.

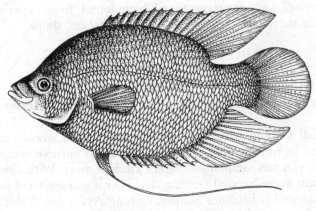

Gurami (see page 106)

Beef

Beef in Java comes from animals which anyone would instantly recognize as cows. In Sumatra, however, it comes from buffaloes. Perhaps this is one reason why Sumatran recipes often require cooking times of several hours, to make the meat tender; or perhaps the thoroughness of the cooking is simply to make the dish keep better. Javanese food, as a rule, is cooked very quickly indeed. In any case, almost all Indonesian meat dishes require the meat to be sliced or cut up thin before cooking starts, and a weekend joint—in the English sense—is quite unknown. The cuts of meat that you buy in the market are in any case different from those found in Europe, and most of them, as far as I know, have no special names. When you go shopping in the *pasar*, you simply pick up or point to the piece that you want, or discuss your requirements with the seller. The cuts that are mentioned here are those that I have found, from experience, are the most satisfactory from British butchers' shops.

SAMBAL GORENG DAGING
Diced beef in a rich coconut sauce   to serve four

Sambal Goreng is really a general name for a whole class of dishes. In other words, this is a kind of all-purpose recipe, in which you can use many different kinds of meat. With chicken, you can make Sambal Goreng Ayam, or if you use hard-boiled eggs as well it becomes Sambal Goreng Ayam dan Telur. My own favourite is Sambal Goreng Udang, made with large prawns (page 111). Sambal Goreng Daging is the traditional dish for Lebaran, the end of Ramadan (the Moslem fasting month), when it is served with Ketupat (page 95) or Lontong (page 95).

500 g (1 lb) topside or
  silverside
100 g (3 or 4 oz) mange-tout or
  sugar peas
50 g (2 oz) fresh peté, or *peté*
  asin (optional)
3 ripe tomatoes
5 shallots, or *1 large onion*
3 cloves garlic
4 kemiri (candlenuts)
2 tsp chilli powder
1 tsp paprika
1 slice terasi (page 41)

1 tsp ground ginger
1 tsp ground coriander
a pinch of ground laos
  (galingale)
a pinch of powdered lemon grass
1 tsp brown sugar (optional)
2 Kaffir lime leaves, or *bay-*
  leaves
salt
1 cup water
1 cup thick santen (coconut milk)
vegetable oil

Cut the beef into small cubes. Top and tail the mange-tout or sugar peas, and cut the peté beans in two. Peel, seed and chop the tomatoes. Pound the kemiri, onion, garlic and terasi in a cobek or mortar until they become a smooth paste. (You can also make this paste in a food processor, using the meat-mincing blade, but do not put terasi in the machine; crush the terasi into the paste with a spoon afterwards.)

In a wok or saucepan, heat about 4 tablespoonfuls of oil and fry the diced beef for 4 minutes. Drain and keep warm, wrapped in some absorbent paper. Reduce the oil in the pan a little, and fry the kemiri and terasi paste for 1 minute, stirring continuously. Add the chilli powder and paprika, along with the rest of the ground ingredients and the salt. Stir; then put in the meat, peté and tomatoes. Stir again, and add the water and the Kaffir lime leaves or bay-leaves. Cover the pan and simmer for ten minutes. Uncover, and add the mange-tout, the sugar, and some more salt if necessary. Simmer for another 3 minutes, then add the santen. Continue cooking until the santen is on the point of boiling. At this point, lower the heat and stir continuously for about 2 minutes. Serve hot.

DAGING GULUNG
A rolled beef dish   to serve six

In this dish, slices of beef are rolled and stuffed, rather like beef olives.

1 kg (2 lb) topside or rump steak	*¼ tsp chilli powder*
2 small aubergines	*1 slice terasi (page 41)*
1 big Spanish onion	*2 tomatoes*
4 cloves garlic	*vegetable oil*
1 tsp brown sugar	*spring onions and gherkins for garnishing*

for the marinade:
1 tbs olive oil

for the tomato sauce:
2 shallots, sliced thin
4 very ripe tomatoes or 120 g (4 oz) canned tomatoes

¼ tsp black pepper
1 tsp soya sauce

salt and pepper to taste
¼ tsp brown sugar

Cut the beef into as large and as thin slices as possible, and marinate for 1 hour. Slice the aubergines, sprinkle them with salt, and let them stand for at least half an hour. Slice the onion. Crush the garlic and terasi into a paste. Peel the tomatoes and cut them up small. Then fry the onion in a frying-pan with a tablespoonful of oil until it is transparent, and add the garlic and terasi paste, the chilli powder, and the sugar. Stir the contents of the pan well and put in the aubergines; continue stirring for 1 minute, then add the tomatoes, cover, and simmer for 5 minutes.

Use this mixture to fill the slices of meat, rolling each slice and fastening it with a cocktail stick. Arrange the rolls on a plate which can be put into a steamer, pour the tomato sauce over them (see below), and steam for 50 minutes. (Alternatively, put the rolls in a casserole, cover with the sauce, and cook in the oven for 50 minutes at gas mark 5 or 375°F.) Serve hot, garnished with chopped spring onions and gherkins sliced lengthwise very thin.

To make the tomato sauce, fry the shallots in a little butter until slightly browned. Sieve the tomatoes into the shallots. If you are using fresh tomatoes, boil them first for about 2 minutes. Add salt, pepper and sugar, stirring well.

You may like to experiment, as I often have, with variations in the filling, using materials that are to hand in whatever part of the world you happen to be. Bulb fennel, for example, is hardly ever eaten in Indonesia, but I discovered it and developed a taste for it when I came to England. If you use two fennel instead of the aubergines, and add two tablespoonfuls of desiccated coconut to the other ingredients, you will find the result very good. You can use the same sauce for this as for the 'regular' Daging Gulung.

SOTO DAGING
A spicy meat soup   to serve four

500 g (1 lb) brisket	*2 tsp lemon juice*
120 g (4 oz) shrimps	*2 tbs vegetable oil*
6 shallots	*salt*
3 cloves garlic	*fried onions, seledri (flat-leaved*
¼ tsp ground ginger	*parsley), and wedges of lemon*
a pinch of chilli powder	*(optional) for garnishing*
¼ tsp turmeric	

Boil the brisket with a little salt for 1 hour. Chop the shrimps and shallots and garlic, and mince them finely.

Cut the meat into small cubes, and save the stock for use later. Sauté the minced shrimps and shallots in 2 tablespoonfuls of oil for 1 minute, and add to them the meat and half a cup of the stock. Put in ginger, chilli powder, turmeric and salt, cover, and simmer for 10 minutes. Then put the meat into another saucepan and strain the liquid over it, throwing away the solids that are left in the strainer. Add two more cups of stock and go on cooking for 20 minutes more. Then add 2 teaspoonfuls of lemon juice.

Serve hot as a soup; garnish with fried onions and chopped seledri, and with wedges of lemon if desired.

DENDENG PEDAS
'Hot' fried beef   to serve six

Remember that *pedas* = hot—spicy hot! This is fried beef, with a robust flavour of chilli.

1 kg (2 lb) topside

for the marinade:
1 tbs olive oil   *1 tbs dark soya sauce*
⅓ tsp black pepper

Cut the beef fairly thin and trim it into small, square pieces. Marinate it for 1 hour or longer.

for the bumbu:
10 shallots   *salt*
2 green chillis   *1 tbs lemon juice* or *fresh lime*
2 tbs vegetable oil   *juice*

Slice the shallots finely. Seed and slice the chillis. Fry them in a tablespoonful of oil, in a wok, stirring all the time until they are golden brown. Add salt to taste. Keep hot.

Put a tablespoonful of oil in a thick frying-pan, and fry the slices of meat a few at a time. Three minutes on each side will be ample.* When all the pieces are cooked, put them into the wok with the onions and chilli. Heat, and mix well. Sprinkle over the mixture 1 tablespoonful of lemon juice, or, better still, fresh lime juice. Stir, and add more salt if necessary. Serve hot, with rice.

RAWON
Diced beef cooked in a spicy black sauce   to serve four

Like gulé, Rawon is halfway between a meat dish and a soup—so do not thicken the sauce. Unlike gulé, Rawon does not have

* *Note:* In Indonesia, the meat is usually fried until crisp. You can even buy sun-dried dendeng which only needs coating with bumbu and frying. Crisp dendeng can be rather tough, and I prefer it as described above; however, a purist might say that my recipe is not 'genuinely' Indonesian.

a warm golden colour but is very nearly black, as if the sauce had been made with Bovril. This colour comes from the keluwek nuts that are a small but important part of the dish. This nut looks from the outside like a large Brazil nut; inside, it has a soft black flesh. At the time of writing, it is not yet obtainable in Britain, but dried keluwek can be bought in Holland. They usually break up into small pieces in the packet, so 2 keluwek can mean 4 or 5 good-sized pieces. Dried keluwek must be soaked in cold water for an hour or so and then boiled for about 10 minutes so that they become soft. Without keluwek, these ingredients will make a pleasant-tasting dish, but it will not be Rawon. The ingredients listed will be enough for four people.

500 g (a little over 1 lb) beef—
  brisket or silverside
3 red chillis
1 slice terasi (page 41)
6 shallots
1 tsp ground coriander
6 shallots
1 tsp ground coriander
¼ tsp turmeric
¼ tsp laos (galingale)

¼ tsp powdered, or 1 blade fresh,
  lemon grass
1 tbs vegetable oil
2 keluwek
a little tamarind—a piece about
  the size of a walnut, which
  must be grilled for about 1
  minute on each side before use
salt

Boil the beef, all in one piece and with a little salt, for about 1 hour.

Seed the chillis and chop them finely; chop the shallots. Then crush the chillis, shallots, terasi, and keluwek to a smooth paste. Mix in with this the coriander, turmeric, laos, and lemon grass. Sauté this paste in 1 tablespoonful of vegetable oil for 1 minute. Cut the boiled beef into small cubes. Strain the stock into the wok or saucepan that the spices were sautéed in, and add the cut-up meat and the grilled tamarind. Simmer for 40–50 minutes. Take out the tamarind before serving.

Rawon is served with plain boiled rice, and it is usually accompanied by raw beansprouts, Sambal Terasi (page 221) and Krupuk (page 239). This is a good supper dish.

Beef

BESENGEK DAGING
Boiled silverside in a spicy sauce   to serve four

500 g (1 lb) silverside	*salt and sugar to taste*
1 onion	*2 tbs tamarind water*
1 slice terasi (page 41)	*1 cup stock*
a pinch of chilli powder	*2 cups thick santen (coconut milk)*
1 tsp ground coriander	*2 tbs vegetable oil*
¼ tsp turmeric	

Boil the meat for 1 hour. Leave it to cool, and keep 1 cupful of the stock. Slice the meat into serving pieces.

Slice the onion and crush the terasi, then sauté both for about 1 minute. Add to them the turmeric, chilli powder, coriander, tamarind water and a pinch of sugar and salt. Sauté this mixture for a few seconds before adding the meat and the stock. Then cover the pan and cook for 5 minutes. Uncover, and pour in the santen. Cook until the sauce becomes thick, stirring from time to time. Serve hot.

SEMUR DAGING
Slices of cooked beef in soya sauce   to serve four

Roast or boiled beef, sliced thin, may be used. This is a splendid way of cooking leftovers from a Sunday joint, or you can use meat from the cooked meat counter of your supermarket.

If you want to make Semur from uncooked meat, however, use fillet steak or topside; this makes it into much more of a party dish.

You can, of course, make Semur in very small quantities, but these ingredients will serve four people, with vegetables and rice:

500 g (1 lb) roast or boiled beef,	*2 hard-boiled eggs*
sliced thin	*1 large potato*
2 shallots	*1 large tomato*
1 clove garlic	*4 spring onions*
2 tbs dark soya sauce	*white or black pepper*
2 tbs clarified butter	*a pinch of grated nutmeg*

Slice the shallots and crush the garlic. Peel the potato and slice it very thin. Peel and chop the tomato. Fry the shallots and garlic in the butter until lightly browned. Add the meat and potato slices, and sauté for 1 minute. Add the chopped tomato, the soya sauce, pepper and nutmeg. Mix well, cover, and cook gently for 5 minutes. Taste. Put in the boiled eggs, cut into halves. Cook for another 5 minutes.

Put in the chopped spring onions just before serving, and garnish with fried onions.

If you use topside, cook a few minutes longer and put the potatoes in a few minutes after the meat.

This, incidentally, is one of the very few Indonesian dishes that you can cook with pork. Choose a good fillet, or use cold roast pork—but *not* pork with stuffing, because the stuffing will ruin the taste of the sauce.

DAGING BUMBU BALI
Slices of cooked beef in chilli and
tamarind sauce   to serve four

Like Semur, this is a good way to use leftovers, and is very easy to cook.

500 g (1 lb) sliced roast beef	*¼ tsp ground ginger*
1 slice terasi (page 41)	*1 tbs dark soya sauce*
2 onions	*¼ cup tamarind water*
2 cloves garlic	*2 tbs vegetable oil*
3 red chillis, seeded and crushed	*salt*

Crush the terasi and the garlic, and slice the onion. Fry the onion in oil until slightly browned, then add the terasi and garlic paste. Fry, stirring continuously, for half a minute or so, and add all the other ingredients, finishing with the meat. Stir well and let everything simmer very gently for 5–8 minutes. The mixture must not go dry, but the sauce should be very thick. Serve hot, with vegetables and rice.

Hard-boiled eggs are also good when cooked in this way.

DAGING ASAM MANIS
Beef, sweet and sour   to serve four

The English title above is a literal translation of the Indonesian
one; but remember that this dish is sweet and sour in the Indonesian, not the Chinese, sense.

800 g (1¾ lb) topside of beef, or   *1 tsp ground ginger*
   rump steak   *1 tsp salt*
2 green chillis   *1 cup tamarind water*
2 onions   *60 g (2 oz) butter, melted*
3 tsp brown sugar

Cut the beef into small, thin slices. Seed and slice the green
chillis and slice the onions. Dissolve the sugar in the tamarind
water and add to it the ground ginger and salt.

Put a layer of slices of meat on the bottom of a thick saucepan
then a layer of onion and chilli (with a little salt), then another
layer of meat, another of onion and chilli, and so on—with a
top layer of meat. Pour the tamarind water and melted butter
over this. Cover the pan and simmer for 35 minutes. Take the
lid off the pan and go on cooking until the sauce has almost
gone. Stir well, so that all the pieces of meat are coated with
the melted butter. Serve hot with rice.

EMPAL
Slices of boiled beef simmered   to serve four
in a rich stock and then fried

500 g (1 lb 2 oz) beef,   *a little tamarind*
   silverside or topside   *1 tsp brown sugar*
salt   *1 cup thick santen (coconut milk)*
3 red chillis (optional)   *made from half a coconut or*
3 cloves garlic   *from 180 g (6 oz) desiccated*
1 tsp ground coriander   *coconut*
1 slice, or a pinch of ground,   *vegetable oil, for frying*
   laos (galingale)

Boil the beef, with a little salt, for 2 hours. At the end, there should
be only about 2 cupfuls of stock left with the beef in the saucepan.

Seed and slice the chillis (but reduce or omit these if you do not want the dish to be hot). Crush the garlic.

Cut the boiled beef into, say, 8 slices. Beat the slices with a meat beater to flatten them. Put all the ingredients except the oil into the stock, ending with the meat, and the santen. Simmer until most of the stock has been taken up into the meat. Take the meat out of the pan and let it cool. Then fry the slices of meat in a frying-pan with a little oil, as if you were frying steak. (Alternatively, deep-fry.) Serve hot.

DENDENG RAGI
A 'dry' beef dish, cooked in grated coconut

250 g (8 oz) topside of beef
grated meat of half a coconut or
   250 g (8 oz) desiccated
   coconut
3 shallots
2 cloves garlic
1 tsp chilli powder
1 tsp ground coriander
¼ tsp ground laos (galingale)

1 slice kencur (page 69)
1 tsp brown sugar
2 tbs tamarind water
salt
2 Kaffir lime leaves
   (if obtainable)
1½ cups water
1 tbs vegetable oil

Grate the coconut. Slice the meat thin and cut into small squares. Slice the shallots and crush the garlic. Put the meat, with all the other ingredients except the coconut and vegetable oil, into a wok. Cover and boil for 40 minutes. Then add the coconut; stir, and taste. Let the mixture bubble until all the water has been absorbed by the coconut, then stir continuously until dry. Add 1 tablespoonful of vegetable oil and go on stirring and cooking until the coconut has become golden brown. Serve hot or cold, as a side dish.

Beef

RENDANG—*A traditional West Sumatran dish*

This dish is from the district in West Central Sumatra known as Minangkabau.

Minangkabau means 'Victorious Buffalo', and indeed the people of the area eat buffalo meat more often than beef, for cows are scarce. Buffalo meat is delicious but very tough, so Rendang is cooked for an unusually long time. Once cooked, it will keep, in an airtight jar, for up to a month, even in a tropical climate. But buffalo meat, apart from being tough, is hard to come by in most western countries, and beef is a very fair substitute for it. As it takes so long to cook, and keeps so well, it is worth making a large quantity.

*1¼ kg (3¼ lb) brisket or good
  stewing steak
6 shallots
3 cloves garlic
salt
1 tsp ground ginger
1 tsp turmeric*

*3 tsp chilli powder
¼ tsp laos (galingale)
7½ cups (3 pints) santen from 2
  small coconuts, made very thick
1 salam leaf or bay-leaf
1 fresh daun kunyit (turmeric
  leaf—optional)*

Cut the meat into biggish cubes. Crush the shallots and garlic with some salt; add ginger, turmeric, chilli, and laos. Mix them and put them into the santen. Add the meat and the various leaves. Cook in a wok, letting the mixture bubble gently and stirring it occasionally until it becomes very thick. This should take 1½ to 2 hours. Taste, and add salt if necessary. When the mixture is thick, the slow cooking must continue, but now the meat and sauce must be stirred continuously until all the sauce has been absorbed into the meat and the meat itself has become a good golden brown. This will take at least half an hour, perhaps as much as 1½ hours. Serve the Rendang hot, with plain boiled rice or Nasi Ketan (page 97).

Rendang will keep for many months in a deep-freeze; even though it contains santen, this becomes oil in the course of cooking and will not go bad.

Lamb

This is, I think, the best-liked kind of meat in most parts of Indonesia—certainly in my own part of West Sumatra, where any big family feast will have at its centre a lamb spitted and roasted whole. Indonesian cooks nevertheless regard lamb as an undisciplined, highly-flavoured meat, which needs plenty of garlic to keep it under control.

KAMBING BUMBU BACEM
Spicy boiled lamb   to serve six to eight

1 shoulder or leg of lamb—
    about 1½ kg (3¼ lb) of meat
1 onion
5 cloves garlic
¼ tsp chilli powder
2 tsp brown sugar

a little tamarind—about 10 or
    15 g (½ oz)
2 tsp ground coriander
1 tsp ground ginger
a pinch of laos (galingale)
1 salam leaf or bay-leaf
salt

Slice the onion and crush the garlic. Put these with the whole piece of meat in a deep saucepan. Add enough water to cover, and put in all the other ingredients. Boil slowly for 1¼ hours.

Take out the meat and let it cool, then cut it into good large slices. Put the slices into another pan, and strain over them the stock from the first pan. Taste, and adjust the seasoning. Cook over a high flame until the sauce has been reduced to half its original quantity. Serve hot.

PANGGANG KAMBING
Spit-roasted or oven-roasted lamb   to serve eight

This, to my way of thinking, is one of the very best ways of roasting and grilling lamb. You can do it with either a whole joint or chops. The quantities suggested here for the marinade will be sufficient for a leg or shoulder or about 16 good-sized chops.

for the marinade:
2 cups tamarind water
3 tsp brown sugar

1 tsp chilli powder
2 tsp salt
1 tsp ground coriander

Marinate the meat for at least 5 hours, or overnight, turning it several times. Just before you are ready to start cooking, prepare a sauce with the following ingredients:

2 tbs lemon or *lime juice*
4 cloves garlic, crushed
3 tbs dark soya sauce

1 tbs saté powder or *ground*
roast peanuts (optional)
¼ tsp ground ginger
1 tbs olive oil or *melted butter*

The traditional way to cook the meat is to grill it on a spit over a charcoal fire, which takes a long time if you are grilling the whole sheep in one piece. There is no reason, though, why a leg or shoulder should not be spitted over charcoal in a barbecue. When the meat is half-cooked, score it deeply with a knife, brush it well with the sauce, and continue cooking until the meat is tender. The whole process is likely to take up to 2 hours.

There is, of course, an easier, less picturesque method, which gives just as good results. Preheat your oven to 350°F (gas mark 4) and roast the lamb for 80 minutes (less if you are using chops). Score the joint deeply, brush it with the sauce and grill it, turning it over and brushing it with sauce several times. When the meat is nicely browned all over, it is ready to serve.

Eat it with Bumbu Saté (page 144) or Sambal Kecap (page 222).

KAMBING ASAM MANIS
Lamb, sweet and sour   to serve six to eight

The name does not mean sweet and sour in the Chinese style, but cooked with sugar and sweet soya sauce to balance the sharpness of vinegar and lemon juice.

If this is to be the main dish, these ingredients will be enough for six or eight; otherwise it will do for twelve or more.

1½ kg (3–3½ lb) leg of lamb, i.e. about 1 kg (2 lb) meat	juice of ½ a small lemon
1 medium-sized onion	1 tbs brown sugar
2 cloves garlic	1 tbs dark soya sauce
1 green chilli	1 tbs olive oil or other vegetable oil
1 tsp ground coriander	1 dozen chopped chives
1 tsp gound ginger	salt
1 tbs white malt vinegar	

Trim any fat and sinew from the meat and cut the meat into small pieces. Chop onion and crush garlic. Remove the seeds from the green chilli, then slice it very small. Fry the onion in the oil until slightly browned; add the crushed garlic, chilli, coriander and ginger, and finally the meat. Mix well in the pan, cover, and simmer for 10 minutes. Then add the vinegar, lemon juice, sugar and soya sauce. Taste, before adding salt. Simmer for a further 20 minutes, adding a little water if necessary. Just before serving, sprinkle with chopped chives.

Eat sweet and sour lamb with plain boiled rice and French beans—see the recipe for Tumis Buncis on page 191. If you want a hot, spicy relish, use Sambal Terasi (page 221).

GULÉ KAMBING
Lamb stew   to serve six

This is a liquid lamb stew—or you can think of it as a very meaty soup. Do not use flour to thicken the sauce; if you want it thicker, use thick santen or less water.

The best way to eat gulé is to put some boiled rice in a soup-plate, ladle the gulé over it, and eat it with a spoon. This is really a main course, and very satisfying for a small lunch party or a family supper; but a moderate helping of it makes a good first course, to be followed perhaps by fish.

If you serve gulé as a main course, these ingredients will be enough for six people:

1 kg (2 lb) lamb, leg or shoulder	*1 tbs vegetable oil*
1 onion or 4 shallots	*1 tsp brown sugar*
2 cloves garlic	*2 tsp ground coriander*
4 kemiri (candlenuts)	*a small stick of cinnamon*
¼ tsp chilli powder	*3 cloves*
¼ tsp white pepper	*1 salam leaf or bay-leaf*
¼ tsp cayenne pepper	*¼ teacup tamarind water*
¼ tsp ground ginger	*2 cups water*
¼ tsp ground laos (galingale)	*salt to taste*
¼ tsp turmeric	*3 cups of fairly thick santen*
¼ tsp powdered, or 1 stick fresh,	*(coconut milk)*
lemon grass	

Cut the lamb into small pieces. Chop the onion and garlic very small, or, better still, crush them in a mortar; add the kemiri and crush into a paste. To this, add the chilli, pepper, cayenne pepper, ginger, laos, turmeric, and lemon grass. Mix well. Fry the paste in oil for about 1 minute. Add the meat, and fry, stirring continuously, for about 2 minutes. Now add all the other ingredients *except* the santen. Cover, and simmer until the meat is tender. Then add the santen, and stir continuously until the liquid is very hot or just boiling. (Be careful here, because santen can curdle, just as a cheese sauce can. If you are in doubt, don't allow the liquid to come quite to the boil.) Taste; take out the salam or bay-leaf, the cinnamon and the cloves before serving.

A little fried chopped onion floating on the surface makes a good garnish, and if you like hot spices you can stir in a little Sambal Cuka (page 223) or Sambal Terasi (page 221) or use the sambal as a relish. Vegetables should be served as a separate course.

If you are fond of tripe, which most Indonesians love, try Gulé Babat. (*Babat* = tripe.) The recipe is exactly the same, except that you will need more garlic.

Gulé can be prepared and cooked up to 3 or 4 days in advance, and kept in the refrigerator until it is needed; but do not add the santen until you are ready to heat and serve the dish. You can keep gulé in a freezer for at least three months, as long as the santen has not been added to it.

KAMBING KECAP
Lamb cooked in soya sauce   to serve four

700 g (1½ lb) lamb, preferably
   from the leg, cut up into small
   cubes
1 tsp ground ginger

2 cloves garlic, crushed
a bunch of spring onions, or
   fresh chives, chopped
2 tbs dark soya sauce

for the marinade:
1 tbs dark soya sauce
a pinch of chilli powder

¼ tsp vinegar

Put the meat in a bowl and pour the marinade over it. Mix well and let stand for half an hour.

Fry the meat in 2 tablespoonfuls of vegetable oil, stirring it continuously, for 3 minutes. Lower the heat, cover the pan, and go on cooking for 3 more minutes. Take the lid off, add the soya sauce, ginger and garlic, stir, and simmer very slowly for 8 minutes. You can add 3 tablespoonfuls of water if the mixture looks as if it is becoming too dry; but this dish is only intended to have very little sauce. Put in the chopped spring onions or chives 1 minute before you finish cooking. Serve hot.

GULAI BAGAR
Lamb curry   to serve six to eight

In West Sumatra, where I was born, this lamb curry was often cooked for big feasts and celebrations. We always had it, for instance, when one of my boy-cousins was circumcised, because this was a major family event and huge numbers of people used to gather for it. Half-a-dozen or more sheep would be slaughtered and cut up into quite large chunks—Gulai Bagar is a chunky dish, and even the daily meal of a largish family might require half of a lamb, bones and all, to make the food tastier. On ordinary days, when there might be no more than fifteen or twenty of us in the house, my grandmother used to cook Gulai in a large earthenware pot over a wood fire outside the kitchen door.

However, you can make excellent Gulai Bagar inside your own kitchen, using quite an ordinary joint of lamb, and it is still delicious.

1 leg or *shoulder of lamb*
7 tbs freshly grated coconut or
   desiccated coconut
2 tsp coriander seed
5 kemiri (candlenuts)
2 aubergines (optional)
8 shallots, or *2 large onions*
4 cloves garlic
5 red chillis or *2 tsp chilli powder*
4 cloves
pinch of grated nutmeg
2 tsp ground ginger
1 tsp turmeric

1 stick cinnamon
4 cardamoms
¼ tsp ground cumin
pinch of powdered lemon grass
3 Kaffir lime leaves or *bay-*
   leaves
500 ml (1 pint) thin santen
   (coconut milk)
250 ml (½ pint) thick santen
   (coconut milk)
salt
2 tbs tamarind water
3 tbs oil

Cut the leg or shoulder of lamb, with the bone, into 4 or 5 pieces (ask the butcher to do this for you if necessary).

In a wok or frying-pan, roast the grated or desiccated coconut until brown. This will take only a few minutes. Then roast the coriander seed in the same way, stirring continuously, for about 2 or 3 minutes. Pound the coconut, coriander seed and kemiri in a mortar. Alternatively, grind them all together in a mixer or food processor, using equipment that is suitable for grinding nuts.

Peel and slice the shallots and garlic finely. Seed and slice the red chillis. Now heat the oil in a large saucepan, and fry the shallots, garlic and chillis for 2 minutes, stirring all the while. Add the meat and cover the pan for 2 to 3 minutes. Uncover, put in the kemiri and coconut mixture, stir, and cover the pan again for another 2 to 3 minutes. Then it is time to add all the remaining ingredients except the thick santen, tamarind water and salt. Simmer for 50 minutes and put in these final three. Continue cooking for 20 to 30 minutes, or until the sauce is beginning to thicken.

At this point, in Indonesia, we would throw in 8 or 10 small round aubergines, called 'terung gelatik'. What I do in London is to cut two ordinary greengrocer's aubergines into 6 or 8 thick pieces. The Gulai then goes on simmering until the aubergines are cooked, which should not take more than about 5 or 6 minutes.

To serve, take out the chunks of meat and slice or carve them as you please. Arrange the meat in a flame-and-oven-proof casserole, and the aubergines on top of the meat. Extract from the sauce all the unwanted solids—cloves, cardamoms, cinnamon and leaves. Pour away the excess oil, which is floating on top of the sauce, and pour the sauce over the meat. Keep the dish hot on a low flame or in a moderate oven until everyone is ready to start eating it, then bring it to table very hot. The best thing to eat with it is plain boiled rice.

By the way, this is the only recipe in the book which calls for cardamoms, *Elettaria cardamomum*. They are grown in Indonesia and have various Indonesian names, but in my experience are so rarely used that they have not been given an entry in the Introduction.

SATÉ KAMBING
Lamb saté   to serve four to six

Saté Kambing can be eaten with plain boiled rice, but it is especially good with Lontong (page 95). If you are eating informally out of doors, this has the extra advantage that you can eat entirely with your fingers, without getting too messy; and the lontong, of course, is always eaten cold, so you have no worries about keeping things hot while the saté is cooking. Indoors, you can serve saté with any kind of rice or vegetables, and it will always be a big success at any party.

1 kg (2 lb) lamb, leg or shoulder

for the marinade:	*1 tsp ground coriander*
2 shallots, or ½ onion, sliced	*1 tsp ground ginger*
1 clove garlic, crushed	*2 tbs tamarind water,*
2 tbs dark soya sauce	*or 1 tbs vinegar*
a pinch of hot chilli powder	*1 tbs olive oil, or vegetable oil*

for the sauce (bumbu saté):	*1 slice terasi (page 41)*
120 g (4 oz) peanuts	*1 tbs lemon juice*
2 shallots	*1 tsp brown sugar*
1 clove garlic	*1 tbs vegetable oil*
chilli powder and salt to taste	*1½ cups water*

Cut the meat into small pieces—each one the size of a reasonable mouthful. Marinate for at least 2 hours or overnight. Put the pieces on to bamboo or thin wire skewers, about 5 on to each skewer. Grill for 5 to 8 minutes, then turn over and grill on the other side for the same length of time. If you barbecue your saté, of course, it will not usually take so long to cook.

To make the sauce, fry the peanuts in oil, and then grind them into powder (a liquidizer can be used for this). Crush the shallots, garlic and terasi, and add the chilli powder and salt. Heat a little oil in a pan, and fry the shallots etcetera in it for a few seconds; then quickly add the water. As soon as the water is boiling, put in the ground peanuts, lemon juice and sugar, stirring well. Taste, and add salt if necessary. Continue boiling and stirring until the sauce is thick; this should not take more than about 3 minutes. Pour the sauce over the saté on the serving-dish, and sprinkle a little fried onion over it if desired.

An alternative sauce for those who do not like peanuts:

2 shallots or ½ small onion,
  sliced thin
3 tbs dark soya sauce
1 tsp white malt vinegar or
  juice of ½ a lemon

a pinch of chilli powder or, if
  you want it really hot, a sliced
  green chilli

Mix all the ingredients, and pour over the saté before serving. Alternatively, brush the sauce on to the saté as it is being cooked over charcoal.

A smiling vendor
offers Saté Kambing
in the market-place

SATÉ GODOG
Lamb in saté sauce   to serve six to eight

This kind of saté is better if you have one of the less expensive cuts of meat. Although you can, if you wish, put the pieces on to a skewer and heat them under the grill just before serving, Saté Godog is more often put straight from the pan into a serving-dish.

For a main course, these ingredients will serve six to eight people:

1 kg (2 lb) shoulder of lamb, cut into small cubes or small lamb chops—which need not be cut up	*1 slice terasi (page 41)*
	5 shallots or 1 medium-sized onion
⅓ tsp cumin	*2 cloves garlic*
2 tsp ground coriander	*1 cup ground peanuts*
⅓ tsp ground ginger	*¼ cup tamarind water*
⅓ tsp chilli powder	*1 tsp brown sugar*
	salt

Crush all the spices—that is, the cumin, coriander, ginger, chilli, and terasi—with the garlic and shallots to make a smooth paste. Fry this in oil for 1 minute. Add the meat, and continue frying for about 3 minutes, stirring all the time, until the meat is well coated with the spices. Add the tamarind water, and enough water to cover the meat. Add sugar, and salt to taste. Cover and simmer until the meat is tender. Taste; add ground peanuts. Mix well, and serve. (Alternatively, skewer the meat and put under the grill to brown. If you are using lamb chops, by all means brown them under the grill before serving; this is an excellent way to cook lamb chops, though not strictly Indonesian, as Indonesians do not cut up lambs in this way.)

You can also make Saté Godog Sapi with beef. Use stewing steak or brisket.

Saté Godog is best eaten with boiled or yellow rice and with carrots and French or runner beans. A little Sambal Terasi (page 221) is a good relish.

Pork

I have never thought of pork as properly belonging to Indonesian cuisine, because I was brought up in quite an orthodox Moslem family and spent my early life in predominantly Moslem communities. Even in Central Java, however, there are large numbers of Catholics and Protestants, with a fair sprinkling of Buddhists and Hindus and representatives, I suppose, of every other major and minor religious faith. Most people eat pork from time to time if their religion allows them to, and will order it in a restaurant even if they do not fancy cooking it at home. You can always buy pork at any market-place in Java; you might find it harder to get in Sumatra, though in big cities like Medan the Chinese will always see to it that there is a good supply. In Bali you see pigs everywhere, free-ranging individualists who all end up the same way: packed in cylindrical baskets, one pig to a basket, they are stacked up on the back of a truck for their last ride.

All the recipes in this section show some Chinese influence, except Saté Pentul, which I think is pure Balinese. As well as the dishes described here, another delicious way to cook pork is with tauco (salted yellow beans, see page 44). Follow the recipe for Ayam Tauco (page 165) and simply use pork instead of chicken.

BABI ASAM PEDAS
Pork in hot-and-sour sauce   to serve four

Indonesians who eat pork—most of them presumably non-Moslems—generally find it rather too fatty and rich. The sauce in this dish is intended to make the meat more digestible.

In addition to the meat, which I suggest should be ½ kg (1¼ lb) fillet of pork, you will need the following ingredients.

for the marinade:
¼ cup tamarind water
2 cloves garlic, crushed
1 tsp chilli powder
2 tsp cornflour
¼ tsp ground ginger
¼ tsp salt

1 cup chopped spring onions, or leeks
3 green chillis
3 ripe tomatoes
3 tbs dark soya sauce
2 tsp lemon juice (optional)
¼ cup water
6 tbs oil

Cut the pork into small thin slices, and marinate these in the tamarind water with crushed garlic, chilli powder, ground ginger, cornflour and salt for at least 30 minutes. Seed the green chillis, then cut them into thin rounds. Peel and seed the tomatoes, then chop them.

Heat the oil in a wok or thick frying-pan and fry the pork, half of it at a time, for about 5 minutes. When all the meat has been fried, reduce the quantity of oil in the pan to about 2 tablespoonfuls. In this, fry the chopped chillis and spring onions or leeks for about 2 minutes, stirring continuously. Add the meat, the chopped tomatoes and soya sauce. Cook for 3 minutes or so. Add water if you think this is necessary. Increase the heat for the final minute. Taste, and add more lemon juice if you want the dish to be sourer. Serve hot.

SEMUR BABI
Pork and transparent vermicelli   to serve four

Use thinly sliced pork for this dish, preferably leg—either raw
or cold roast pork. The vermicelli is the transparent kind, made
from green bean starch, that is common in Japan and all over
south-east Asia. In Indonesia we call it by its Chinese name,
so-un.

500 g (1¼ lb) sliced pork
a bunch of spring onions
3 cloves garlic
3 green chillis or *freshly ground*
    black pepper

1 piece of ginger or *1 tsp ground*
    ginger
3 ripe tomatoes
60 g (2 oz) vermicelli
4 or 5 tbs dark soya sauce
1 tbs oil

Clean and cut the spring onions into pieces about 2 cm (nearly
1″) long. Seed the chillis and cut into very fine sticks, and cut
the ginger in the same way. Peel and seed the tomatoes, then
chop them. Peel the garlic and slice it thinly. Soak the vermicelli
in cold water for 30 minutes, then drain.
    Heat the oil in a wok or saucepan, and quickly fry the sliced
garlic and ginger. Add the meat and chilli. Stir for a minute
or so, then add the tomatoes. Cover the wok or pan, simmer for
4 minutes, uncover and add the soya sauce. Simmer for 1 to 2
minutes longer before you add the vermicelli, and finally
increase the heat for a few seconds and stir. Serve immediately.

BABI KECAP
Pork cooked in soya sauce   to serve four

This, as its name suggests, is pork cooked in soya sauce. It is a particular favourite with my own husband and children, who always know when it is about to appear on the table because the ginger and garlic frying in the sauce smell so deliciously savoury.

½ kg (1¼ lb) fillet of pork or leg of pork	3 tbs dark soya sauce
1 tbs clear soya sauce	pepper or a pinch of chilli powder
2 tbs plain flour	2 tbs boiled water
½ tsp powdered ginger	2 tbs medium dry sherry or rice wine (optional)
120 g (4 oz) button mushrooms	2 tsp lemon juice
4 cloves garlic	6 tbs oil or pork fat
1 slice of root ginger, about 2 cm (1") across and ½ cm (¼") thick	

Cut the pork into small cubes. Put the flour into a bowl and add the clear soya sauce and ginger powder, mixing them well together. Coat the pork with the mixture and then let it stand for at least 30 minutes.

Clean and slice the mushrooms. Peel the garlic and ginger and slice them very thin; you can use these thin slices as they are, or cut them again into very tiny sticks.

Heat the oil or fat in a wok or thick frying pan and fry the meat, half of it at a time, turning it from time to time, for 5 minutes. Repeat the process for the remaining half of the meat. The flour that coated the meat will tend to stay in the pan or stick to the bottom of it, but leave it there—it will thicken the sauce later. Now take most of the oil out of the pan, leaving only about two tablespoons which you then heat again. In this, fry the tiny slices of garlic and ginger and the mushrooms, stirring continuously, for 1 minute. Add the soya sauce, the meat and the water. Mix well, season with pepper or chilli powder, and stir continuously for 1 or 2 minutes. Just before serving, add the sherry or rice wine and the lemon juice. Serve hot.

This dish keeps extremely well in the freezer, and it is worth making a large quantity from, say, half a leg of pork, which is much cheaper than buying pork fillet. If you are going to freeze your Babi Kecap, however, do not add the sherry or lemon juice at the time of cooking. To serve from the freezer, thaw the meat out completely and heat quickly on a high flame for 2–3 minutes, stirring or shaking the pan well all the time. Add the sherry or rice wine and lemon juice just before serving.

SATÉ BABI
Pork saté   to serve four

An important difference between this and other kinds of saté is that we do not usually eat pork with peanut sauce. We eat it by itself, or with Sambal Kecap (page 222).

¾ kg (1¾ lb) fillet	for the marinade:
of pork	*2 tbs clear soya sauce*
1 tbs melted pork fat or	*2 cloves garlic, crushed*
butter	*1 tsp ground ginger*
1 clove garlic, crushed	*1 tsp 'five spices'*
2 tsp dark soya sauce	*1 tbs clear honey*
2 tsp lemon juice	*¼ tsp white pepper*

Cut the pork into small thin squares and marinate for 2 hours. Push on to bamboo or metal skewers. Put these on a rack or in a roasting tin and cook in a preheated oven at 350°F (gas mark 4) for 30 minutes, turning them over several times.

Mix the fat (or butter) with the crushed garlic, soya sauce and lemon juice. Just before serving, brush the saté with this soya and lemon mixture, and grill for 2–3 minutes. Serve immediately.

Most readers will know that the 'five spices' used in this recipe are a Chinese ingredient, the mixture being composed of star anise, fennel, cloves, cinnamon and pepper.

SATÉ PENTUL
Minced pork saté   to serve four

The first time I ate Saté Pentul was in Bali, at a little warung in the central square of Den Pasar. My husband said, however, that he had tasted it on a previous visit, before our marriage, when he had wandered into the preparations for a big festival and been given generous sticks of saté from the hundreds that were grilling over a shallow trench filled with charcoal. In Lombok, which is the next island to the right as you look at the map, they make Saté Pentul with beef and a little terasi and call it Saté Pusut. I have tried both, and both are good, but I find the pork recipe slightly simpler to cook (no terasi) and tastier. Like all saté, this makes an equally good main course or snack with drinks before the meal.

½ kg (1 lb 2 oz) pork, leg or fillet	1 tsp brown sugar
	2 tsp soya sauce
½ or 1 tsp sambal ulek (crushed chilli, see page 224)	1 tbs tamarind water
	2 tbs grated or desiccated coconut
3 cloves garlic	1 duck egg or hen egg
¼ tsp ginger powder	salt
1 tsp coriander seed, roasted and crushed	6 tbs thick santen (coconut milk)

Mince the pork, including some of the fat. Crush the garlic and mix it with the sambal ulek. To this add the ginger powder, crushed coriander, sugar, soya sauce and tamarind water. Put about half a teaspoonful of this mixture into the santen in a bowl, and keep this in a cool place until the saté is ready for grilling.

Beat the egg well. Mix the remainder of the spices with the minced meat, and add the grated coconut, beaten egg and some salt. Mix everything well together and shape into small balls the size of a walnut. Put four meat balls on to a bamboo skewer just before you are ready to grill. You can make the mixture up to 24 hours before, but don't mould it or put it on to skewers until the last possible moment; if you do, the balls will tend to split and fall off. Grill slowly, turning carefully from time to time. After 4 or 5 minutes, when the mixture should be half-cooked and pretty firm, brush the balls with the spiced santen and carry on grilling until they are golden brown. If you brush on the santen too soon, the meat will again tend to fall to pieces. Eat immediately, with Bumbu Saté (page 144) or Sambal Kecap (page 222) or simply by themselves.

If you want to get Saté Pentul ready beforehand for a dinner-party, make them earlier in the day and bring them up to the half-cooked stage. Then, just before serving, brush them with the santen and finish them off with a few minutes under the grill. Once grilled, they can if you wish be kept hot for quite a long time in a well-buttered electric frying pan. This allows you to take out a few at a time if you are serving them as appetisers before the meal. For this, use single balls and cocktail sticks instead of skewers.

Variety Meats

All Indonesians love offal, with the result that pieces of the animal that you might expect to buy fairly cheaply in England turn out to be relatively expensive over there. The best saté of all is Saté Padang, in which different kinds of offal are skewered together. I have not included a recipe for it here, because the sauce is difficult to make and I cannot get all the ingredients for it in Europe. If, however, you are in Indonesia and have a chance to eat Saté Padang, take it.

JILABULO
Chicken livers with sago and coconut   to serve two

This recipe from Sulawesi is an excellent way to cook chicken liver. The result is not entirely unlike a coarse pâté, and although I would not like to push the resemblance too far it did suggest to me that this would be a good first course for a dinner party, perhaps with some French toast and a little parsley to garnish it, or simply by itself. The taste and texture are not like pâté at all, but they seem to be acceptable to English palates. At home we would cook Jilabulo in banana-leaf packets, and just undo them and eat them when we felt like it.

5 chicken livers
3 tbs sago
1½ cups thick santen (coconut milk)
¼ tsp pepper

2 shallots
2 cloves garlic
1 tsp ground ginger
salt

Clean the liver and slice it thinly. Peel, slice and crush the shallots and garlic, or pound them until smooth. Add salt and pepper and ground ginger. Mix all these in a saucepan with the sliced liver. Stir the sago into the santen and add this to the liver. Cook slowly for about 5 minutes or until the sago becomes thick, stirring occasionally. Then get ready to steam it. In Indonesia we get some good-sized squares of banana leaf, drop a large spoonful from the pan on each square, and fold it over and under. These little parcels are then steamed for 15–20 minutes. Where there are no banana leaves, I use a small soufflé dish or several individual dishes to hold the mixture, and steam it in my rice steamer for 20 minutes. Serve hot or cold.

KELIA HATI
Liver in a spiced coconut sauce   to serve four

This is usually made with ox liver, but lamb liver is a good substitute.

700 g (1½ lb) ox liver
2 tbs white vinegar
4 shallots
2 cloves garlic
800 ml (1½ pints) thick santen (coconut milk)
1 or 2 tsp sambal ulek (page 224), or 1 tsp chilli powder

¼ tsp ground coriander
a pinch of powdered lemon grass
a pinch of laos (galingale)
1 tsp ground ginger
¼ tsp turmeric
1 salam leaf, or bay-leaf
salt

Clean the liver by soaking it for about 20 minutes in a bowl of cold water with the 2 tablespoonfuls of white vinegar. Then cut it into small slices about 1 cm (½″) thick.

Peel and slice the shallots and garlic finely. Put all the ingredients (except the liver) into a wok or saucepan to make a thick, spiced santen. Add a little salt and boil for about 30 minutes. Put in the liver and continue cooking for another 30 or 40 minutes, stirring occasionally. The sauce ought to be good and thick.

Taste, and add salt if necessary. Serve hot.

GORENG BABAT ASAM PEDAS
Hot sour fried tripe   to serve four

Hot sour fried tripe is the literal translation. When I was a child we always had tripe cooked this way at home, and we all regarded it as a great treat. Tripe is a popular delicacy in, I think, most parts of Indonesia, and I am pleased to find that it is highly thought of in at least some parts of Britain. If you like tripe, you will like Goreng Babat, and if you don't like tripe, then I think it's a pity.

1 kg (2 lb) tripe	*a pinch of powdered lemon grass*
5 shallots	*(optional)*
3 cloves garlic	*1 tsp brown sugar*
5 green or red chillis	*1¼ tsp salt*
¼ teacup tamarind water	*2 salam leaves* or *bay-leaves*
1 tsp powdered ginger	*oil for frying*
¼ tsp ground coriander	

In Indonesia tripe is sold raw, so it has to be boiled for 30–45 minutes in salt water, scraped, and rinsed in cold water before use. In Britain, Australia and the USA tripe has usually been cleaned and boiled before you buy it.

Put this clean boiled tripe into a large saucepan. Cut the unpeeled shallots into quarters, slice the garlic thinly, seed the chillis and cut them into halves. Put all these into the saucepan with the tripe. Dissolve the powdered ginger, ground coriander, powdered lemon grass, sugar and salt in the tamarind water, and pour this over the tripe. Add the salam or bay-leaves and boil the tripe for half an hour. Leave it to cool, still in the tamarind water. When cool, discard all the remaining juice and the solids and cut the tripe into small squares. Heat about a cupful of oil in a wok or frying pan, and fry the tripe, a few squares at a time, until nicely brown. Serve hot.

GULAI OTAK
Brains cooked in a spicy coconut sauce

This is a traditional Sumatran recipe for cooking brains, which we always mix with daun mangkok (see page 53). I have made it in London with curly kale, however, and it both looked and tasted good.

3 pairs of sheep brains	*1 tsp ground ginger*
10 daun mangkok or about 180 g (6 oz) young leaves of curly kale	*½ tsp turmeric*
	3 asam kandis or 3 slices asam gelugur (page 47)
3 kemiri (candlenuts)	*2½ cups thick santen (coconut milk)*
4 shallots	
4 cloves garlic	*salt*
1 tsp sambal ulek (page 224)	*1 salam leaf or bay-leaf*

Wash the brains several times in cold salted water and boil them for 5 minutes. Wash the daun mangkok or curly kale, and shred it finely. Pound the shallots, kemiri and garlic in a cobek or mortar until they become a smooth paste. Add the sambal ulek and the other ground ingredients, and mix well.

In a saucepan, put half of the daun mangkok or kale, and on top of this put the brains, cut in halves. Then add the rest of the greenstuff together with the asam kandis or gelugur and salam leaf. Dissolve the pounded ingredients into the santen and add this to the contents of the pan. Cook slowly on top of the stove for 25 minutes or until the sauce is quite thick.

Discard the pieces of asam kandis or gelugur and salam leaf before serving. Serve as hot as possible.

SEMUR LIDAH
Boiled tongue in soya sauce   to serve four

500 g (1¼ lb) ox tongue	*2 tbs dark soya sauce*
3 shallots	*1 tbs oil or butter*
1 clove garlic	*salt and pepper*
¼ tsp ground ginger	*¼ cup water*
a pinch of nutmeg	*1 cup chopped spring onions and*
1 tsp tomato purée	*parsley (optional)*

If you buy the tongue from the butcher raw, boil it first for 2 hours and leave it to cool in the stock. When it is cool, skin the tongue and cut off, in slices, the 500 g that you need for this dish.

Peel and slice finely the shallots and garlic. Heat the oil in a wok or saucepan, and fry the shallots or garlic until soft. Add the ground ginger, nutmeg, tomato purée and the sliced tongue. Stir, then add the soya sauce and a little salt and pepper, and the water. Simmer for 3 or 4 minutes. Stir in the chopped spring onions and parsley just before serving. Serve hot.

Chicken

Indonesian chickens are not only free range but, in many cases, are left pretty well to run wild. Any car journey involves numerous attempts to avoid them as they step unconcernedly into the road. This sort of existence makes them scraggier and tougher than European chickens, but much tastier—and infinitely superior to the average broiler. However, even a battery bird can be made delicious. Indonesian chicken dishes should, in my opinion, be eaten with the fingers, except for the very wet ones, which obviously call for a spoon. The meat ought not to fall from the bone too readily; the cooking times suggested here are for soft English chickens. Tough little Indonesian birds need longer.

TERIK AYAM
Chicken in thick candlenut sauce   to serve two to three

6 drumsticks and 6 wings, or   ¼ tsp ground cumin
  6 whole chicken legs   1 slice terasi (page 41)
3 shallots   salt
3 cloves garlic   3 cups santen (coconut milk)
5 kemiri (candlenuts)   2 tbs vegetable oil
1 tsp ground coriander

Grill the terasi, peel and chop the shallots, and pound these together with the kemiri and garlic. Add the coriander, jinten, and salt, and mix all well together into a thick paste. Put this in a wok, pour the santen over it, and put in the chicken pieces. Simmer, uncovered, until the sauce is thick. Then add 2 tablespoonfuls of oil. Continue cooking, stirring constantly, until the sauce is really thick; then serve hot.

SOTO AYAM
Indonesian chicken soup   to serve four to six

This can be eaten as soup, or as a supper dish with rice. If you serve it as a main course, these ingredients will feed four to six people.

2 chicken breasts	5 kemiri (candlenuts)
120 g (4 oz) shrimps	1 cabé rawit (page 51) or
120 g (4 oz) beansprouts	¼ tsp chilli powder
¼ tsp ground ginger	a pinch of turmeric
2½ cups chicken stock	1 tsp salty (clear) soya sauce
4 cloves garlic	salt and pepper

for the garnish:

4 spring onions (chopped)	1 potato, sliced thin and fried
several sprigs of seledri	until crisp
(flat-leaved parsley)	fried onions
wedges of lemon	1 hard-boiled egg (optional)

Season the chicken breasts with 1 crushed clove of garlic and salt and pepper, and boil them for 30–40 minutes. Take out the chicken and allow to cool. Clean the beansprouts (page 206).

Pound the kemiri and garlic, and cabé rawit into a paste, and fry this in a little vegetable oil for 1 minute. Add the shrimps, turmeric, ginger and soya sauce. Shred the boiled chicken and add this to the sauce. Pour on 1 cup of stock, cover, and simmer for 5 minutes. Add the rest of the stock, adjust the seasoning, and simmer for another 10 minutes. Just 2 minutes before serving, put in the beansprouts.

Arrange slices of hard-boiled egg and fried potato in soup-plates and sprinkle with chopped spring onions and seledri. Top with slices or wedges of lemon. Bring the soto to table in a large serving-bowl and ladle it on to the plates. Sprinkle on top with fried onion. This should be served very hot.

If you eat soto as a supper dish, make some plain boiled rice to go with it; you may also want to add a little more chicken. If you think the cabé rawit, or chilli powder, will make the dish uncomfortably hot, then leave this ingredient out. If you are cooking for people who disagree amongst themselves on how hot their food should be, then make your soto without chilli but provide a side-dish of hot sambal for the spice-lovers; for example, Sambal Kecap (page 222) or Sambal Cuka (page 223).

AYAM PANGGANG BUMBU BESENGEK
Roast and grilled chicken in coconut sauce   to serve two

1 spring or *small roasting chicken*	*1 tsp ground coriander*
1 slice terasi (page 41)	*¼ tsp ground laos (galingale)*
4 shallots	*¼ tsp powdered,* or *1 blade fresh*
2 garlic	*lemon grass*
3 kemiri (candlenuts)	*500 ml (1 pint) santen (coconut*
¼ tsp chilli powder	*milk)*
¼ tsp turmeric	*1 tbs vegetable oil*

Cut the chicken into two, lengthways, and wash and dry the halves.

Crush the terasi, kemiri, garlic and shallots into a smooth paste. Mix into it all the other ground spices. Heat the oil in a wok and sauté the paste for half a minute. Brown the chicken halves in this oil and paste. Pour in the santen and let it bubble, turning the chicken from time to time. When the sauce has become thick, take out the chicken. The sauce can be left in the wok or poured into a small saucepan; it will be heated up before serving. The chicken halves must now be grilled on a charcoal stove (or under a gas or electric grill, if a charcoal stove is out of the question).

Serve hot, with plain boiled rice, and heat up the sauce as gravy. A good vegetable dish to accompany this is Acar Campur (page 205); or you can serve any plain boiled vegetable, such as beans or carrots, with Sambal Bajak (page 226).

To freeze, pack the chicken halves in the sauce. Thaw out completely before serving; heat the sauce, and grill the chicken on charcoal.

AYAM PANIKÉ
Chicken in aromatic sauce   to serve four

1 medium-sized chicken
6 shallots
1 tsp chilli powder
4 cloves garlic
4 kemiri (candlenuts)
1 slice terasi (page 41)
2 cups water
1 tsp brown sugar
¼ tsp ground ginger or small
  slice of root ginger

¼ tsp powdered, or 1 blade fresh
  lemon grass
2 cups santen (coconut milk)
2 Kaffir lime leaves (these are not
  absolutely necessary, but it will
  not be a real Ayam Paniké
  without them)
vegetable oil
salt and pepper

Clean and cut the chicken into serving pieces and rub with salt
and pepper. Brown the pieces in hot oil. Keep them warm
until required.

Crush the shallots, garlic, kemiri and terasi into a paste, and
mix with this the chilli, ginger, lemon grass and sugar. Fry this
mixture in a little oil for half a minute; then add the water and
the Kaffir lime leaves. Put in the chicken; cover the pan, and
boil gently until the pan is almost dry. Then add the santen.
Cook until the sauce is good and thick, stirring from time to
time.

KELIA AYAM
A Sumatran chicken curry   to serve three to four

'Kelia' is pronounced k'-lee-o.

1 small boiling chicken, cut up
  into serving pieces
4 cups thick santen (coconut milk)
6 shallots, or 1 onion
3 cloves garlic
3 kemiri (candlenuts)

1 tsp ground ginger
1 tsp chilli powder
¼ tsp laos (galingale)
1 salam leaf or bay-leaf
1 tsp turmeric
salt

Pound the shallots, garlic and kemiri into a paste (or, if you are
using onion, slice the onion very finely). Mix all the ingredients

with the santen, adding the pieces of chicken last. Simmer until the sauce is thick; this will take 1–2 hours. Taste, to make sure there is sufficient salt. Serve hot.

This dish will freeze well, but freeze it before the sauce is too thick. There should be enough sauce to cover the chicken when it is packed. To serve Kelia Ayam from the freezer, let it stand an hour or two to begin thawing, then put it straight into a pan or wok and heat until the sauce is thick.

TUMIS AYAM DENGAN JAMUR
Chicken cooked with mushrooms   to serve two

You can make this dish with chicken breasts straight from the shop or, if you have the sort of family that only eats the wings and legs of a roast chicken, you will find Tumis Ayam an excellent way of using the leftovers.

2 chicken breasts	1 tbs tauco (salted yellow beans,
120 g (4 oz) mushrooms	page 44)
4 shallots	1 tsp ground ginger
2 green chillis	2 cloves garlic
6 spring onions	6 tbs boiled water or clear stock
	2 tbs vegetable oil

If you use cooked chicken, shred it into small pieces. Uncooked chicken should be diced or cut into small, thin slices. Shred or slice the mushrooms. Peel and slice the shallots. Seed the chillis, and cut lengthwise into thin strips: cut these in half across if they are more than 4 or 5 cm long. Cut the spring onions into pieces of about the same length. In a cobek pound the garlic and yellow beans to a smooth paste and add the ground ginger.

Fry the sliced shallots in a wok until lightly browned, and quickly add the yellow-bean paste and the chillis. Stir the mixture for a minute or so, then add the chicken and mushrooms. Stir again, and add the water or stock. Cook gently for five minutes. Add the spring onions, increase the heat and stir for one minute. Serve immediately.

AYAM BUMBU ACAR
Chicken in yellow piquant sauce to serve four

1 small chicken or *chicken pieces*	*a pinch of chilli powder* or *2*
sufficient for 4 people	*green chillis, if you like it hot*
3 kemiri (candlenuts)	*2 tbs vegetable oil*
2 cloves garlic	*salt*
1 shallot	*3 tbs white vinegar*
¼ tsp turmeric	*1 tsp brown sugar*
a pinch of ground ginger	*¼ tsp dry mustard*
10 pickling onions	*8 tbs chicken stock*
¼ cucumber	

Boil the chicken for 50 minutes with a little salt.

Pound together the kemiri, garlic, and shallot, and add to them the turmeric and ginger. Mix all these well. Peel the pickling onions; peel the cucumber and cut it lengthwise into 4 or 6 pieces, throwing away the seeds. Then cut the cucumber sticks into chunks about 1 cm (½″) long. If you are using chillis, seed them and cut them lengthwise, then cut each half into two quarters.

Bone the boiled chicken and cut it into small pieces. Heat a tablespoonful of vegetable oil in a wok and sauté the paste of kemiri, garlic etcetera for half a minute. Put in the pickling onions, chillis and salt; stir for 1 minute while cooking, then add the vinegar. Cover the wok with a saucepan lid and let it all simmer for 5 minutes. Uncover, and put in the chicken pieces, the sugar, mustard, and stock. Cover again for 6–8 minutes. Uncover for the second time and add the cucumber; then go on cooking, stirring occasionally, for another 4 minutes. Serve hot.

AYAM GORENG
Indonesian fried chicken to serve four

The name means simply 'fried chicken', and that is all it is. The marinade, however, gives it a characteristically Indonesian flavour.

1 medium-sized chicken or chicken portions for 4 people

for the marinade:

¼ cup tamarind water	*1 tsp ground coriander*
1 tbs clear soya sauce	*1 clove garlic, crushed*
a pinch of chilli powder	*a pinch of turmeric*
1 tsp ground ginger	

Marinate the pieces of chicken in this mixture for 2 hours, turning them from time to time.

Strain the chicken, so that the marinade drips away from it. Then deep-fry the portions, 4 or 5 at a time.

Chicken fried in this way is excellent with Nasi Goreng (page 100).

AYAM TAUCO
Chicken cooked with salted yellow beans to serve four

1 medium-sized roasting chicken	*½ tsp chilli powder*
2 onions	*1 tsp paprika (optional)*
4 cloves garlic	*1 tsp ground ginger*
2 tsp dark soya sauce	*2 tbs vegetable oil*
1 tbs tauco (salted yellow beans, page 44)	*¼ cup tamarind water*
	1 cup water
1 tsp brown sugar	

Cut the chicken into serving pieces; wash, and dry. Slice the onions. Pound the garlic and the tauco into a smooth paste.

Fry the onions in the oil for half a minute. Add the tauco, then the chicken. Stir well, so that every part of the chicken is coated with tauco. Put in the soya sauce and the rest of the ingredients. Cover, and simmer very gently for 45 minutes. Then take the lid off, and cook for a further 5 minutes to reduce the sauce. Serve hot.

AYAM PANGGANG
Roast and grilled chicken with soya sauce   to serve two

1 small chicken will be sufficient. Wash and dry it, inside and out, and rub with salt and pepper and butter. Roast for 30 minutes. When the chicken has cooled a little, cut it in half lengthways. Beat the flesh with a meat-beater to tenderize it— but carefully, so as not to bring it off the bone.

for the bumbu:

1 tsp chilli powder	*1 tsp brown sugar*
a pinch of pepper	*2 tbs soya sauce*
1 clove garlic	*juice of ¼ a lemon*

Mix all the above ingredients thoroughly, and coat the two halves of the chicken with the mixture. Then grill the chicken slowly, turning it several times and brushing it with the remainder of the bumbu. When you do this for the last time, brush the chicken also with melted butter. Grill until golden brown.

    Ayam Panggang is very good if it is done under a gas or electric grill; but for perfection it should, of course, be done over a charcoal stove.

GORENG AYAM MBOK BEREK
mBok Berek's fried chicken   to serve two to four

Back in the early sixties, about the time when I was first married, it was a regular treat for my husband and me to drive fifteen kilometres or so out of Yogyakarta along the Solo road to the neighbourhood of the great Hindu-Javanese temple complexes that rise out of the plain between Merapi volcano and the sea: Kalasan, Candi Sewu, and Prambanan itself, where now they dance the story of the Ramayana in the cool nights of June and July. Very close to one of the smaller temples, Candi Sari, was a large restaurant set among the fields and bamboo groves. It was a pleasantly informal place, with terraces and canopies pushing out from the main building to make extra dining-space as the business grew. Its fame rested, and as far as I know still rests, on one superlative dish: chicken boiled in the water of young coconuts and then fried. Before I left Indonesia, baskets of mBok Berek's chicken (*mBok* is the Javanese word for 'mother' or 'Mrs') were being flown to Jakarta from the nearby airport, and today, so I have heard, you can buy them in the United States if you know who to ask. Certainly, if you go to Yogya, you will be able to try the excellence of this chicken for yourself; but you can imitate it quite faithfully in your own kitchen. The only ingredient that may present problems if you are in Europe is the coconut water, and this is absolutely essential. Water out of a hairy, thick-shelled old coconut from the supermarket will do well enough, but you do need three cups of it—the contents of several nuts. Ideally, the water should be from *kelapa muda*, the young nut (see page 37) that grows profusely all over Java and can be had for the taking—if you know how to shin up a sixty-foot palm trunk to get it.

1 chicken, cut in half
5 shallots
1 piece of root ginger or *1 tsp*
  ginger powder
1 piece laos (galingale) or
  ¼ tsp ground laos

salt and pepper
2 salam leaves or *bay-leaves*
3 cups coconut water
coconut oil or *vegetable oil for*
  frying

Chop the shallots coarsely. Peel and bruise the ginger and laos. Put these into the coconut water in a deep saucepan. Put in the chicken halves, season with salt and pepper and boil for 40 or 50 minutes until tender. By this time most of the coconut water will have evaporated or been absorbed into the chicken; if there is any left, throw it away and allow the chicken to cool. Then deep-fry the chicken in a wok until it is golden brown. This dish can be eaten hot or cold; it tastes good indoors, but it is equally splendid as the foundation of a real gourmet picnic.

GUDEG
Chicken with jackfruit

to serve six

This is perhaps the most famous of the traditional recipes of central Java. This area is one of the most densely populated in the world, fertile, intensively farmed, and very beautiful. It has been the seat of empires and sultanates; its courts and wealthy merchant houses refined and perfected the arts of music, poetry, philosophy—and cooking. Gudeg, however, is a popular rather than a courtly dish. The best Gudeg is to be had in the old royal city of Yogyakarta, or so the people there will tell you; citizens of other towns have been heard to say that the Yogyanese make their Gudeg too sweet. Whatever town you are in, the most pleasant surroundings in which to eat Gudeg are certainly those of a warung—a stall, more or less permanent but open on all sides to the air, where the proprietor cooks and serves his food and gossips with his customers. A good warang fills much the same social function, and has much the same atmosphere, as a small French pavement café. When I was at high school and university in Yogya, and lived in a boarding-house full of young girls on the north side of the town, our favourite place for eating out was a warung near the market-place, called Gudeg Krang-

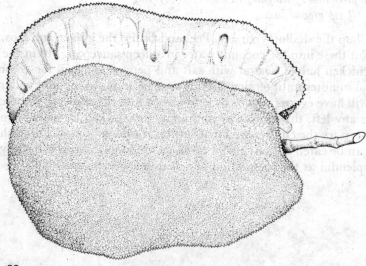

Nangka—Jackfruit

gan. Probably it is still there. I cannot say positively that my recipe is the same as that used in Gudeg Kranggan, because every good warung-owner has his secrets.

One of the traditional ingredients may be difficult to get in Europe. This is nangka or jackfruit. You can sometimes buy it fresh in Holland, but rarely in England. Canned nangka, however, is good. Otherwise, use canned bamboo shoots; the result is still very close to an authentic Gudeg.

1 chicken	*3 tsp ground coriander*
salt and pepper	*1 small piece kencur (page 69)*
3 cups of very thick santen, from	*a small jackfruit weighing about*
one medium coconut or 300 g	*500 g (1 lb) or about 400 g*
(10 oz) desiccated coconut	*(14 oz) canned jackfruit*
1 tsp chilli powder	*drained and rinsed or 240 g*
6 shallots	*(8 oz) canned bamboo shoots,*
1 slice terasi (page 41)	*sliced thin*
3 cloves garlic	*2 salam leaves or bay-leaves*
4 kemiri (candlenuts)	*1 Kaffir lime leaf (optional)*
¼ tsp laos (galingale)	*hard-boiled eggs (optional)*
1 tsp cumin	

Well season the chicken with salt and pepper, coat it with butter, wrap it in aluminium foil, and roast it.

Crush the shallots, garlic, terasi and kemiri into a paste, mix this thoroughly with the other ingredients, adding the santen last, and stir well. Taste the mixture to make sure that there is enough salt—remembering that there is also a certain amount of salt in the chicken.

Cut the chicken into serving pieces and put these, with the juice of the chicken, into the santen and spices. Simmer, in a fairly deep saucepan, until the sauce becomes thick, about 50–60 minutes. Stir occasionally, and take great care that the chicken does not burn.

If you wish, put some whole hard-boiled eggs into the sauce at the same time as the chicken. Slice these thin before serving; they will have become very hard, and will taste superb, impregnated as they are with the heavy sauce and the spices.

Serve with plain boiled rice.

Chicken

LAPIS AYAM
Layered steamed chicken   to serve four

'Lapis' in this case refers to the layers of chicken which, in Indonesia, we usually steam in a neat square parcel made from a banana-leaf. Lapis Ayam cooks just as well, however, wrapped in aluminium foil and either steamed or baked in the oven.

4 chicken breasts, boned	*1 egg*
225 g (½lb) beef (brisket)	*1 can (4 oz) bamboo shoots*
3 shallots	*2 green chillis*
3 cloves garlic	*2 tbs soya sauce*
2 tsp ground coriander	*2 tbs rice flour* or *plain flour*
1 tsp ginger powder	*1 tsp cornflour*
1 slice terasi (page 41), grilled	*salt*
a pinch of laos (galingale)	*pepper*
a pinch of powdered lemon grass	*1 tbs oil* or *butter*

Rub the chicken with 1 tablespoonful of soya sauce and a little pepper. Mince the beef, with a little of the fat. Put it aside while you pound 2 shallots and 2 cloves of garlic with the terasi in a mortar. To this add the coriander, ginger, laos, lemon grass and some salt. Mix these with the minced beef, add the egg and the flour and knead well.

Cut the bamboo shoots into small cubes or dice, and peel and slice the remaining shallot and the garlic. Seed the green chillis and slice them into very thin rounds. Heat the oil in a saucepan, fry the sliced shallot, garlic and chillis until soft, then add the diced bamboo shoots. Dissolve the cornflour in the remaining 1 tablespoonful of soya sauce, and add this to the contents of the saucepan. Stir while cooking for 2 minutes and let the mixture cool.

Now take a piece of aluminium foil (or a banana-leaf, if you have one) big enough to wrap the meat. Lay on it a piece of the chicken breast, and spread over this one third of the minced beef and one third of the bamboo shoots and spices, mixing them all well together and making sure that the chicken is entirely covered. Repeat the process, layer on layer, so that you finish up with 3 layers of minced meat and bamboo shoots in between 4 layers of chicken, with chicken on top. Rub the top surface of the pile with a little oil or butter, wrap the whole lot tightly in the aluminium foil (or leaf) and either steam it for 1 hour or bake it in a preheated oven for 1 hour at gas mark 5 (375° F).

To serve, unwrap the parcel carefully and pour the small quantity of sauce at the bottom of it into a bowl. Slide the meat on to a serving dish and slice it vertically downwards so that the alternate layers are revealed. Pour the sauce over it. Lapis Ayam can be eaten straight away, stored and re-heated later, or eaten cold.

SEMUR AYAM
Chicken in soya sauce   to serve four

4 chicken breasts

Boil these for 20 minutes in 2 cupfuls of water, to which have been added: 1 tablespoonful of sweet soya sauce, a pinch of grated or powdered nutmeg, half a teaspoonful salt, and a little pepper.

1 onion	*4 spring onions*
2 cloves garlic	*2 tbs clarified butter*
1 green chilli	*1 tbs dark soya sauce*
2 ripe tomatoes	

Slice the onion and crush the garlic. Take out the seeds from the chilli and shred it finely. Boil the tomatoes for 2 minutes in a little water.

Fry the onion in the butter until transparent, then add the chilli and the crushed garlic. Stir for half a minute before putting in the chicken. Then sieve the tomatoes into the pan, add soya sauce and chicken stock. Taste. Let everything simmer for 10 minutes. Chop the spring onions and put them in 1 minute before cooking ends. Serve at once.

GULAI AYAM DENGAN REBUNG
Chicken cooked in sauce with bamboo shoots to serve four

This is a simple but delicious way of cooking chicken pieces. The chicken is cooked in santen with thinly sliced bamboo shoots, so you have your meat and vegetable in one dish. All you need to go with them is plain boiled rice.

chicken pieces (enough for 4)
1 225 g (8 oz) can bamboo shoots
1 cup good chicken stock or a chicken cube
4 shallots
1 slice terasi (page 41)
4 kemiri (candlenuts)
2 cloves garlic
a pinch of powdered laos (galingale)
a pinch of cumin
2 salam leaves or bay-leaves
1 tbs vegetable oil
salt and pepper
500 ml (about 1 pint) santen, made from half a coconut or 180 g
* (6 oz) desiccated coconut*

Clean the chicken, rinse the bamboo shoots in cold water and slice them thinly. Peel and slice the shallots finely. Peel the garlic and pound it up with the kemiri and terasi to make a smooth paste. Make the santen.

Now, in a wok or a saucepan, heat the oil and fry the shallots until soft. Add the kemiri paste, stir for half a minute and add the laos and cumin. Put in the sliced bamboo shoots and the chicken stock (or dissolve the chicken cube in a cup of boiling water and add that). Cover the pan and simmer for 4 minutes. Uncover it, put in the chicken pieces, put the lid back on and continue simmering for 2 minutes. Add the santen and salam leaves and a little salt and pepper, and simmer gently with the lid *off* for 40 to 50 minutes or until the chicken is tender, stirring from time to time. Serve hot.

PINDANG AYAM DAN DAGING
Chicken and beef in tamarind sauce   to serve four to six

2 chicken breasts
500 g (1 lb) beef—brisket or
  silverside
1 slice terasi (page 41)
2 shallots
1 red chilli or a pinch of chilli
  powder
6 cabbage leaves or a small
  cabbage heart

3 cloves garlic
a pinch of ground laos (galingale)
2 tbs dark soya sauce
a piece of tamarind about the size
  of a walnut
2 cups stock
salt and pepper

Boil the beef, seasoned with a little salt and pepper, for ¾ hour. Add the chicken breasts and continue boiling for 20–30 minutes more. Let the meat cool; keep the stock.

Slice the shallots and garlic very finely (and the chilli, if you are using whole chilli). Grill the terasi and tamarind for about 1 minute on each side, and pound and crush the terasi. Cut the beef and chicken into large slices. Discard the cabbage stalk from the centre of each leaf, so that each leaf becomes two half-leaves; or, if you are using a cabbage heart, cut this into 4 or 6 pieces.

Put the beef and chicken into a saucepan with 1 cup of stock, and then add all the ingredients except the cabbage. Taste the mixture, and add salt if necessary (remember that the soya sauce is already very salty). Cover the pan, and simmer slowly until the pan is almost dry. Now transfer the meat to another saucepan, and strain over it what is left of the stock which you have just been cooking the spices in—by straining, you will get rid of the lump of tamarind and other solids, the flavours of which have now gone into the meat. Add the other cup of stock, and the cabbage. Cover the pan again and cook for 15 minutes. Serve hot.

ABON AYAM
Fried shredded chicken

This is very tasty as a garnish or accompaniment to Nasi Rames (page 174). It can be served hot or cold. You can keep it, in an airtight jar, for several weeks.

4 chicken breasts	*1 tbs tamarind water*
salt	*2 tsp brown sugar*
2 cloves garlic	*vegetable oil*

Boil the chicken, with a little salt and 2 crushed garlic cloves, for 40–45 minutes. Let the pieces cool, skin them, and shred the meat finely. Season with salt, tamarind and sugar. Put about 3 tablespoonfuls of vegetable oil into a wok, and when the oil is good and hot throw in a handful of shredded chicken. Stir it all the time as it cooks, until it is golden brown and crisp. Go on like this until all the chicken is fried.

AYAM GORENG JAWA

to serve four

This is a favourite Javanese way to fry chicken.

1 chicken, about 1½ kg (3–3½ lb)	*a pinch of powdered, or 1 blade*
6 shallots	*fresh, lemon grass*
¼ tsp ground coriander	*salt and sugar to taste*
3 kemiri (candlenuts)	*1½ cups santen (coconut milk)*
a pinch of turmeric	*vegetable oil for deep-frying*
a pinch of ground laos (galingale)	

Cut the chicken into small portions. Crush the kemiri and shallots, mix the other ingredients except the oil. Put the santen in a saucepan with the kemiri, shallots, and spices, and mix thoroughly. Put the chicken into this sauce and boil for 45–50 minutes, or until all the sauce has been taken up by the meat. Allow to cool, then deep-fry in vegetable oil.

OPOR AYAM
Chicken in white coconut sauce   to serve four

1 medium-sized roasting chicken
¼ a red chilli or a pinch of chilli
   powder
1 slice terasi (page 41)
¼ a lemon
5 shallots or 1 medium-sized
   onion
3 cloves garlic
5 kemiri (candlenuts)
1 tsp ground coriander
¼ tsp cumin

a pinch of ground laos (galingale)
2 Kaffir lime leaves or bay-leaves
a piece of rhubarb, about 8 cm
   (3–4″) long (rhubarb is the
   best alternative to the original
   Indonesian ingredient: cermé
   or belimbing wuluh, pages 52
   and 49)
3 cups thick santen (coconut milk)
salt and pepper

Wash and dry the chicken, and rub it inside and out with salt and pepper and lemon juice. Roast for 1 hour at gas mark 5 (375° F). Leave to cool, and cut into serving pieces.

Make santen from half a fresh coconut or 320 g (12 oz) desiccated coconut. Peel and slice the shallots or onion. Seed the chilli and grill or fry the terasi. Crush the garlic, terasi, kemiri and chilli together in a mortar; then mix well all the ground ingredients. Slice the rhubarb. Put all these, with the cumin and the bay-leaves or Kaffir lime leaves, into the santen in a deep saucepan. Mix, and season with salt. Put in the chicken pieces and cook on top of the stove until the sauce is thick. Serve hot.

If you want to freeze Opor Ayam, stop cooking before the sauce thickens: you will need enough sauce to cover the chicken pieces when you pack them. When you want to serve, let the package thaw out completely before heating, and then heat thoroughly until the sauce is thick.

Eggs

This is a very short section, because we do not often use eggs as the principal ingredient of a dish. They play important parts in several recipes in this book, for example Gudeg and Sambal Goreng; and we eat just as many boiled eggs, fried eggs and omelettes as anybody else does. Generally speaking, we use duck eggs in savoury cooking more often than hen eggs because in many areas they are more plentiful; there are more ducks among the flooded rice-fields than there are chickens at home in the village.

ACAR TELUR
Eggs in piquant sauce to serve four

Duck eggs or hen eggs are equally good for this sauce.

4 or 6 hard-boiled eggs	1 tbs clear soya sauce
3 shallots	3 tbs vinegar
2 cloves garlic	2 tsp brown sugar
4 kemiri (candlenuts)	1 tsp dry mustard
1 tsp ground ginger	1 cup water
¼ tsp turmeric	salt
2 or more green chillis	1 tbs vegetable oil
½ cucumber	

Peel and slice the shallots and garlic and pound them in a mortar with the kemiri until they become a smooth paste. Add the ground ginger and turmeric. Seed the green chillis and chop them finely. Peel the cucumber and slice into thin rounds.

Peel the eggs and cut each into four.

In a wok or saucepan, heat the oil and fry the kemiri paste for 1 minute. Add the chillis, soya sauce and vinegar, stir, and let the mixture simmer for a minute or two. Then add the sugar, mustard and water, and some salt, stirring well. Let this sauce simmer for 5 minutes. Taste, and put in the eggs and cucumber, spooning the sauce carefully over the eggs. Keep the heat on under the eggs for another 3 or 4 minutes, then serve immediately with rice.

TELUR ISI
Stuffed eggs

These can be used to garnish Nasi Kuning (page 102), or as a side dish or a party snack.

12 hard-boiled eggs	*3 tbs fresh grated*, or *desiccated,*
3 shallots or *1 onion*	*coconut*
2 cloves garlic	*salt*
a pinch of ginger powder	*3 tbs boiled water, still hot*
a pinch of chilli powder or	*1 tbs vegetable oil* or *clarified*
freshly ground black pepper	*butter*

Peel and slice the shallots or onion finely. Peel and crush the garlic. Heat the oil or butter in a wok or saucepan, fry the sliced shallots until soft, and add the crushed garlic, ginger, chilli powder and coconut. Mix well in the pan. Add salt and 2 table-spoons of hot water. Cook and continue stirring for 4 minutes. The mixture should be moist, so add the remaining 1 tablespoon of hot water to it before you put it into a bowl to cool.*

Now halve the hard-boiled eggs and scoop out the yolks. Mix the yolks with the other prepared ingredients, fill the whites, and garnish with parsley.

* Not everyone likes the chewy, flaky consistency of grated coconut. If you want the mixture to be smooth, blend it in a liquidizer, moistening it with a little extra water or, better still, with a little curry sauce or tomato sauce.

TELUR BUMBU BALI
Eggs in tomato and chilli sauce   to serve four to six

Most Indonesian egg dishes that I know of consist of hard-boiled eggs in one or another of a wide range of sauces—all the way from mild combinations of soya sauce and tomatoes (as in Semur, see Semur Ayam, page 171, and Semur Lidah, page 158) to explosive concoctions of the hottest chilli. At home in Magelang, where I lived with my parents and my five sisters, whichever sister was cooking that day would call to the other members of the family and ask if they wanted their eggs in Bumbu Bali, Bumbu Acar, Bumbu Rujak . . . These bumbu, or sauces, can be used, with variations, to cook meat or fish or vegetables. In Java we did not consider any one sauce to be essentially superior to any other, though I suppose everyone had his own favourites. I have noticed, however, that in Indonesian restaurants in Holland Bumbu Bali seems to be especially popular. Perhaps the name has something to do with it—but it does taste good, and it is easy to make.

12 hard-boiled eggs	*4 ripe tomatoes*
6 shallots	*2 tbs dark soya sauce*
2 cloves garlic	*1 cup boiled water*
3 red chillis or 2 tsp Sambal	*salt*
Ulek (page 224)	*1 tbs vegetable oil*

Peel and slice the shallots and garlic and seed the chillis. Pound these in a cobek or mortar until smooth. Peel, seed and chop the tomatoes.

Heat the oil in a wok or saucepan and stir-fry the shallot-garlic-chilli paste for a minute or so. Add the chopped tomatoes, soya sauce and water. Let the mixture come to the boil and add the eggs, whole or halved, and simmer for 8 minutes. Taste, and add salt if necessary. Serve hot, with boiled rice.

TELUR DADAR PADANG
Duck egg omelette with coconut   to serve four

This savoury omelette is thick and satisfying, and can be eaten either as a main dish with rice and vegetables or as a snack with salad.

3 duck eggs
2 shallots
1 clove garlic
1 red chilli or ¼ tsp chilli powder
1 or 2 fresh grated, or desiccated, coconut
salt
1 tbs cold water
2 tbs vegetable oil

Peel the shallots and garlic and seed the chilli. Chop them finely, or better still pound them together. Mix them with the coconut and the water, and add a little salt to taste. Then beat the mixture thoroughly with the eggs. It needs more beating than an ordinary plain omelette and should become quite fluffy.

Heat the oil in a wok, and spoon it over the sides or tilt and turn the wok so that the sides are well coated with oil. Pour the omelette mixture into the hot wok, and while it is still liquid, swirl it around so that the omelette is not too thick in the centre. Let it cook for 2 or 3 minutes. Turn it over carefully (it should be perfectly circular) and cook slowly for another 3 or 4 minutes, until the middle, which of course is still the thickest part, is firm and the whole omelette is lightly browned. The edges should now be delicately crisp.

Serve hot or cold, cut up into slices like a cake.

Duck

In the rice-growing areas, where the flooded fields abound in frogs and small fish, flocks of ducks are to be found in every village. They march out in the morning to the fields, usually in the care of a boy or an old man with a small flag on a pole. Towards dusk they reassemble around the flag for the journey home. They are, naturally, highly regarded as food, provided that the sauce is thick enough and the garlic sufficient to match the strong flavour of the meat.

Rich food of this kind needs plenty of rice to go with it—preferably plain boiled rice.

BEBEK BUMBU CABÉ I
Duck in chilli sauce (without coconut)   to serve four

1 duck, cut into 10 or 12 pieces
1 cup white malt vinegar
1 large onion
1 stick cinnamon
6 shallots
6 cloves garlic
1 green chilli
1 tbs vegetable oil
1 green pimiento
¼ tsp cayenne pepper

1 small piece root ginger
1 pinch laos (galingale)
¼ tsp powdered, or 1 blade fresh, lemon grass
1 salam leaf or bay-leaf
1 Kaffir lime leaf (optional)
juice of 1 orange
juice of ½ a lemon
salt
a handful of chives

Soak the duck in vinegar for 2 minutes, then wash and dry. Put in a large saucepan with the onion, which should be cut into big chunks, the stick of cinnamon, and some salt. Cover with water, bring to the boil, and simmer for 1 hour. Allow to cool, then take out the duck, strain the stock, and remove all the fat.

Pound together the shallots, green chilli, and garlic. (It is advisable to remove the seeds of the chilli.) Fry the paste that is thus made in a tablespoonful of vegetable oil until it is just beginning to change colour; then add the cayenne pepper, the lemon juice and orange juice, and then the pieces of duck, with half a cup of stock. Next, put in the ginger, laos, Kaffir lime leaf (if you have one), salam and powdered lemon grass (or their alternatives). Cover, and simmer for 5 minutes.

Cut the pimiento into narrow strips and add these to the mixture. Stir and taste, and regulate the seasoning if necessary; it should taste good and hot, slightly sour, and there should be just enough salt. Stir, and continue cooking for 8 minutes. Sprinkle with plenty of chopped chives. At this point you can, if you wish, add another half cup of stock, but this dish should have only a little sauce. Remove the salam leaf and lemon grass before serving. Serve very hot, with plain boiled rice. A suitable vegetable dish to go with your duck is Tumis Buncis (page 191).

BEBEK BUMBU CABÉ II
Duck in chilli sauce (with coconut)   to serve four

1 duck, cut into 10 or 12 pieces	*6 cloves garlic*
1 cup white malt vinegar	*2 tsp ground ginger*
1 large onion	*2 green chillis*
1 stick cinnamon	*¼ tsp cayenne pepper*
salt	*1 salam leaf or bay-leaf*
500 ml (1 pint) very thick	*1 Kaffir lime leaf (if available)*
santen (coconut milk)	*1 blade, or a little powdered,*
6 shallots	*lemon grass*

Boil the duck as you would for Bebek Bumbu Cabé *without* coconut—but only for half an hour.

Pound the shallots, garlic and chillis to a paste, and add to this the ground ginger. Put all the ingredients into the santen, and stir them. Put the boiled duck, with half a cup of stock, into a wok. Pour the spiced santen over it. Boil, stirring occasionally, until the sauce is very thick and oily. This will take about 1½ hours. If, at the end, you think there is too much oil, remove some of it before serving.

Duck

OPOR BEBEK
Duck in white coconut sauce   to serve two

Roast a small duck in the oven at about 400° F (gas mark 6)
until it is golden brown. This should take a little over an
hour, depending on the size of the duck. Then cut it in half
lengthwise.

Meanwhile you will have been at work on the numerous
other ingredients, listed below. The last of these, rhubarb, may
be a surprise. In Indonesia we would use about 6 cermé or 3
belimbing wuluh; but a stick of rhubarb is a highly satisfactory
alternative.

4 *shallots*	1 *tsp ground ginger*
1 *slice terasi (page 41)*	2 *tbs vegetable oil*
4 *cloves garlic*	2 *cups santen, made from 1 fresh*
4 *kemiri (candlenuts)*	*coconut or 350 g (12 oz)*
salt	*desiccated coconut*
¼ *tsp chilli powder*	1 *bay leaf*
¼ *tsp laos (galingale)*	1 *stick rhubarb about 10 cm*
¼ *tsp powdered, or 1 blade fresh,*	*(4") long*
lemon grass	*some melted butter*
1 *tsp ground coriander*	

Pound the shallots, terasi, garlic, kemiri and a pinch of salt into
a paste, and add to it the chilli, laos, lemon grass, coriander, and
ginger. Fry it in 2 tablespoonfuls of oil for 1 minute. Put in both
halves of the duck, and cover them with santen. Add the bay-
leaf, and the rhubarb cut up small. Boil for 1 hour or until the
pan is almost dry, taking care not to burn it. Taste, and add salt
if necessary. Put the duck into an oven-proof dish, brush with
melted butter, and put under a high grill until golden brown.
Serve immediately.

The remaining sauce can be served separately, if you eat the
Opor with boiled rice. Alternatively, top it up with half a cup
of stock or water, and boil in it a few potatoes—preferably new
ones—to eat with the duck. You can still serve the sauce as
gravy.

BEBEK HIJAU
Duck in green chilli sauce

This is sometimes called Gulai Bebek Padang, and is another well-known West Sumatran dish. It improves if it is kept for 24 hours so that the fat can be skimmed off. Bebek Hijau needs a lot of green chilli to give it colour, and this of course makes the taste hot and strong. You can moderate it somewhat by using the largest possible chillis, on the principle that the big ones are always gentler.

1¾ kg (4¼ lb) duck	3 tbs tamarind water
12 green chillis	1 stalk lemon grass (bruised)
10 kemiri (candlenuts)	or ¼ tsp sereh powder
12 shallots or 2 large onions	3 Kaffir lime leaves (optional)
5 cloves garlic	1 bay leaf
3 tbs vegetable oil	freshly-ground black pepper
2 tsp ginger powder	salt
¼ tsp turmeric	1¼ cups cold water
¼ tsp ground laos (galingale)	2 tbs chopped chives

Clean and cut the duck into 8 pieces, and discard most of the skin. Seed and chop the chillis, and blend them into a smooth paste with the kemiri; alternatively, mince and then pound them together. Slice the shallots and garlic finely.

Heat the oil in a saucepan. Fry the shallots and garlic until slightly browned, then add the chilli-and-kemiri paste. Stir for 1 minute, and add the ginger powder, turmeric, laos and lemon grass (or sereh powder). Stir this mixture, and put into it the duck, tamarind water, Kaffir lime leaves, bay leaf, pepper and salt. Stir again and cover the pan. Cook on a low heat for 45 minutes. Take the lid off the pan, add the water, increase the heat and let the dish bubble for 10 minutes, stirring occasionally. Add the chives and continue cooking for another 15 minutes. Remove the lemon grass, Kaffir lime leaves and bay leaf before storing in a covered dish in the refrigerator. Next day, skim off the fat, re-heat and serve hot.

Duck

BEBEK TAUCO
Duck with salted yellow beans   to serve four

1 duck, cut up into serving pieces	*1 piece of root ginger, about 1 cm*
1 cup vinegar	*(½") long*
2 tbs tauco (salted yellow beans,	*1 tsp brown sugar*
page 44)	*1 tbs vegetable oil*
1 tbs dark soya sauce	*2 cups water*
2 green chillis	*a handful of chives or fresh*
5 cloves garlic	*spring onions*
6 shallots or 1 onion	

Put the vinegar into a saucepan, pour in about 4 cups of water, and soak the pieces of duck in this for about 4 minutes. Wash them afterwards in cold water.

Pound the tauco until it becomes a smooth paste, or else put it in a liquidizer for a few seconds. Seed the chillis and slice them finely. Slice the shallots or onion finely. Peel the root ginger and slice it thin; crush the garlic.

Heat the oil in a pan, and sauté the shallots and garlic for 1 minute. Add the ginger and chillis, stir while frying for another minute, then add the tauco and soya sauce. Stir-fry for a minute longer before putting in the duck and the sugar. Mix everything well together so that the pieces of duck are coated with the tauco, then add 2 cups of water or just enough to cover the duck. Put the lid on the pan and simmer for 60–80 minutes, taking care not to boil dry or burn. For the last 5 minutes, uncover the pan. Ladle out the excess oil, and stir. The sauce should now be thick. Put in the chopped chives or spring onions, and serve very hot.

Vegetables

Any Indonesian can live well as a vegetarian—when he has to. As well as the more elaborate dishes described here, I must also mention *lalab*: a plate of raw or lightly-cooked vegetables which are treated rather like an undressed salad, with each mouthful being dipped in sambal before it is eaten.

SAYUR BAYEM
Spinach soup   to serve six

This is an excellent soup, especially if the spinach is fresh and young. It can be made with either corn on the cob or sweet potatoes. You will need:

500 g (1 lb) young spinach leaves	*½ green chilli, or a pinch of chilli powder*
2 young corncobs, or 120 g (4 oz) sweet potatoes	*a pinch of ground ginger*
	a small slice of kencur (page 69)
2 shallots	*1 salam leaf or bay-leaf*
	salt

Wash the spinach and chop it coarsely. Cut each corncob into three pieces; or peel and cut the sweet potatoes into small cubes.

Slice the shallots and chilli finely and put them into a saucepan with 1 cup of water. Add the ginger, kencur, salam and salt, and bring to the boil. When the water boils, put in the corn or sweet potatoes, cover the pan, and simmer for 15 minutes. Uncover, add the chopped spinach and another half cup of water. Taste, and add more salt if necessary. Cook until the spinach is tender (about 5–7 minutes), remove the kencur and the leaf and serve hot.

OSENG-OSENG WORTEL
Stir-fried carrots   to serve two

These are carrots, cut into matchsticks and cooked in a little oil or butter. The word wortel doesn't sound Indonesian and isn't. It is borrowed from the Dutch name for the carrot, since it was the Dutch who introduced this vegetable to Indonesia.

250 g (8 oz) carrots
4 shallots
1 clove garlic
¼ a green or red chilli or a
 pinch of chilli powder

4 tbs good stock or 1 tsp dark
 soya sauce and 4 tbs water
2 tbs vegetable oil or clarified
 butter

Peel, wash, and cut the carrots into small sticks. Slice the shallots and chilli. Crush the garlic. In a wok, heat 2 tablespoonfuls of vegetable oil or clarified butter. Sauté the sliced shallots and chilli for 1 minute, then add the garlic and the carrots. Stir continuously for a minute or so and then put in the stock, or soya sauce and water. Cover and continue to cook for 4 minutes. Uncover, taste, and add salt if necessary. Cook for a further 2 minutes, stirring all the time. Serve hot.

OSENG-OSENG CAMPUR
Stir-fried mixed vegetables   to serve two

This is similar to Oseng-Oseng Wortel, except that a variety of vegetables is used. I find the following combination very satisfactory, but in Indonesia I would use kacang panjang instead of runner beans, and waluh jipang instead of cauliflower.

60 g (2 oz) carrots
60 g (2 oz) runner beans
60 g (2 oz) cauliflower, or
 courgettes
60 g (2 oz) beansprouts
2 shallots

1 slice terasi (page 41)
a pinch of chilli powder
1 tsp dark soya sauce
2 tbs vegetable oil
6 tbs water
salt and pepper

Peel, wash, and cut the carrots into sticks lengthwise; cut each stick into 3 or 4 shorter pieces. Cut the beans about the same length as the carrots. Wash and cut the cauliflower into small flowerets, and clean the beansprouts. If you are using courgettes, cut them up in the same way as the carrots, so that all the pieces of vegetable are about the same size.

Crush the shallots and terasi and fry them together in a little oil for about half a minute. Add the chilli powder, carrots, cauliflowers, and beans. Stir continuously for 2 minutes while frying, then add the soya sauce and 6 tablespoonfuls of water. Cover for 10 minutes, then take the lid off again and go on cooking for 2 minutes. Add the beansprouts and a little salt and pepper. Stir for another 3 minutes. Serve immediately.

This oseng-oseng is good for freezing; when you want to serve it, thaw it out completely, then re-heat it, stirring continuously until it is really hot.

ORAK ARIK
Shredded quick-fried cabbage with egg   to serve four

This is a quick and easy way to cook cabbage. It tastes excellent, and the cabbage is in the pan for so short a time that it loses none of its goodness.

1 medium-sized white or green cabbage	*2 tbs vegetable oil* or *clarified butter*
1 medium-sized onion	*2 standard eggs* or *1 large egg*
salt and pepper	

Shred the cabbage finely and chop the onion. Heat the oil or butter in a heavy frying-pan. Fry the onion until soft; add the shredded cabbage, and salt and pepper to taste. Stir continuously while frying for 2 minutes, then cover and continue cooking for not more than 5 minutes. Stir again. Break the eggs into a bowl, season with salt and pepper, and beat thoroughly. Let the cabbage fry for another 8–10 minutes, stirring occasionally; add water only if absolutely necessary, and then in very small amounts. When the cabbage is cooked, pour in the beaten egg and scramble it with the cabbage. Serve immediately.

GORENG TERONG
Fried aubergines   to serve two to four

2 medium-sized aubergines   ½ tsp brown sugar (optional)
1 large onion   salt
2 tsp paprika   vegetable oil
½ tsp chilli powder

Cut each aubergine into six, lengthwise, and then cut each piece across into two. Sprinkle with salt and let stand for 30 minutes; then wash, drain and dry.

Slice the onion finely. In a heavy frying-pan, heat about 5 tablespoonfuls of oil. Fry the aubergines carefully, five or six slices at a time, until they are cooked. Put them on kitchen paper and keep them warm while you fry the sliced onion until soft (you need less oil for this; a tablespoonful will be enough). Add paprika, chilli, and sugar to the onion, and go on frying for another 2 minutes, stirring continuously. Season with salt. Just before serving, add the fried aubergines to the onion, stir everything up together, and serve hot.

SEMUR TERONG
Aubergines cooked in soya sauce   to serve two to four

2 medium-sized aubergines   ½ tsp vinegar or lemon juice
1 onion   ½ tsp brown sugar
2 cloves garlic   2 tbs vegetable oil
2 red tomatoes   salt
2 tbs dark soya sauce   chilli powder or pepper

Wash the aubergines and cut them into halves; then cut each half lengthwise into four. Sprinkle these with a little salt and let them stand for half an hour. Slice the onion. Peel, seed and chop the tomatoes. Sauté the sliced onions in the oil for 1 minute, add the crushed garlic and the aubergines; then lower the flame, and turn the aubergines several times. Put in the soya sauce, chopped tomatoes, sugar, vinegar, and chilli (or their alternatives). Stir the mixture once, and taste. Cover the pan and let it simmer for 7 minutes. Uncover and go on cooking for

3 minutes more—turn the aubergines once in the course of these 3 minutes. Serve hot.

LAWAR JANTUNG PISANG
Sliced banana heart   to serve four

This is a very simple everyday vegetable dish in Alor (Nusa Tenggara Timur), where of course you can pick your jantung pisang whenever you like in your back garden.

Jantung means 'heart', and the 'heart' of a banana is the long heavy spike of the withered flower, cut after the combs of young fruit have become firmly set. Lawar means 'sliced thinly'.

1 jantung pisang (see above)
3 shallots, sliced
1 cup thick santen, from half a coconut or 180 g (about 6 oz)
   desiccated coconut
salt and white pepper

Discard the outer petals of the jantung until you get into inner layers of petals which are paler in colour. Then put the whole flower-spike into a large saucepan half-filled with boiling water, bring it back to the boil and cook for 15 minutes. Take it out of the saucepan to cool while you make the santen. Put the santen in a saucepan with the sliced shallots and salt. Bring these ingredients very slowly to the boil while you slice the jantung pisang into small flat quarter-rounds. Do this by splitting the spike lengthwise into four, then slice each quarter. When the santen boils, put in the jantung pisang slices. Lower the heat and simmer for 10 minutes, stirring often so that the santen does not get a chance to curdle. Serve hot with rice and a meat or fish dish.

GULAI PUCUK LABU
Squash or courgette shoots cooked in
coconut sauce   to serve four

Labu is a general name for plants of the squash family, including pumpkins and musk melons. In this recipe from West Sumatra, however, we are concerned with a plant which is related to the squashes. It is sometimes called labu Siam, or Siamese pumpkin; the Sundanese of West Java call it gambas; in South America, where it originated, and the West Indies it is choco or chayote. See the entry for Waluh Jipang on page 88, and the drawing on the next page.

Pucuk here means the young shoots of the plant. Gambas grows either vertically on a trellis or horizontally on a wooden frame just high enough to lift the fruit clear of the ground. It puts out enormous numbers of shoots, as most plants of this family do, and many of these have to be thinned out so that the rest will produce good solid fruit. Fortunately the shoots are very good to eat, and indeed it is well worth while experimenting with the shoots of similar plants; I have cooked this gulai in London with shoots from my own courgettes (a bit rough-textured, but not at all bad) and gem squash (much smoother and very like the real thing). In any case, you can use either the shoots alone or shoots with fruit.

1 chayote, or *6 small courgettes*	*a pinch of laos (galingale)*
½ kg (1 lb) young shoots of the	*1 salam leaf or bay-leaf*
plant	*1 cup water or stock*
2 shallots	*2 cups thick santen (coconut milk)*
1 clove garlic (optional)	*salt*
1 green chilli	

If you are using chayote, peel it and cut it lengthwise into four pieces, discarding the seed in the middle. Then slice the pieces across, about ½ cm thick. Soak these slices in cold water while you prepare the other ingredients. Small courgettes need only be washed and chopped into rounds. Wash the shoots in cold water.

Peel and slice the shallots and garlic finely; seed and chop the chilli. Boil the water or stock in a saucepan and add the shallots, garlic, chilli, laos and salam leaf. Simmer for 2 minutes before adding the sliced chayote or courgettes. Simmer for a further 2 minutes and put in the shoots and the santen. Add salt; let the santen come to the boil, then immediately lower the heat and stir continuously (to prevent the santen from curdling) for about 4 more minutes or until the shoots are tender. Serve hot, in its own sauce.

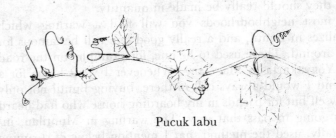

Pucuk labu

TUMIS BUNCIS   to serve four

An excellent way to cook French beans.

500 g (1 lb) French beans
3 shallots or *1 small onion*
a pinch of chilli powder, or
    pepper
a pinch of ground nutmeg

a pinch of ground ginger
6 tbs good stock or *1 chicken*
    cube
2 tbs vegetable oil or *clarified*
    butter

Wash, top and tail, and slice the beans. Slice the shallots or onion finely, and sauté them in oil or butter for 1 minute. Add the beans, the chilli or pepper, nutmeg and ginger; go on stirring for 2 minutes. Pour in the stock, or use a chicken cube and 6 tablespoonfuls of water. Cover the pan and simmer gently for 8 minutes. Uncover, and let the vegetables continue to cook for another 2 or 3 minutes while you stir them. Serve hot.

BUNTIL
Taro leaves and spiced coconut filling

Buntil are 'bundles'—the English and Javanese words are strangely alike—made of layers of taro leaf and spiced coconut filling. Buntil are very popular in Central Java, but most people would rather buy them ready-made than cook them at home. Their preparation is a tedious business, taking about 4 hours of cooking time, and although they are worth a good deal of effort they should really be made in quantity.

In most neighbourhoods you will find a warung which specializes in Buntil, and a really good one will be famous for miles around. There used to be one, for example, on the road from Yogyakarta to Magelang. Whenever I went home for a weekend I would always call in there, buying Buntil not only for myself but for friends in my boarding-house who had heard I was going to pass that way. The warung in Muntilan, incidentally, used the method that I mention below of steaming the Buntil in a woven kukusan and pouring the santen over them.

If you are going to make Buntil, therefore, make a fairly large quantity; they will keep in the refrigerator for up to 5 days, or you can simply reheat them each day. Unfortunately, taro leaves are not, in my experience, available in Europe and I know of no substitute. The taro plant originated in South-East Asia, but it has since become of great importance in the West Indies and Central America, where its tubers, called eddo or dasheen, are eaten like potatoes and its leaves may be referred to as callaloo after the soup of that name. See page 194 for a drawing of them.

20 large taro leaves (*daun talas*)
1 young coconut (*kelapa muda,*
    see page 37—the younger the
    better so long as its flesh is
    firm enough to be grated)
120 g (4 oz) ikan teri (*tiny*
    dried anchovies, page 124)
6–8 peté beans
salt
1 tsp brown sugar (*optional*)

4 cups thick santen (*coconut milk*)

and to be crushed:
15 cabé rawit (*page 51*), *the*
    stalks removed
4 cloves garlic
1 slice terasi (*page 41*)
4 red chillis
1 piece of kencur (*page 69*)

Grate the coconut and mix it together with all the crushed ingredients. Discard the heads of the ikan teri. Slice the peté very thinly. Mix the ikan teri and peté in with the coconut, etcetera; season with salt (and sugar, if desired).

The taro leaves should be washed and put out in the sun, for a few minutes only, so that they become limp and supple; they must not dry out. Each bundle, or packet, requires two leaves. Divide the mixture into 10 portions, spread each portion on the surface of a leaf, and lay another leaf on top. Roll or fold this leaf-sandwich, not too tightly, starting from the stem-end of the leaves. Then fold the sides in towards the centre so that the packet is one-third of the original width of the leaf—it usually ends up about 8 cm square. Tie the packet to keep it from unfolding; this is normally done with a length of dried rice-straw, which is fibrous and surprisingly strong.

When everything is bundled up, arrange the packets in a rice-steamer and steam for 2 hours, remembering to add water to the pan when necessary. Then, if you were using a traditional kukusan, you would start to pour the santen slowly over the Buntil, a cupful at a time, while steaming continued. The closely woven kukusan would retain most of the santen, and what trickled through into the water would give a rich flavour to the steam. Assuming that you are not using a kukusan, transfer the Buntil to a thick saucepan (or to an earthenware pot lined with banana leaf) and pour all the santen over them. Boil them in the santen until all the liquid has been absorbed, which will take about another 2 hours.

Serve hot or cold. Cut the tie-strings and slice the packets, which should be firm but should still show the internal layers of leaf and filling. Eat as a main dish, with boiled rice.

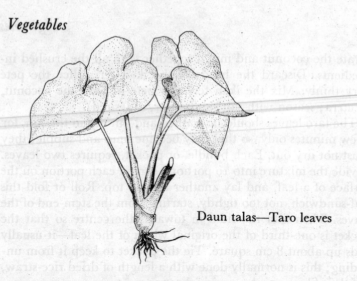

Daun talas—Taro leaves

LAWAR MANGGA MUDA
Mango slices cooked in coconut milk to serve four

Literally, 'sliced young mangoes'. Surprisingly, this fruit makes
a delicious vegetable dish cooked in santen or, when cold, a
salad. Like most dishes from Alor, it uses no garlic. Try it with
unripe apples—they make a good substitute.

2 large unripe mangoes	*salt*
3 shallots, sliced finely	*a pinch of ground white pepper*
1 cup thick santen (coconut milk)	

Make ready a saucepan half-filled with cold water with 1 teaspoon of salt. Peel the mangoes and slice them thinly. Put them
into the salted water and keep them there while you slowly boil
the santen and shallots for about 2 to 3 minutes, stirring all the
time. Add salt and pepper. Drain the mangoes, put them into
the boiling santen, and simmer for 3 minutes.

Serve hot in its own sauce as a vegetable. Alternatively, drain
off the sauce, allow the mangoes to cool, and eat as a salad.

URAP PANGGANG
Vegetables baked with coconut and egg to serve four

I used to make this dish in Indonesia from fresh bamboo shoots.

I still use bamboo shoots in England—canned ones, of course— but courgettes and cauliflowers also taste very good if they are cooked this way.

When you open a can of bamboo shoots, you will find chunks of bamboo immersed in liquid. These shoots have been boiled without salt at the time they were packed; the water is put in to stop them getting dry. Throw the water away, rinse the shoots in warm water, then slice them very thinly. Finally, cut each slice into small sticks.

If, however, you use courgettes, simply wash them and slice them thinly, then sprinkle them with salt and leave them to stand for half an hour. Rinse them and let them dry. With a cauliflower, all you need do is to cut it into small flowerets.

1 300 g (10 oz) or 250 g
(12 oz) can of bamboo shoots
or courgettes or a cauliflower
of the same weight
180 g (6 oz) desiccated coconut
or half a fresh coconut,
grated, without the brown rind
¼ tsp chilli powder
1 tsp paprika
¼ tsp ground ginger

¼ tsp ground coriander
2 tsp tomato ketchup
¼ tsp brown sugar
salt to taste
1 onion
2 cloves garlic
2 tbs vegetable oil
1 or 2 eggs
1 cup water

Prepare the bamboo shoots or courgettes or cauliflower, as described above. Slice the onion and crush the garlic. Heat the oil in a wok or deep frying-pan, then fry the onion and garlic for 1 minute. Add the bamboo shoots or courgettes or cauliflower and sauté for 1 minute. Then put in all the other ingredients, except the eggs and water. Sauté for 2 more minutes and add water. Cover, and simmer for 5 minutes. Uncover, and continue cooking, at the same time stirring well, until all the water has been absorbed by the coconut. Taste. Now beat the egg or eggs, and season with a little salt and pepper. Put the vegetables in an oblong ovenproof dish. Pour the beaten eggs evenly over the top, and cook in the oven at gas mark 4 (about 350° F) for 30–40 minutes or until the egg sets. Serve hot.

GADO-GADO
Mixed vegetable salad with peanut sauce **to serve six**

This is a very popular vegetable dish, not expensive, and very good for you. In my student days, my usual lunch was a plate of Gado-Gado, and it makes an excellent lunch just by itself. It can also accompany a full meal, with meat and rice; or you can follow the Indonesian custom of eating it either before or after the main course.

To take the vegetables first, you might select the following.

90 g (3 oz) cabbage	*120 g (4 oz) beansprouts*
90 g (3 oz) French beans	*a quarter of a cucumber*
90 g (3 oz) carrots	*1 medium-sized potato*
90 g (3 oz) cauliflower	

Lettuce and watercress may also be added. In Indonesia, the yard-long bean (kacang panjang, page 65) would often be used in addition to or instead of the French beans.

The ingredients for the bumbu, or sauce, and for the garnish are as follows.

for the bumbu:	*2 cups water*
120 g (4 oz) peanuts	*30 g (1 oz) creamed coconut*
vegetable oil	*(optional)*
1 slice terasi (page 41)	*juice of half a lemon*
1 clove garlic	
2 shallots	for the garnish:
salt	*1 hard-boiled egg*
⅓ tsp chilli powder	*fried onions*
⅓ tsp brown sugar	*krupuk (prawn crackers)*

First, prepare the vegetables. Slice the beans and carrots, and shred the cabbage. Cut up the cauliflower into small flowerets. Clean the beansprouts (see note in recipe for Urap, page 206).

Next, make the bumbu. Fry the peanuts in a cupful of vegetable oil for 5 to 6 minutes. Drain, and let them cool. Then pound or grind them into a fine powder. Crush the terasi, garlic and shallots into a rough paste, adding a little salt. Fry this paste in 1 tablespoonful of oil for 1 minute. Add the chilli powder, sugar and more salt; then add 2 cupfuls of water. Let all this come to the boil, then add the ground peanuts. Stir the mixture well and let it simmer, still stirring occasionally, until it becomes thick. This is the moment to put in the creamed coconut, if you want it; stir it until it dissolves. This bumbu can be re-heated quickly when the vegetables are ready. Don't add the lemon juice until just before serving.

Boil each vegetable separately, for not more than 5 minutes. Beansprouts and watercress should be boiled for 3 minutes at the most. Boil the potato and slice it thinly.

When the vegetables are done, heat up the bumbu, not forgetting to stir in the lemon juice. Serve Gado-Gado on a round or oval dish which is big enough to spread the vegetables out on. Put the cabbage first, round the edge (with the lettuce, if you are using lettuce—uncooked, of course) but leaving room for the potato and cucumber slices around the outside. In the centre, put the carrots, cauliflower and beansprouts, with the sliced hard-boiled egg on top. Pour the bumbu over all this, and garnish with fried onion and with krupuk broken into small pieces.

In Indonesia, if Gado-Gado is your whole lunch, you will probably want to smuggle some rice into it in the form of Lontong (page 94) sliced and put round the edge with the potato and cucumber.

Incidentally, you may be told that you can make bumbu Gado-Gado with crunchy peanut butter. You can, after a fashion, but it is not very satisfactory. If you find the preparation of the bumbu tedious, you can buy 'instant' bumbu in powder form, from many 'Indische' shops in Holland, and from various stores in London, Sydney, New York and other cities. A very good bumbu, which you can use with Gado-Gado or with Saté, can be made from 'satay powder', which you should be able to get from any good Chinese provision merchant. With these powders, simply boil a cupful of water, stir in the powder, and simmer for a few minutes until the mixture thickens. Pour this over the vegetables (or the saté) in the usual way.

PETOLA DAGING
Stuffed bottle gourd, or marrow   to serve four to six

This recipe is from Sulawesi. Petola is a relative of cucumbers and vegetable marrows, and is what in Java we would call oyong (under which name it appears in the descriptive catalogue of fruit and vegetables, on page 76) or emes. In English, it is usually called a bottle gourd. I have never come across them in Britain, where they could only be grown in hot-houses, but I have often made Petola Daging with small marrows or large courgettes, with excellent results. A real petola needs to be thinly peeled, and I find that the marrow is also better if it is peeled before being stuffed.

5 bottle gourds (petola) or 2 small vegetable marrows
120 g (4 oz) prawns, shelled
250 g (½ lb) minced beef, or chicken—preferably breast
5 shallots or 1 onion
2 green chillis or ½ tsp chilli powder
4 eggs
1 tbs vegetable oil
salt and pepper

Thinly peel the petola or marrows, cut them in half lengthwise and discard the seeds from the centre of each. Leave them in cold salted water while you prepare the stuffing.

Chop the prawns and mix them with the minced beef or chicken. Peel and slice the shallots finely. Seed the chillis and cut them into thin rounds. Separate the white of 1 egg and keep it on one side; beat all the rest of the eggs, season with salt and pepper, and make into several thin omelettes. Leave these to cool.

Heat the oil in a wok or saucepan and fry the sliced shallots and green chillis until soft. Add the mixture of meat and prawns and stir-fry for about 3 minutes. Season with salt and pepper, leave to cool a little and then add the egg-white. Mix well.

Take the petola or marrow pieces from the water, dry them with a paper towel. Roll up your thin omelettes and slice them into thin coiled strips; mix these with the meat. Use the mixture to fill one-half of each petola or marrow, then put the other half on top as a lid. These can then be steamed in a rice steamer for 30 minutes. Alternatively, put them in an oven-proof dish and bake in a medium oven (350° F) for 40–50 minutes. Serve hot or cold, cut into thick round slices.

SAYUR KUNING
A turmeric-coloured meat and
vegetable stew   to serve four to six

This stew is cooked in santen. The turmeric gives it its yellowish colour.

250 g (8 oz) brisket   *a pinch of ground laos (galingale)*
salt   *a pinch of powdered lemon grass*
3 kemiri (candlenuts)   *¼ tsp ground ginger*
6 shallots   *1 tsp turmeric*
1 small vegetable marrow   *1 salam leaf or bay-leaf*
1 medium-sized potato   *60 g (2 oz) broad beans (in*
2 carrots   *Indonesia we would use*
1 cup water   *kacang pagar, Lima beans)*
¼ tsp chilli powder   *1 cup thick santen (coconut milk)*

Boil the brisket with a little salt for 60 minutes. Keep a cupful of the stock, and cut the meat into small pieces.

Pound the kemiri and shallots into a smooth paste. Peel the marrow, potato and carrots, and chop them into small cubes.

Put the cupful of water into a saucepan, and in it put the kemiri paste, chilli, laos, lemon grass, ginger, turmeric and salam (or bay) leaf. Stir this mixture and bring it to the boil. When it is boiling, add the carrots, potato, broad beans, and the meat. Cover, and simmer for 5 minutes. Put in the stock and the marrow; season with salt, cook for 6 or 7 minutes on a high flame, then pour in the santen. Simmer very gently until the mixture is almost boiling again, then stir for 2 or 3 minutes. Adjust the seasoning and serve hot.

This dish is meant to have a runny, soupy sauce, so don't put any thickening agent into it.

SAYUR LODEH
A rich, spicy vegetable stew   to serve four

1 medium-sized aubergine	*6 shallots or 1 onion*
salt	*1 cup water or stock*
120 g (4 oz) very young French	*30 g (1 oz) ebi (dried raw*
beans (in Indonesia we would	*shrimps, page 44)*
use kacang panjang, 'yard-long	*¼ tsp brown sugar*
beans')	*1¼ tsp ground coriander*
120 g (4 oz) bamboo shoots	*¼ tsp powdered, or 1 stalk of*
60 g (2 oz) very young spring	*fresh, lemon grass (optional)*
greens (optional—in	*2 Kaffir lime leaves or bay-leaves*
Indonesia we use melinjo	*2 cups thick santen (coconut milk)*
leaves, page 73)	
1 slice terasi (page 41)	
4 kemiri (candlenuts)	
3 cloves garlic	
1 green chilli or ¼ tsp chilli	
powder	

First, prepare the vegetables. Slice the aubergine, sprinkle with
salt, and let it stand for 30 minutes; then rinse and leave to dry.
Cut up the beans into pieces about 1 cm (½″) long. Slice the
bamboo shoots very thin (page 195). Chop the spring greens
coarsely.

Grill the terasi and kemiri for about 1 minute—say half a
minute each side. Pound these into a paste with the garlic. Seed
the chilli and slice it finely; slice the shallots or onion as thin as
possible.

Put all the vegetables, except the greens, into a saucepan with
a cup of water or stock. Cover the pan and cook for 5 minutes.
Add the ebi, salt, sugar and all the spices, and continue cooking
for a further 4 minutes. Put in the santen and the greens, and
simmer very gently until the santen is just about to boil—now
stir continuously for 2 minutes to prevent the santen from
curdling. Take out the stalk of lemon grass, if used, and Kaffir
lime leaves or bay-leaves before serving.

Serve hot; like Sayur Kuning, this has a wet, soupy sauce
which should not be too thick.

SAYUR ASAM
'Sour vegetables'   to serve four

The sourness announced in the recipe title comes chiefly from the tamarind. Make sure that enough tamarind water is used, and that it is good and strong. In some dishes, tamarind can be replaced by lemon juice, but not here. An acceptable substitute, however, is rhubarb. You need a piece of rhubarb about 10 cm (4″) long, chopped into small pieces and put in together with the aubergine.

Several of the vegetables shown here are, in fact, European or American substitutes. They are perfectly suitable; but I have shown the original Indonesian ingredients in brackets. All quantities are approximate, and may be varied to suit your own taste.

1 small aubergine
2 medium-sized courgettes
salt
2 cups water
4 leaves of white cabbage (or melinjo leaves, page 73)
120 g (4 oz) runner beans (yard-long beans, page 65)

2 kemiri (candlenuts)
1 small green chilli
2 shallots
a pinch of laos (galingale)
1 salam leaf or bay-leaf
¼ tsp sugar
4–6 tbs thick tamarind water

Slice the aubergine and courgettes, sprinkle them with salt, and leave to stand for half an hour. Boil the peanuts in a cupful of water for 10 minutes. Slice the cabbage leaves, top and tail the runner beans and cut them into pieces about 1 cm (½″) long.

Put half a cup of water into a saucepan. Crush the kemiri, chilli and shallots, and add them all to the water. Boil for 5 minutes and add the laos, the salam or bay-leaf, the sugar and the remaining half-cup of water. Bring back to the boil and put in the cabbage and beans. Simmer for 3 minutes. Add the aubergine, courgettes, and cooked peanuts. Simmer for another 5 minutes, and put in the tamarind water and salt. Simmer for 4 or 5 minutes longer, and serve hot.

Sayur Asam can also be eaten as a soup. It looks like a cloudy, thick vegetable soup; the sourness makes it very refreshing.

GULAI NANGKA
Cooked jackfruit   to serve four

In the market-place at home you can buy a whole nangka (jack-fruit) if you have a large family, or a half, or a quarter of one, raw. You can also buy cooked slices of nangka. In London I have used canned nangka, and find it very satisfactory, though not cheap.

400–450 g (14 oz–1 lb) nangka (jackfruit)
salt
250 g (8 oz) brisket or good stewing steak
2 cups water
500 ml (1 pint) thick santen (coconut milk)
4 kemiri (candlenuts)
3 tbs desiccated coconut
2 onions
1½ tsp ground ginger
¼ tsp turmeric
¼ tsp ground laos (galingale)
2 tsp Sambal Ulek (crushed chillis, page 224)
1 daun kunyit (turmeric leaf), optional
2 Kaffir lime leaves or a bay-leaf

If you are using fresh nangka, peel it (the peel or skin is very thick), slice it, and soak the slices in plenty of cold water. (See the note on page 74.) Boil the slices in slightly salted water for 15 minutes. For canned nangka, you need only rinse the slices before use—the canners have cooked them for you.

Cut the meat into small thin strips and boil it, in about 2 cupfuls of water with a little salt, for 30 minutes. While the meat is boiling, make the santen and prepare the other ingredients. In a heavy-bottomed frying-pan, roast the kemiri and desiccated coconut until brown. This will take about 5 minutes. Then pound them in a mortar to make a thick paste; or put them in your food processor, using the meat-mincing blade. Peel and slice the onions, and crush or process these into the kemiri and coconut paste. Mix this paste with the santen, and add all the other powdered ingredients and the sambal ulek. When the meat has cooked for 30 minutes and the water is very much reduced, pour in the spiced santen and add the slices of nangka, the Kaffir lime leaves or bay-leaf, the kunyit leaf (if used) and some salt. Simmer for 40 minutes, or longer if you want your Gulai to be quite thick. Take out the leaves before serving. Serve hot with plain boiled rice.

RUJAK KANGKUNG
Water spinach, or watercress, in a spicy sauce   to serve four

Kangkung (see page 66) is one of my favourite vegetables, and in South-East Asia it is so common and grows so easily that it is also one of the cheapest. My husband never got a chance to taste it for the first year or so that he was in Indonesia, because he was still a bachelor and his Javanese cook considered kangkung to be beneath the dignity of a foreigner, particularly if he was also a teacher. In fact, it has an excellent flavour and is also good for you; but the only way you can buy it in Britain is in cans, imported from Malaysia and unpoetically labelled 'swamp cabbage'. (I find its other English name, water spinach, a more accurate description.) There is really no substitute for kangkung, but this recipe is also very successful with watercress—another vegetable that is so common in Java that my husband was not allowed to get near it.

¼ kg (1¼ lb) kangkung
1 tsp Sambal Ulek (crushed
  chillis, page 224)
2 shallots
1 clove garlic
1 slice terasi, grilled (page 41)
1 tsp brown sugar
1 tbs dark soya sauce

If you use fresh kangkung, trim and clean it as if it were watercress, boil it in salted water for 4 minutes, then drain it. If you use canned kangkung, drain and rinse it in cold water.

Peel and slice the shallots, then pound them in a cobek or mortar with the terasi, brown sugar and sambal ulek to make a paste. Put this paste into a saucepan with the soya sauce, heat it on a low flame for a few seconds and add the kangkung. Stir for a minute or so. Can be served hot or cold; with rice.

PELECING PERIA
Bitter cucumber stir-fried in a chilli and
lime sauce   to serve four

A friend of mine from Lombok tells me that Pelecing is just a
simple way of cooking vegetables or chicken, but that if you ask
for Pelecing by itself you will invariably find that it is made with
kangkung (water spinach or swamp cabbage). If you want
some other kind of vegetable you will have to name it—for
example, Pelecing Peria. (A peria is a kind of rather bitter
cucumber: see page 78 and the drawing below.) Chicken
cooked this way is of course Pelecing Ayam. The most important
ingredient in Pelecing, according to my friend, is terasi (page
41), and the better the terasi the better the Pelecing will be. But
Pelecing must also be chilli-hot, and cabé rawit (page 51) is
much the best kind of chilli to use for it. I find the bitterness of
the peria, mingled with the flavour of the terasi, the hot chilli
and plenty of lime juice, quite irresistible; you would certainly
never mistake it for anything else.

Peria—Bitter cucumber

3 or 4 peria (bitter cucumbers)	2 cloves garlic
salt	1 piece terasi (page 41)
6 cabé rawit (page 51)	1 tbs vegetable oil
3 kemiri (candlenuts—optional)	juice of 1 lime or lemon

If you use fresh peria, cut them lengthwise in half so that you
can take out the seeds. Slice them like cucumbers, put the slices
into a colander, sprinkle them liberally with salt and leave them
for at least 30 minutes. Then wash them under cold running
water and boil them for 3 minutes with a little salt. If you use
canned peria, just rinse them in cold water and slice them.
 Pound the cabé rawit, kemiri, garlic and terasi in a cobek or

mortar until smooth. Heat the oil in a wok or frying-pan and fry the pounded ingredients for a minute or so. Add the peria and stir-fry for 2 minutes; season with salt and lime juice. Serve hot or cold.

ACAR CAMPUR
A cooked vegetable salad   to serve six to eight

250 g (8 oz) carrots
1 cucumber
250 g (8 oz) French beans
250 g (8 oz) cauliflower
1 red pimiento (optional)
1 green pimiento (optional)
1 red or green chilli
10 pickling onions
3 kemiri (candlenuts)
1 shallot

2 cloves garlic
2 tbs vegetable oil
¼ tsp turmeric
¼ tsp ground ginger
4 tbs white malt vinegar
salt
1 cup water
2 tsp brown sugar
1 tsp dry English or French
    mustard

Wash all the vegetables. Peel the carrots and the cucumber. Top and tail the beans, and cut each one into, say, three pieces. Cut the carrots and cucumber into pieces about the same size as the beans, and cut the pimientos into strips. Take out the seeds from the chilli and cut it into four. Peel and wash the pickling onions.

Crush the kemiri, shallot and garlic to a paste, and sauté this in the vegetable oil for 1 minute. Add the turmeric, ginger, chilli, and pickling onions. Stir everything together for a few seconds and put in the vinegar and a little salt. Cover and cook for 3 minutes. Then put in the carrots, cauliflower, beans, and pimientos. Pour the cup of water over these, cover again, and go on cooking for 8 minutes more.

Uncover for the second time to add sugar, dry mustard, and cucumber. Cover, and cook for 2 minutes. Then take the lid off for the last time and stir continuously as the vegetables cook for another 3 minutes.

Acar Campur can be served either hot or cold. In an airtight jar, it can be stored for several weeks.

URAP
Vegetable salad with coconut dressing　　　　to serve four

Although Urap can properly be called a vegetable salad, it is not like an occidental one. It can be made out of almost any combination of vegetables that you like, and these may be either cooked or raw. So the recipe is divided into three parts: first, a section on cooked vegetables; secondly an alternative section on raw vegetables; and thirdly the ingredients for the bumbu, or sauce, and the instructions which apply to it.

Whether you use cooked or raw vegetables, it is advisable to use fresh coconut, freshly grated. See the note on the next page.

COOKED VEGETABLES
A good mixture would be 90 g (3 oz) of each of the following:

cabbage, shredded, but not too
  finely
French or runner beans, cut
  up into pieces about
  1 cm (¼″) long
carrots, cut into rounds
beansprouts, or cauliflower

Tauge—Beansprouts

(Note on cleaning beansprouts.
A beansprout has a very small
greenish-yellowish leaf, a white stem and a little brown root. The whole thing is perfectly edible, root and all, but if you cook a quantity of them the brown pigment from the root tends to make the final result look a bit messy. Therefore, unless you are in a hurry, it is worth spending the time to twist off each root from its stem.)

Boil each vegetable separately for not more than 5 minutes (and the beansprouts for not more than 3 minutes). Then serve them as explained in the last part of the recipe.

RAW VEGETABLES
Do not mix cooked and raw vegetables. If you are going to use raw, the selection given at the top of the next page would be a

good one, but it can of course be varied in accordance with what is available and fresh.

1 bunch watercress
90 g (3 oz) raw carrots, chopped
90 g (3 oz) raw white cabbage,
*   shredded*
about 6 radishes, sliced

¼ cucumber, sliced
spring onions, chopped
mint (in Indonesia, kemangi),
*   chopped*

THE BUMBU

¼ a small coconut*
1 slice terasi (page 41)
¼ tsp chilli powder
1 clove garlic

a pinch of sugar
juice of ¼ a lime or 1 tbs very
*   thick tamarind water*
salt to taste

Break open the coconut and remove the flesh. Peel the brown rind from it, so that you have pure white coconut. Grate this. Then fry in oil (or grill) the slice of terasi for 1 minute on each side. Pound the terasi with the garlic, salt, sugar and chilli into a coarse paste, and mix this paste with the grated coconut. Add the lime juice, or the tamarind water.

Take all the vegetables that you have prepared and put them into a fairly deep bowl. Put in the spiced coconut bumbu, and mix the whole lot together by tossing them as if you were dressing a salad. Serve in an oblong or oval dish.

*NOTE ON POSSIBLE USE OF DESICCATED COCONUT
Desiccated coconut can be used for the bumbu, although it does not taste quite as good as fresh coconut. If you do use desiccated, then you will need to boil the mixture (of coconut, terasi, garlic, chilli, salt and sugar) in a cupful of water for 5 minutes. Stir continuously while it boils. Then, if you are using *boiled* vegetables, put them into the pan also and stir well while you let everything cook for a minute or two longer. If you are using *raw* vegetables, of course, don't put them into the pan; let the bumbu cool before you add it to your salad.

KAREDOK
A mixed salad with peanut dressing   to serve four to six

This is a Sundanese recipe—that is to say, it comes from West Java. The combination of vegetables varies somewhat from place to place, but the ones that you will come across most often are listed here. French beans may be used instead of the first ingredient—the difference is not great. But the small round eggplants, although not exclusive to South-East Asia, are not so easy to find elsewhere and do not really have a substitute.

120 g (4 oz) 'yard-long beans'	*for the dressing:*
(kacang panjang)	*120 g (4 oz) peanuts*
120 g (4 oz) bean sprouts	*1 clove garlic*
120 g (4 oz) sweet potatoes	*1 piece terasi (page 41)*
120 g (4 oz) white cabbage	*1 small piece kencur (page 69)*
4 small round eggplants (terung	*3 cabé rawit (page 51)*
gelatik)	*1 tsp brown sugar*
¼ cucumber	*2 tbs tamarind water, or juice of*
2 tbs chopped fresh mint (or, in	*¼ lime*
Indonesia, kemangi)	*salt*
	1 cup boiling water

First, prepare the vegetables. Cut the yard-long beans into pieces about 1 cm (½″) long. Clean the beansprouts (see page 206). Peel the sweet potatoes, cut them into very tiny matchsticks and soak them in cold water with a teaspoonful of salt until you are ready to dress the salad. Shred the cabbage finely, cut the round eggplants each into four pieces, and peel and slice the cucumber.

Roast or fry the peanuts in a thick cast-iron wok or frying-pan; then grind them up or pound them well in a mortar. Fry or grill the terasi (see page 41). Peel the garlic and kencur and pound them into a smooth paste along with the terasi, cabé rawit and a little salt. Mix this with the ground-up nuts in the saucepan, and pour on the boiling water. Add the sugar and tamarind water or lime juice, and heat the mixture, stirring continuously for 2 minutes. Then leave to cool.

Arrange the raw vegetables on a bowl or plate. Pour the

peanut sauce over them, add the kemangi, and toss this salad just before serving. Like Gado-Gado (page 196), Karedok can be eaten by itself or as a vegetable dish with rice and meat.

ASINAN CAMPUR
A fruit and vegetable salad   to serve four

This is a sharp, clean-tasting salad, to be eaten before, with, or after the main meat course.

4 leaves white cabbage
¼ cucumber
2 medium-sized hard apples, e.g. Granny Smith or Cox's or,
  in Indonesia, 2 kedondong
6 radishes or 1 medium-sized Chinese radish (lobak)
2 carrots or 1 medium-sized bengkuang

for the dressing:
2 tbs white malt vinegar
1 tsp white sugar
2 tsp salt
a pinch of cayenne pepper
1 tbs water

Mix thoroughly the vinegar, water, salt, pepper and sugar.

Shred the cabbage finely. Peel and cut the apples (or kedondong) into four; remove the core and slice thinly. Peel the cucumber, cut it in half lengthwise, scoop out the seeds, and slice into very thin semicircles. Peel the carrots (or the bengkuang) and cut into short thin 'matchsticks'. Slice the radishes (or lobak).

Put all these vegetables and fruit into a salad bowl. Pour the vinegar dressing over them, and mix well. Let the salad stand for at least 1 hour before serving, and turn or toss it from time to time.

Incidentally, I find that in practice there is very little difference, except in size, between the two kinds of radish. They are both varieties of *Raphanus sativus*.

Tahu and Tempe

Tahu and tempe are both made from soya beans. This fact by itself puts off some westerners, and even Indonesians from outside Java find tempe an acquired taste. My father, from Central Sumatra, never acquired it, but I started eating tempe when I was twelve or thirteen years old and came to live in Central Java. Tahu is a Chinese invention, but well-known and generally popular all over Java and on many other islands, at least in the neighbourhood of large towns—that is to say, wherever there is a large Chinese population.

Tahu, or bean curd, is a soft cake prepared from soya beans by grinding them, extracting the casein and pressing it into slabs which are then cut up into cubes about 5 cm on a side. In Chinese shops in England, these cubes are sealed into plastic bags with a little water to keep them moist and are sold for more or less immediate consumption. Tahu will keep, in cold water in a refrigerator, for a couple of days at most. Alternatively, the white cubes are fried before being sold. This makes them smaller, rather drier, yellowish, and gives them a thick soft crust. Fried tahu can also be kept in the refrigerator for about two days. Tahu cannot be frozen.

Tempe is becoming, in Britain, one of those things that people have vaguely heard of but cannot quite place. Even in Holland, where it is quite easy to buy, and in North America, where making tempe at home is a popular hobby for health-food lovers, it cannot yet be called a household word. Whether it will become one before the end of this century may depend on how well world food supplies hold out and on commercial food manufacturers' response to rising prices. Of all Indonesian soya bean products, tempe is the one which is of the greatest potential importance as an item of everyone's diet. Soya beans are easy to grow, very cheap and packed with proteins, carbohydrates and vitamins. Unfortunately they are not easy for the human digestive system to cope with. The purpose of the fermentation and other chemical processes which produce tahu, tempe, tauco, kecap and so on is to break down the constituents that human enzymes can't tackle by themselves.

Soya beans become tempe through the action of certain enzymes produced by a small number of yeasts or moulds (*ragi* in Indonesian). Much the most suitable micro-organism for the production of tempe in non-tropical countries appears to be *Rhizopus oligosporus*, though intensive research into the whole tempe-making process is going on in the United States and Britain. *R. oligosporus* does for us what we cannot do properly ourselves: it breaks down the tissues of the beans without affecting in any way their nutritional value. It also helps to bind the beans together into a solid slab or sausage which can be cut or bitten into easily and which has a pleasantly crunchy texture and a nutty flavour. The colour, too, is attractive. A slab of tempe can look very like a good Brie cheese, but with the individual beans still keeping their shapes inside it.

This desirable food is fairly easy to make, even in temperate countries (which I take to mean cold, wet places like England). The beans are soaked in water so that they swell and their skins split and loosen. The skins are rubbed off and thrown away, and the beans split into two halves, either by hand or with some sort of simple rolling-machine, or in Java by treading the beans as if they were grapes for wine-making. They are then steamed or boiled for about 20 minutes and allowed to cool. A powdered culture of *R. oligosporus* is then sprinkled over them and stirred well in. The beans are packed in plastic bags (banana or teak leaves, if you want to be a traditionalist) pierced with small holes every centimetre or so, or in plastic tubes, or in aluminium foil trays with foil covers. The important thing is that there should be a reasonable supply of air to the mould-spores. The mass of beans should not be too thick, and every bean should be within about 2 cm of the surface so that oxygen can penetrate to it. Then the tray or package is incubated at a temperature between 25° and 30° C for 20–48 hours, and the tempe is ready. Temperature and air supply are critical; *R. oligosporus* is fussy, wilts in excessive heat or cold, needs oxygen but may be overcome by air-borne rogue yeasts if these are wafted in.

Those are the usual instructions for making tempe in the west. You can do it at home if you can find a supply of *R. oligosporus*, and we must hope that this will become easier as tempe becomes more popular. In theory, you can transfer one healthy colony of mould from one batch of tempe to the next, but in practice it is impossible to prevent contamination from other yeasts and you end up with something rather evil-smelling. In Java itself, surprisingly perhaps, more can be left to nature. The skinned and cracked beans are spread out in shallow trays, a little of the fungus is scattered over them, and they are covered for about two days. If they were left any longer, continuing fermentation could give rise to poisonous substances, though as overdone tempe smells strongly of ammonia it is not likely that anyone would try to eat it. A slightly bigger risk comes from the cost-cutting procedures of Javanese manufacturers who mix grated coconut with the beans. This *ampas kelapa* has previously been used for the extraction of santen (coconut milk); it has little food value and easily succumbs to airborne bacteria. Food poisoning can sometimes result from eating tempe made in this way, though cases are rare. Anyone buying tempe in Java is recommended to avoid *tempe bongkrek* and buy only *tempe murni*—literally, 'pure tempe'.

Nutritionists and cooks must agree that tempe has a lot going for it. It contains about 40 per cent protein—more than any other plant or animal food. It has carbohydrates but no starch and unsaturated oil without cholesterol. It has all eight essential amino acids, or so I am informed by the literature (see the Bibliography on page 249). It contains Vitamin A and several B-complex vitamins, iron, calcium, zinc, phosphorous and magnesium. It can be frozen at almost any stage in its manufacture or preparation. The one-pound bag of soya beans that (at the time of writing) costs 20p in a supermarket will make 2½ lb of tempe. However, I have chosen and included these tempe recipes here simply because they are easy to cook and good to eat.

GADON TAHU
Steamed bean curds, with coconut
and chilli   to serve six to eight

If everyone in the family likes bean curd, try this on them. It is a very popular dish in Central Java, and a very easy and convenient way of cooking bean curd. Use the fresh white kind, not the fried.

10 pieces of bean curd
30 g (1 oz) minced beef or *chicken*
4 shallots, or 4 tbs chopped spring onions
2 cloves garlic, crushed
1 tsp ground coriander
1 tbs lime juice or *juice of Kaffir lime*
about 1 tbs small pieces of salam leaf or *bay-leaf*
1 cup thick santen (coconut milk)
1 tsp brown sugar
4 green chillis, seeded and chopped (optional)
2 eggs
salt

This dish must be steamed, and it should of course be wrapped in banana leaf; but I have cooked it very satisfactorily in a soufflé dish, or in individual small dishes.

Mash the bean curd in a bowl with a spoon, and add all the other ingredients, except for the fragments of bay-leaf. If you don't like your food chilli-hot, replace the green chilli with freshly ground black pepper. Spoon the mixture into the dish or dishes, put a few pieces of bay-leaf on top, and steam in a rice- or fish-steamer for 30 to 45 minutes. Serve hot as a side dish with rice.

SEMUR TAHU
Bean curd in soya sauce   to serve two to four

4 pieces of bean curd
30 g (1 oz) so-un (vermicelli
   made from green bean starch)
1 small onion
2 cloves garlic
4 tbs dark soya sauce

1 tbs tomato ketchup
fried onions and parsley for
   garnishing
1 cup water
vegetable oil or butter

Cut each piece of bean curd in half. Soak the so-un in cold water for 30 minutes. Slice the onion finely and crush the garlic.

Put 3 tablespoonfuls of oil or butter in a frying-pan, and fry the tahu for 3 minutes on each side. Keep the pieces warm.

Put another tablespoonful of oil or butter in the pan, and fry the onion for about 2 minutes. Add the garlic, soya sauce and tomato ketchup. Put in the bean curd and water, and simmer slowly for 4 minutes. Then add the so-un and turn the heat a little higher; go on cooking for 3 minutes more. Serve hot, garnished with chopped parsley and fried onions.

TAHU GORENG
Fried bean curd   to serve two to four

These ingredients, to my way of thinking, are about right for two people; but if you are not sure yet how much you like bean curd, they could be enough for four.

4 pieces of bean curd
2 cloves garlic
4 tbs tamarind water
salt
vegetable oil

Cut each piece of bean curd in half. Crush the garlic, put it in the tamarind water, and season with salt. Dip the bean curd pieces into this water before deep-frying them until golden brown.

You can eat Tahu Goreng as a snack, or as a first course with

Sambal Kecap (page 222) or as just another side dish in a rijsttafel. Alternatively, you can make it into Tahu Campur, as follows:

TAHU CAMPUR
Bean curd with vegetables   to serve two

4 *Tahu Goreng (see previous page)*
120 g (4 oz) beansprouts
2 medium-sized potatoes

¼ cucumber
seledri (flat-leaved parsley)
8–10 emping melinjo (page 235)

for the sauce:
1 *cabé rawit (page 51) or a pinch of chilli powder (use more chilli if you like your food hot)*
2 cloves garlic (optional)
3 heaped tbs Kacang Goreng (page 228)
1 tbs dark soya sauce

1 *tsp Bovril (This is not as un-Indonesian as it may sound. At home I would use petis udang, which looks rather like Bovril and tastes very similar; it is made from shrimps.)*
juice of ½ a lime or ½ a lemon
2 tbs hot boiled water

Clean the beansprouts (as described on page 206) and put them in boiling water with a little salt. Cover and leave them for 6 minutes, then drain and keep them warm. Peel the potatoes, slice them thin, and fry them till crisp. Peel and slice the cucumber, chop the seledri, and fry the emping.

Now make the sauce. Pound the cabé rawit or chilli powder, the garlic and the Kacang Goreng into a fine powdery paste. Put this in a bowl with the soya sauce, Bovril and lime juice; mix well together and add the water. Mix well again.

To serve: arrange the Tahu Goreng on serving plates with the fried potatoes, slices of cucumber and beansprouts. Top with chopped seledri. Pour over this as much sauce as you like, and crush or break the emping over it.

Like Tahu Goreng in the previous recipe, this is good as a snack or small lunch dish. It can be a first course or you can serve it as a side dish with plain boiled rice and other meat or vegetable dishes.

Tahu and Tempe

TAHU ISI
Bean curd with savoury stuffing   to serve two to four

The bean curd may be either the white fresh variety or fried. The quantities shown are for 4 people, to be eaten with rice and vegetables; but if you are fond of tahu there will be enough here for 2 people for a good snack lunch, with no other food on the table.

6 pieces of white bean curd or 12–15 pieces of yellow fried bean curd

for the filling:
4 shallots or a bunch of spring onions, chopped
1 tbs chopped seledri (flat-leafed parsley)
  or coriander leaves
3 cloves garlic, sliced finely
30 g (1 oz) minced beef or pork or, if you want this to be a
  vegetarian dish, 1 cup finely diced carrots and potatoes
2 tsp cornflour
pepper and salt
2 tbs water
1 small egg
oil or butter

If you are using white bean curd, scoop out a little of it with a teaspoon to make a hole in the middle of the block about the size of a small egg-cup. With the yellow bean curd, which comes in smaller chunks, you will need to cut away the 'skin' on one side and scoop out the hole with a small knife. In either case, chop the bean curd that you have removed and mix it with the meat, or the carrots and potatoes.

Now heat about 2 tablespoons of oil or melted butter in a saucepan. When it is hot, put in the chopped shallots or spring onions and the garlic. Stir-fry for a minute or so and add the bean curd mixed with the meat or carrots and potatoes. Continue stir-frying for another 4 or 5 minutes. Add cornflour, salt and pepper, chopped seledri or coriander leaves, and water. Mix well. Turn the heat down and let everything cool a little before adding the egg, well beaten. Stir everything together thoroughly with a spoon and then fill the holes in the bean curd with the mixture.

If you are using white bean curd, steam it by itself for 20 minutes in order to make it firmer and then cut each block diagonally into 2 triangles. Let these cool and then fry them in deep oil or butter in a wok for 4 or 5 minutes on each side. If you are using the ready-fried bean curd, however, all this steaming and cutting is unnecessary; simply fill them, and deep-fry them in a wok, but only for 2 minutes on each side.

Tahu Isi can be eaten hot or cold, by themselves or with rice or with any salad you choose. At home, we usually eat them with Sambal Kecap or Sambal Tauco, or with saté sauce, or just as a snack with raw cabé rawit—the really hot kind.

TAHU GORENG BACEM
Bean curd boiled with spices, then fried to serve four

Four chunks of bean curd, just as they come from the shop. Cut each chunk into two and boil them all with the same ingredients that you would use for Tempe Goreng Bacem (page 220)—but for 30 minutes only. Then fry and serve in the same way.

TEMPE GORENG
Fried tempe to serve four

350 g (12 oz) tempe   *vegetable oil*

for the marinade:
2 cloves garlic   *¼ cup tamarind water*
2 shallots   *salt and pepper*

Cut the tempe into thick slices. Crush the garlic and shallots and mix these well with the tamarind water; add salt and pepper. Marinate the tempe in this for at least 50 minutes, turning the slices over several times.

Deep-fry the tempe slices until golden brown, and serve hot.

KERING TEMPE
Crisp fried tempe   to serve four

350 g (12 oz) tempe	¼ tsp chilli powder
8 shallots	2 tsp paprika
2 cloves garlic	a pinch of brown sugar
vegetable oil	salt

Cut the tempe into thin small squares. Crush the shallots and garlic into a fairly smooth paste. Deep-fry the tempe in oil until it is golden brown and crisp; drain the slices, and keep them warm.

Put 2 tablespoonfuls of oil in a wok, fry the shallots and garlic paste for 1 minute, and add chilli powder, paprika, sugar and salt. Stir-fry for another minute, then put in the fried tempe and stir well until the slices are well coated with the bumbu.

The tempe can be served hot or cold. The slices can be stored in airtight jars.

TERIK TEMPE
Tempe in thick candlenut sauce   to serve four to six

500 g (1 lb) tempe	¼ tsp cumin
1 slice terasi (page 41)	salt
5 shallots	1 salam leaf or bay-leaf
5 kemiri (candlenuts)	3 cups santen (coconut milk)
2 cloves garlic	2 tbs vegetable oil
1 tsp ground coriander	

Cut the tempe into thick slices. Grill the terasi, peel and chop the shallots, and pound these together with the kemiri and garlic. Add the coriander, cumin and salt, and mix all well together into a thick paste. Put this, with the salam or bay-leaf, into a wok, pour the santen over it, and put in the tempe slices. Simmer, uncovered, until the sauce is thick. Then add the 2 tablespoonfuls of vegetable oil. Continue cooking, stirring constantly, until the sauce is really thick. Serve hot.

KERIPIK TEMPE DAN TERI
Crisp-fried tempe with dried anchovies

500 g (1 lb) tempe
250 g (½ lb) ikan teri (tiny dried anchovies, page 124)
5 shallots
3 cloves garlic
1 tsp ground ginger
1 tsp chilli powder or 1 tsp Sambal Ulek (page 224)
salt
vegetable oil

for the marinade:
1 cup tamarind water
2 cloves garlic, crushed
1 tsp salt

Slice the tempe slab into thin pieces, then cut these into tiny squares. Put the crushed garlic and salt into the tamarind water, and marinate the tempe in this for 30 minutes. Discard the heads of the ikan teri. Peel and slice the shallots and garlic.

Drain the tempe and dry the pieces with kitchen paper. Heat the oil in a wok and deep-fry the tempe until crisp and golden brown. Don't try to fry all the tempe at once; do it little by little, keeping the pieces you have fried warm, wrapped in absorbent paper. When you have finished frying the tempe, start frying the ikan teri, stirring continuously until crisp. This will take about 2 minutes. Drain and keep warm. Discard the oil you have used for frying the teri, and put 2 tablespoonfuls new oil into the wok. Fry the sliced shallots and garlic until slightly coloured, add the ground ginger, chilli powder or Sambal Ulek, and some salt. Stir for a few seconds and put in the tempe and ikan teri. Continue stirring for a few more seconds. This dish can be served hot, to be eaten with rice. When cool, it can be stored in an airtight jar. This keripik will stay crisp for several days.

Tahu and Tempe

TEMPE GORENG BACEM
Tempe boiled with spices and fried   to serve four

350 g (12 oz) tempe	1 heaped tsp brown sugar
1 small onion	½ tsp chilli powder
2 cloves garlic	1 cup tamarind water
1 tsp ground coriander	salt
½ tsp ground ginger	1 cup water
1 salam leaf or bay-leaf	vegetable oil
a pinch of ground laos (galingale)	

Cut the tempe into thick slices and slice the onion thinly. Now put all the ingredients (except, of course, the oil) into a saucepan, cover, and cook for 50–60 minutes or until dry. Take care that the contents of the pan do not burn. Leave everything to cool for a few minutes, then fry in hot oil, turning once. When the slices of tempe are nicely brown, serve them hot.

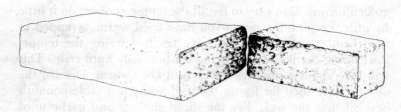

Tempe

Sambal

Sambal (or, in Javanese, sambel) is any kind of hot or spicy relish which is served with food. Some types are much hotter than others, but all are highly flavoured. You can adjust the hotness of your sambal, of course, by putting in more or less chilli. Sambal is usually treated a bit like red-currant jelly: that is, it is served in a small bowl or dish, and people help themselves to as much as they want. In a number of recipes in this book, I have mentioned which sambal I think goes best with a particular dish. As you become more experienced with Indonesian food, you will obviously prefer to make your own choices.

SAMBAL TERASI
Shrimp paste relish

Unlike some other kinds of sambal, this one doesn't keep, so make it in small quantities—just enough for one meal. It is very hot.

5 green chillis
1 shallot
1 slice terasi, grilled (page 41)
1 clove garlic

¼ tsp brown sugar (optional)
salt
juice of ¼ a small lime

Boil the chillis for 6 minutes, seed them, and cut them up small. Then pound them together with the shallot, garlic, and grilled terasi. Season with salt, sugar if desired, and lime juice.

SAMBAL TERONG
Aubergine relish

This is a relish which can be used hot or cold.

2 small aubergines or *1 big one*	*2 tsp chilli powder*
1 big Spanish onion	*1 slice terasi (page 41)*
4 cloves garlic	*1 tsp brown sugar*
1 tbs vegetable oil	*2 big tomatoes*

Slice the aubergine and sprinkle it with salt; leave to stand for half an hour. Cut up the tomatoes and remove the seeds.

Crush the terasi and garlic together. Slice the onion thinly, and fry until slightly brown. Add the garlic and terasi, the sugar and the chilli powder. Put in the aubergine, and mix well. Add the tomatoes, cover the pan, and continue cooking gently for 5 minutes. Taste, and add salt if necessary. Then put the mixture into a pudding basin and steam it for 20 minutes.

If you want this relish to be really hot—spicy hot—then take 4 green chillis, seed them and chop finely, and put them into the frying-pan at the same time as the onions. Alternatively, use dried red chillis: soak them for at least 15 minutes and put them into the mixture, whole, when everything goes into the basin for steaming.

SAMBAL KECAP
Soya sauce and chilli relish

This is a very simple sambal, quick and easy to make. It is ideal for adding just a little piquancy to such dishes as Mie Jawa (page 236), any saté (especially if you don't like peanut butter sauce), and Nasi Goreng (page 100).

2 tbs dark soya sauce	*2 shallots, sliced very thin*
juice of ½ a lemon or *1 lime*	*1 clove of garlic, crushed*
2 cabé rawit (page 51), crushed,	*(optional)*
or ½ tsp chilli powder	*1 tbs boiled water*

Mix all the ingredients well together just before serving.

SAMBAL CUKA
Vinegar relish

This is another very easy sambal, especially good with soto and Tahu Goreng.

15 g (½ oz) peanuts, roasted or
   fried
2 cabé rawit (*page 51*) or ½ tsp
   chilli powder
1 clove garlic

3 tbs white vinegar
½ tsp sugar
1 tbs boiled water
salt to taste

Crush the cabé rawit or chilli powder and garlic, add the nuts, and continue crushing until fine. Add the sugar, salt, vinegar and water. Mix well, and serve.

SAMBAL KELAPA
Coconut relish

This sambal is made from fresh coconut, and should be eaten on the same day.

¼ fresh coconut
1 slice terasi (*page 41*)
1 clove garlic
3 cabé rawit (*page 51*)*
salt

a small piece of gula Jawa (*page
   240*) or 2 tsp brown sugar
1 tbs tamarind water or *the
   juice of 1 Kaffir lime or of
   1 lime*

Separate the white flesh of the coconut from all trace of the brown outer skin, then grate it. Grill or fry the terasi, and then pound it, together with the garlic, cabé rawit and gula Jawa into a paste. Add the tamarind water, or juice, season with salt, and mix the paste thoroughly with the grated coconut. Serve.

---

* This is the minimum amount of cabé rawit; if you like your sambal really hot, put in 6 or 8 cabé rawit instead of 3. But remember that cabé rawit is the hottest and fiercest of all the chilli family.

SAMBAL TAUCO
Salted yellow bean relish

'Tauco' is salted yellow beans (page 44); you can buy them in Britain at Chinese grocery shops, in cans. Sambal Tauco is another hot relish that keeps for a long time. You can make it less hot by using less chilli.

1 6¼ oz (about 190 g) can of
*   salted yellow beans*
5 cloves garlic
1 tsp ground ginger or a piece of
*   root ginger, about 1 cm (¼″) long*
¼ cup tamarind water

1 tsp brown sugar
4 green chillis or 1 tsp chilli
*   powder*
6 shallots or 1 onion
½ cup water
2 tbs vegetable oil

Crush the garlic and the yellow beans together, either by pounding them in a mortar or by means of a liquidizer. Seed the green chillis and slice them finely. Slice the shallots or onion. If you are using root ginger, peel and chop it into very small sticks. Heat the oil and sauté the shallots for 1 minute. Add the chillis and ginger and sauté for another minute; then put in the tauco and garlic paste, sugar, tamarind water and the water. Stir, then simmer for about 8 minutes. Stir again, still cooking, for 1 minute. Serve hot, or allow the sambal to cool before storing it in an airtight jar.

SAMBAL ULEK
Crushed chillis

The ulek-ulek (see drawing on page 35) is the implement you use to crush candlenuts, chillis, etcetera in a cobek. Sambal Ulek is made of chillis that have been crushed this way. This is a very basic sambal, which is useful to keep in quantity, so that you can use it for quite a lot of recipes which specify red chillis as one of the ingredients. As this sambal can be stored for at least 2 weeks in the refrigerator, it is worth while making quite a lot of it. But to crush the chillis in a cobek with the ulek-ulek is very laborious. A food processor is a great help here.

1 kg (2¼ lb) red chillis
3 tsp salt

Seed and chop the red chillis roughly, then put all these into a saucepan and half-fill the saucepan with boiling water. Boil the chillis for 8 minutes. Drain, and put them into the food processor, using the blade for mincing meat. Let the machine run for a minute or so. For Sambal Ulek you don't want the chilli paste to be too smooth. Put this sambal into a jar, stir in the salt, cover the jar tightly and keep in the refrigerator.

SAMBAL IKAN
Fish relish

I find that the easiest and tastiest Sambal Ikan is made with canned tuna fish. Sambal made with eel, however, is also delicious; cut the eel up very small and wash it in vinegar. In Indonesia we make this sambal with ikan teri or ikan bilis (tiny dried anchovies, page 124).

1 can of tuna fish, about 120 g   *3 cabé rawit (page 51) or*
  (4 oz), or 1 eel or 90 g (3 oz)   *2 tsp chilli powder*
  ikan teri   *2 tbs tamarind water or*
1 cup thick santen (coconut milk)   *2 tsp tomato purée*
4 cloves garlic   *1 tsp brown sugar*
3 shallots, peeled and chopped   *salt*
4 kemiri (candlenuts)   *2 tbs vegetable oil*

Pound the garlic, shallots, kemiri and cabé rawit into a paste. Fry this paste in vegetable oil in a wok for about half a minute. Put in the tuna fish, eel or teri; stir-fry for 1 minute and add the tamarind water, or tomato purée, sugar and salt. Stir in the santen, and go on simmering until the mixture becomes thick. This sambal can be served hot or cold.

SAMBAL BAJAK
Mixed spice relish

This is a hot relish, and to make it all the ingredients have to be pounded together. If you do this in a mortar, try to keep the mixture off your fingers as much as possible if you have sensitive skin; it is not only your tongue that can feel the effects of a strong chilli. Sambal Bajak will keep for a long time in an airtight jar, and lose none of its fierceness.

10 red chillis
1 slice terasi (page 41)
10 shallots
5 cloves garlic
3 kemiri (candlenuts)

3 tbs vegetable oil
salt
1 tsp brown sugar
1 cup thick santen (coconut milk)

Take the first five ingredients above—that is, the chillis, terasi, shallots, garlic, and kemiri—and pound them all together into a fine paste. Alternatively, mince them first as fine as you can and then put them in a liquidizer. Sauté them in the vegetable oil for a few minutes, then add the salt, sugar and santen. Simmer gently for 20 minutes, and finish by cooking on a high flame, stirring continuously, for 1 minute.

Let the sambal cool before you store it. It can be served hot or cold, and can be reheated many times without impairing the flavour. If you have used a mincer and liquidizer during the preparation, wash them several times in hot water and with plenty of detergent before you use them for anything else.

Side Dishes

REMPEYEK KACANG
Indonesian savoury peanut brittle

Usually, these are just called 'peyek' for short. Peyek are a crispy, nutty savoury, very good to serve with drinks before a meal.

250 g (8 oz) peanuts
2 kemiri (candlenuts)
2 tsp ground coriander
1 clove garlic

1 tsp salt
1 cup water
120 g (4 oz) rice flour
vegetable oil

Cut each peanut in half. Pound the kemiri and garlic together and add the coriander and some salt. Mix these ingredients (not the peanuts) with the rice flour, and then start to add water, a little at a time, stirring and mixing thoroughly. The batter that is produced should be thick, but should still be able to run. Pour the peanuts into the batter.

For frying peyek, you need a non-stick frying-pan and a wok. Heat a little oil in the frying-pan, and enough in the wok to deep-fry the peyek. Take up a tablespoonful of the batter, with some nuts in it, and pour it quickly into the frying-pan. Fry it there for about half a minute—you will probably be able to do 3 or 4 peyek at a time—and then drop the half-cooked peyek into the hot oil in the wok. Deep-fry them until they are crisp and golden-brown: this will take a minute or a little longer. Carry on like this till all the batter and nuts are used up. Let the peyek cool before putting them into store; in an airtight container, they will keep for up to a fortnight.

REMPEYEK TERI
Dried anchovies fried in batter

120 g (4 oz) teri (ikan bilis, see page 124)	*2 tsp ground coriander*
	a pinch of salt
2 kemiri (candlenuts)	*1 cup water*
1 clove garlic	*120 g (4 oz) rice flour*

Cut off the heads of the teri. Make the batter, and fry, exactly as for Rempeyek Kacang, with 4 or 5 fish in each peyek. You will need less salt here, however, than in Rempeyek Kacang, because the teri are already very salty.

REMPEYEK BAYEM
Fried spinach in batter

'Bayem' is spinach, and these are simply crisp-fried spinach leaves, fried whole in a little batter. Fresh spinach from your own garden is best, but of course not obligatory. You need about 20 good leaves for the quantity of batter described on page 227. Wash them, and leave them to dry.

Make the batter exactly as for Rempeyek Kacang, or perhaps a little thicker—a little less water, or a bit more rice flour. Coat each leaf on both sides in the batter, and fry as before. These Peyek Bayem will only keep for about 24 hours, even in an airtight container.

KACANG GORENG
Fried peanuts

This is the simplest possible way of frying peanuts. You will need 500 g (1 lb 2 oz) of shelled raw peanuts.

Heat a cup of vegetable oil in a wok or deep frying-pan. When it is hot, put in half of the peanuts and stir-fry continuously for 4–5 minutes. Take them out quickly and put them in a colander lined with absorbent kitchen paper. Repeat the process with the remaining peanuts. Dry the excess oil from the peanuts with the kitchen paper, and sprinkle a little salt over them while they are still hot. Let them cool, then store in airtight containers.

KACANG TUJIN or KACANG BAWANG
Fried peanuts, another way

500 g (1 lb) peanuts
2 cloves garlic
salt
vegetable oil

Put the peanuts into a bowl with the crushed garlic and a tea-spoonful of salt. Pour in enough boiling water to cover the nuts. Cover the bowl and let it stand for 30 minutes, then peel off the thin skin from the peanuts—it is usually enough to rub the nut between finger and thumb, the skin will have become very loose. Put the nuts on absorbent paper, and when the peeling is completed heat a cupful of oil in a wok or a deep frying-pan. Stir-fry the peanuts in this, ½ lb at a time, for 5–6 minutes. Let cool before storing in airtight containers.

PANGSIT GORENG
Minced pork and prawns in crisp-fried cases

225 g (½ lb) pork, minced
60 g (2 oz) prawns, shelled and minced
4 shallots, sliced very thin
3 cloves garlic, sliced very thin
1 tbs chives, chopped finely
2 small eggs
1 tsp cornflour
salt and pepper
120 g (4 oz) wun tun skins (see page 233)
oil for frying

Fry the shallots and garlic lightly. Mix them with the pork and prawns, chives, eggs and cornflour, and season. Take about a spoonful of the mixture and roll it into a ball. Put this on a wun tun skin, fold the skin over to make a triangle, and give the two sharp angles a twist. Deep-fry the pangsit in a wok, 4 or 5 at a time, for about 2 minutes so that the skins become brown and crisp. Eat hot or cold, as an appetizer or as a side dish.

PERGEDEL KENTANG
Potato cakes

The name of this recipe, I think, comes from Dutch, but I have never been quite sure whether the recipe itself originated in Holland or in Indonesia. I have always thought of it as a typically Indonesian dish, because my grandmother used to make it so often; and certainly Indonesian cooks, if they did not invent pergedel, have adopted them.

500 g (1 lb) potatoes	*a handful of seledri (flat-leaved*
1 egg	*parsley)*
1 egg white	*salt and pepper*
6 shallots	*a pinch of grated nutmeg*
250 g (8 oz) minced steak	*vegetable oil*
4 spring onions	

Boil the potatoes in their skins, and peel and mash them while they are still hot. Peel and slice the shallots, and sauté them in a little oil until they are soft. Drain them, and add them to the mashed potatoes. Season with salt, pepper, and nutmeg. Chop the spring onions and seledri and mix these well in with the potatoes. Knead the potatoes and minced meat thoroughly together. Beat one egg and mix that, too, with the potatoes; then simply pour in the white of a second egg and stir the whole mixture quickly with a fork. Take a spoonful of it, roll it into a ball, and flatten the ball slightly with the back of a fork—or, if you are going to use the pergedel to garnish another dish, make smaller balls, the size of marbles. When the whole mixture has been used, start frying the balls, a few at a time, in deep oil in a saucepan.

By themselves, pergedel are usually served hot, though many people like them cold as well. They are normally served cold as a garnish—they are very good with, for example, Nasi Kuning (page 102).

PERGEDEL JAGUNG
Sweet corn fritters

In Indonesia these are made of fresh corn on the cob, and if you can buy your corn fresh then there is no doubt that the pergedel look authentically Indonesian. However, I have also made them with canned sweet corn, and although they look rather like ordinary corn fritters they do taste like the real thing. Here I give the recipe for making pergedel with fresh corn. If you use canned corn, then a 326 g can (11½ oz) will be right for these ingredients; all you need to do is to mix its contents with the spices.

6 fresh corn cobs (not too young and not too old)	*90 g (3 oz) prawns, fresh or frozen (optional)*
1 red chilli or ½ tsp chilli powder	*1 tsp ground coriander*
4 shallots	*salt*
2 cloves garlic (optional)	*1 large egg*
	vegetable oil

Grate the corn off the cobs. Put the prawns, peeled shallots, chilli and garlic all together through a mincer. Mix them well in a bowl with the corn, and season with coriander and salt. Break the egg into the mixture and whisk quickly. Heat about 5 tablespoonfuls of oil in a frying-pan. Drop a heaped tablespoonful of the mixture into the pan and quickly flatten it with a fork. You should be able to fry 4 or 5 pergedel at a time, giving each one about 2½ minutes on each side and turning once only. Serve hot.

Pergedel Jagung can be frozen. Thaw them completely before you re-fry them or heat them in the oven at gas mark 4 (about 350° F) for 30–40 minutes.

SERUNDENG
Roasted grated coconut

This is made from grated coconut, which is roasted until golden brown.

180 g (6 oz) freshly grated or	*¼ tsp ground cumin*
desiccated coconut	*¼ tsp ground laos (galingale)*
90 g (3 oz) fried peanuts	*1 tbs tamarind water*
(optional, see page 228)	*¼ tsp brown sugar*
5 shallots	*3 Kaffir lime leaves or 1*
3 cloves garlic	*bay-leaf*
1 tsp ground coriander	*salt*
1 slice terasi (page 41)	*2 tbs vegetable oil*

Pound the shallots and garlic until smooth, or mince them in a meat mincer. Heat the oil in a wok and fry the shallots and garlic for half a minute before adding all the other ingredients except the coconut and fried peanuts. Stir-fry for 1 minute; then add the coconut* and mix well. Continue cooking, stirring from time to time, until the coconut starts to colour. When this happens, stir continuously until the coconut is golden brown. Add the fried peanuts, stir for 1 minute, and serve.

Serundeng will keep in an airtight jar for several months. It is usually served cold, as a side dish or garnish. It is particularly good with Nasi Rames (page 99).

* If you use desiccated coconut, you must put in 1 cup of water at the time the coconut is added to the mixture. Let it just simmer until all the water has been soaked up by the coconut, then start stir-frying. With fresh coconut, of course, this extra water is not needed.

MARTABAK
Savoury meat pancakes

This dish, I believe, originated in India. In towns all over Java, it is sold out of doors in open *warungs* or stalls in the main square —the *alun-alun*—and in street markets. It is the sort of substantial snack that everyone needs to sustain him during an

evening's stroll around town, and the warung that sells martabak is always crowded. Another attraction is to watch the
vendor, usually a man, preparing the dough. He rolls it into a
ball, slaps it on to a wooden table, and starts to pull it very
quickly and skilfully into the thinnest imaginable sheet—without tearing it. When the dough is ready, he spreads the meat
and other filling on to it and folds it over to make a kind of
square pasty, 15 cm (6″) or more each side. At one side of him
is his frying-pan, a large square of iron supported over glowing
charcoal. This iron is mirror-smooth from years of use, and is
kept well greased with olive oil. The martabak vendor drops the
martabak on the iron square and lets it fry for a few minutes on
each side, turning it only once. He works so fast that there are
usually 4 or 5 martabak frying at once. As each one is finished,
he wraps it in a banana leaf, then in a sheet of paper, before
handing it to the customer.

On the table in the warung you will see a big tray of cooked
minced lamb, a tray of chopped spring onions and seledri, a big
bowl of peeled Spanish onions (we call these *bawang Bombay*),
and a basket full of duck eggs. Before he makes each martabak,
the man puts a large spoonful of the minced lamb into a bowl,
then a handful of chopped spring onions and seledri. Then he
starts to slice up an onion; at this point the customer can say
just how much onion he wants. He breaks an egg into the bowl,
adds salt and spices, whisks it quickly, and fills the next sheet
of dough. Fold it over, trim it, drop it on the hot iron; the
martabak is ready to eat, blisteringly hot, in less than 5 minutes.

Now let me try to tell you how you can make excellent Martabak at home. I have made them many times, but I have to confess that I have never succeeded in making this paper-thin
dough; nor is it necessary to do so, though I give the ingredients
and method in case you want to try. I buy my dough already
prepared and trimmed from a Chinese supermarket; it is not
genuine martabak dough, but it does very well. The Chinese
name for it is *wun tun*; probably you have eaten wun tun soup in
Chinese restaurants. In Indonesia we call these little squares of
dough *kulit pangsit*. They are sold in packets of 20–25 pieces,
and they are smaller than the pieces which the warung-owner

uses—about 7 cm (3″) square. They should be kept cool, preferably in a refrigerator.

If you want to make the dough yourself, you will need:

300 g (10 oz) plain flour *salt*
2 standard eggs   *cold water*

Sift the flour and salt into a bowl. Break the eggs into it and mix well with a spoon, then knead thoroughly. Put in enough cold water to make a firm dough, and roll into a ball. Knead again, and roll the dough into a ball again. Sprinkle a pastry-board with cornflour, flatten the ball on this, and carefully pull out the dough into a thin, very thin sheet. Cut this sheet into pieces of whatever size you want your martabak to be, and keep the pieces cool until the filling is ready.

 Whether you make or buy your dough, for the filling you need:

500 g (1 lb) lamb or beef, *1 tsp powdered lemon grass or*
 roasted or boiled   *several sticks fresh lemon*
1 or 2 large onions   *grass, sliced very thin*
2 cloves garlic   *¼ tsp chilli powder or freshly*
1 tsp ground coriander   *ground black pepper*
¼ tsp cumin   *1 cup chopped spring onions or*
¼ tsp ground ginger   *chives*
¼ tsp turmeric (optional—   *¼ cup chopped seledri (flat-leaved*
 sometimes I use 1 tsp curry   *parsley) or ordinary parsley*
 powder instead)   *olive oil*
            2 or 3 eggs

Mince the meat, slice the onions finely, crush the garlic. Put 1 tablespoonful of olive oil into a wok and fry the onion and garlic until soft. Add coriander, cumin, ginger, chilli or pepper, turmeric or curry powder, and lemon grass. Stir-fry for half a minute, then put in the minced meat. Mix well and continue stirring for 1–2 minutes. Leave this mixture to cool before you break the eggs into it and add the chopped spring onions or chives and parsley. Mix well again, and spoon the filling on to your squares of dough. If you are using *kulit pangsit* or *wun tun—*

the small squares—work on a floured board and put 1 heaped tablespoonful of filling on a square. Then put another square of dough on top and seal the edges roughly.

As each martabak is filled, drop it into a frying-pan which has been well oiled with olive oil—say, 2 tablespoonfuls of oil, renewed from time to time if necessary. The oil must be very hot when the martabak goes into it. Press the martabak down with a spatula for a few seconds, so that the thin casing will be moist and will not be fried crisp. Fry for 1 minute, or a little more, on each side, turning only once.

To serve Martabak: I said at the beginning that Indonesians eat martabak mostly in the open air, and obviously it is a very nourishing snack which one can eat with one hand while on the move. But I have also served martabak as a savoury with drinks before dinner; as a first course, accompanied by mango chutney or Acar Campur (page 205) or by itself; and as a main course with Nasi Kuning (page 102) or Nasi Goreng (page 100). Whatever way it is served, I always find it extremely popular.

Freezing: Martabak can be frozen successfully. To serve it from the freezer, thaw thoroughly, put the martabak in an ovenproof dish, cover it and heat in the oven at gas mark 4 (about 350° F) for 20 minutes.

EMPING

Emping have a dry, slightly nutty flavour and in Indonesia are used to garnish dishes like Nasi Goreng (page 100), Gado-Gado (page 196), or Tahu Campur (page 215). They are made from melinjo nuts (page 73), crushed and dried, and you can buy packets of Emping in the shops or market-place.

To cook them, drop a few at a time into hot oil in a wok and let them sizzle for just a few seconds. They will become bigger, but not dramatically so. Take them out, drain them and sprinkle a little salt on them. Let them cool and serve them. Uncooked Emping will keep for several months in an airtight jar; cooked ones in a sealed jar will stay crisp for two to three days.

MIE JAWA
Javanese fried (or boiled) noodles

This started out as a Chinese dish, which in Indonesia is called *bakmie*. It is very popular in Holland, where it is often called *bamie* and appears in many variations in different restaurants. There are basically two kinds: Bakmie Goreng, which is fried noodles, and Bakmie Godog, which is noodle soup. The Javanese adapted these noodles to their own cuisine and they now make Mie Jawa, using beef instead of pork. You can, of course, go back to using pork if you prefer it.

For BAKMIE GORENG, to serve three or four people, you need:

250 g (8 oz) egg noodles	*90 g (3 oz) beansprouts*
90 g (3 oz) topside of beef or pork fillet	*2 cabbage leaves*
4 spring onions	
60 g (2 oz) shrimps or prawns	*vetsin (Accent, or monosodium*
5 shallots	*glutamate)*
2 cloves garlic	*salt and pepper*
3 kemiri (candlenuts—optional)	*vegetable oil or pork fat*
2 tomatoes	*seledri (flat-leaved parsley) and*
3 tsp dark soya sauce	*fried onions for garnishing*
2 medium-sized carrots	

Put the noodles into salted boiling water and boil them for 5 minutes (or according to the instructions on the packet). Turn them out of the saucepan into a colander and hold them under cold running water for a few seconds, then leave to drain. Cut the beef or pork into small pieces. Slice the shallots finely. Crush the kemiri and garlic into a smooth paste.

Clean the beansprouts (see page 206), peel and slice the carrots into thin rounds, and shred the cabbage coarsely. Chop the spring onions. Peel, seed and chop the tomatoes.

In a wok, heat 2 tablespoonfuls of oil or pork fat. Sauté the shallots for 1 minute. Add the kemiri and garlic paste, the cut-up meat, and the shrimps or prawns. Continue stir-frying for 2 minutes, then add the shredded cabbage and carrots and go on stirring for about 4 minutes. Add the noodles and beansprouts and keep on stirring for another 3 minutes; next, add the soya sauce, chopped tomatoes, and spring onions. Season with salt, pepper and vetsin and carry on stirring and frying until the noodles are really hot. Garnish with parsley and fried onions, and serve immediately.

For BAKMIE GODOG, the ingredients will be enough for five or six people, but you will also need about 800 ml (1½ pints) of good stock.

Follow the method for Bakmie Goreng up to the point where the cabbage and carrots have just been put in. Now add the stock, soya sauce and chopped tomatoes. You can transfer the whole lot from the wok to a saucepan if you want to; but the usual practice is to boil up the soup in the wok. Let this soup simmer for 5 minutes. Then add the noodles, beansprouts and chopped spring onions. Season with salt and pepper. Cook for about 3 minutes on a high flame. Serve immediately in soup-plates, garnished with parsley and fried onions.

KRUPUK UDANG
Prawn crackers

The raw Krupuk Udang that you buy in the shop are thin, flat oblong flakes. Every trace of moisture should be removed before cooking, as a damp krupuk will not become crisp. In the tropics you spread your krupuk in the sunshine for an hour or two before you fry them; in London I give them an hour or two in a warm dry cupboard.

To cook them, drop them one at a time into a wok of hot vegetable oil; they swell in a second or two to two or three times their original size, and should then be taken out, drained and cooled.

Like Emping, Krupuk will keep a long time when raw; after cooking, they will keep in an airtight jar for two to three days. Serve them to be eaten with fingers as a side dish, or break one or two into pieces and use to garnish dishes such as Gado-Gado (page 196) or Nasi Goreng (page 100).

Sweets

KOLAK UBI
Sweet potatoes in coconut syrup   to serve four to six

This is a simple way to cook sweet potatoes, to serve as a sweet.

500 g (1 lb) sweet potatoes   *pinch of salt*
2 cups thick santen (coconut milk)   *2 cups water*
90 g (3 oz) brown sugar

Peel and wash the sweet potatoes and cut them into small squares. Boil these in 2 cups of water for 10 minutes, then drain them.

In another saucepan, simmer the santen with a pinch of salt and the brown sugar, stirring often and being careful that the santen does not quite come to the boil. When the sugar is dissolved, put in the sweet potatoes and continue to simmer until the sweet potatoes are cooked. This will take 10 or 15 minutes. Serve hot. Kolak Ubi can also be made in advance, and reheated before serving.

KOLAK LABU
Pumpkin in coconut syrup

This is made in exactly the same way as Kolak Ubi, except that *labu*—pumpkin—is used instead of sweet potatoes.

NAGASARI
Rice cake with banana   to serve four to six

250 g (8 oz) rice flour   *2 cups thick santen (coconut milk)*
60 g (2 oz) cornflour   *4 tbs granulated sugar*
2 large bananas   *pinch of salt*

Sift the rice flour and cornflour together into a mixing-bowl, and add a pinch of salt. Heat the santen in a saucepan with the sugar; stir until the sugar is dissolved, but do not let the santen boil. Peel the bananas and cut each one into three, crosswise. Then cut each piece of banana lengthwise in half. Mix the warm santen into the flour to make a smooth batter.

This is another of those Indonesian dishes that should be cooked in banana leaves. However, you can manage perfectly well with a heatproof soufflé dish or pudding basin. Grease it, and pour into it the batter and the chunks of banana, which should be well covered by the batter. You can either steam this or boil it in a saucepan as if it were a Christmas pudding; it will need 50 minutes or an hour. Let it cool before serving.

To serve, either spoon it out of the soufflé dish on to dessert plates, or turn it out like a blancmange on to a serving-dish.

PISANG GORENG
Fried bananas   to serve four

4 bananas, medium-sized ones   *1 cup santen (coconut milk)*
  which are fairly ripe   *pinch of salt*
90 g (3 oz) rice flour   *clarified butter for frying*
30 g (1 oz) melted butter

Mix the flour, butter, santen and salt into a smooth batter. Cut the bananas lengthwise down the middle, then cut each piece across into two. Coat well with the batter and fry in clarified butter until golden brown.

The bananas can also be cut into round slices, which are fried in the same way, 4 or 5 at a time. One banana is enough for two helpings.

RUJAK
Hot, spicy fruit salad to serve six

At home we use fruit that is not fully ripe, such as a slightly unripe mango, because this has the right sourness and sharpness of taste. The best sugar to use is *gula Jawa*.* However, I also use dark, soft, brown sugar or Demarara sugar, and either of these is quite satisfactory.

1 pomelo or *ugli fruit* or *Texas grapefruit* (in Indonesia *jeruk Bali*, page 59)
¼ cucumber
¼ pineapple

2 apples, Granny Smith or *Cox's* (in Indonesia *kedondong*, page 67)
2 mangoes or *slightly unripe pears*

In Indonesia, we would usually add also *bengkuang* and *jambu*.

Peel and segment the pomelo, ugli fruit or grapefruit. Slice the cucumber; this may be peeled or not, as you prefer. Prepare the other fruit, washing and peeling as required, and cutting everything into small pieces. Put the pieces straight into a bowl of cold water with 1 teaspoonful of salt. When you are ready to serve, drain off this water and pile all the fruit in a plate or bowl.

for the bumbu:
1 cabé rawit (page 51)
1 slice grilled terasi (page 41— optional)
*120 g (4 oz) gula Jawa**

¼ cooking banana (pisang klutuk, page 80—optional)
large pinch of salt
1 tbs tamarind water

Pound all these, except the tamarind water, until they are smooth; add the water and mix well. You may need to add a tablespoonful of tamarind water. This bumbu should look like a fairly thick, sticky syrup.

* Gula Jawa is brown sugar made from juice of the flower of the coconut palm. It is sold in hard cakes; the amount needed is cut off and crushed, or scraped off. Gula aren is similar, but comes from the sugar-palm. A general name for both types is gula merah ('red sugar'), and similar palm sugars are found elsewhere—e.g. jaggery in Burma and gula Malaka in Malaysia.

To serve, pour all the bumbu over the fruit and mix well; then serve and eat as you would an ordinary fruit salad. Alternatively, put the bumbu in its own small bowl, and let everybody help themselves.

ONDÉ-ONDÉ
Small rice cakes rolled in grated coconut

250 g (8 oz) glutinous rice flour	*pinch of salt*
2 tbs cocoa (optional)	*1 cup water*
90 g (3 oz) gula Jawa (page 240) or Demerara sugar	*½ fresh coconut*

In Indonesia ondé-ondé are always a pleasantly fresh green colour, since they are made with the fragrant leaf called *daun pandan*. I have tried making ondé-ondé in England with green colouring, but they didn't look so nice; so, as an alternative, I use cocoa to give the colour, and a mild flavour, of chocolate.

Sift the flour and the cocoa into a mixing-bowl, with a pinch of salt. Add the water a little at a time, mixing and then kneading the pastry until it is soft and smooth. Take a knob of pastry about as big as a small marble, flatten it on the pastry board, and fill with a small piece of gula Jawa or ¼ teaspoonful of demerara sugar. Shape the pastry into a ball, with the sugar inside. Repeat until all the pastry is used up.

Half-fill a saucepan with water, and add a pinch of salt. Bring to the boil, and drop in your ondé-ondé one by one, until there are ten or a dozen in the pan. Boil them for 10–15 minutes, or until they float on the surface. Take them out very carefully and drain them in a colander. When cooking is completed, grate the fresh coconut, having first removed the brown outer rind. Mix ¾ teaspoonful of salt with the coconut, and roll the ondé-ondé in the gratings until all are well covered. Arrange on a serving-dish, and sprinkle any remaining coconut on top. Serve warm or cold.

KUE TALAM
Batter pudding   to serve four

This should have the consistency, more or less, of a soufflé.

90 g (3 oz) rice flour
300 ml (½ pint) thin santen
  (coconut milk) or water

60 g (2 oz) brown sugar
pinch of salt

for the cream:
30 g (1 oz) rice flour
240 ml (8 fl oz) thick santen
  (coconut milk)

salt

Mix the rice flour, thin santen, brown sugar and salt to make a smooth batter. Cook this slowly until it thickens. Pour it into a buttered cake tin, and steam for 8 minutes.

While it is steaming, make the cream by mixing 30 g (1 oz) of rice flour with the thick santen—and it should be very thick santen. Add a little salt to taste. Cook, stirring continuously, until thick. Pour over the brown cake, which is still steaming, and go on steaming for a further 5 minutes, making a total of 13 minutes' steaming.

Let the dish cool, and slice it into serving portions. Kue Talam will keep overnight in the refrigerator, but should be taken out at least 2 hours before serving, so that it can be eaten cold but not chilled.

KUE TALAM PISANG
Banana batter pudding   to serve six to eight

This is similar to Kue Talam, but has thin rounds of banana cooked inside it.

3 large bananas
250 g (8 oz) rice flour
60 g (2 oz) cornflour

3 cups santen (coconut milk)
100 g (3 to 4 oz) brown sugar
pinch of salt

Sift the rice flour and cornflour into a mixing-bowl, and add a pinch of salt. Heat the santen in a saucepan, taking care not to let it boil. Put about half a cup of santen into a small saucepan and use it to dissolve the sugar. Use the rest of the santen, with the flour, to make a smooth, fairly thick batter. Mix the dissolved sugar into this. Peel the bananas and cut into thin rounds. Spoon the batter into small baking cups, leaving room to put several rounds of banana on top of each. Then steam these for 25–30 minutes, until the batter is set and cooked. Serve warm or cold.

DADAR GULUNG
Pancake with a coconut filling   to serve four to six

The batter is exactly the same as for an ordinary pancake, and if you make 300 ml (½ pint) of it you will need the following quantities for the filling:

120 g (4 oz) desiccated coconut	*pinch of salt*
or ¼ a fresh young coconut	*1 tsp lemon juice*
90 g (3 oz) brown sugar	*1 cup water*
1 stick cinnamon	

In Indonesia we would also add a little of the fragrant leaf known as *daun pandan*, but this is not essential. If you use fresh coconut, remember as usual to take off the brown rind before you start grating it.

Put the water and sugar in a saucepan, bring to the boil, and stir until the sugar is dissolved. Add the coconut and the other ingredients—but not the lemon juice. Simmer until the coconut has soaked up all the water. Add the lemon juice, stir for about a minute, and discard the cinnamon stick. Keep the filling warm while you make the pancakes. When they are ready, fill each one, roll it up, and serve immediately.

KUE BUGIS
Small cakes with coconut filling

250 g (8 oz) glutinous rice flour   *pinch of salt*
1½ cups santen (coconut milk)

for the filling:
120 g (4 oz) grated coconut,   *1 tbs glutinous rice flour*
  fresh or desiccated   *1 cup water*
90 g (3 oz) brown sugar

for the cream:
1 cup very thick santen (coconut   pinch of salt
  milk)*

Put the rice flour in a saucepan and pour in the santen carefully, stirring continuously. Add a pinch of salt. Cook this mixture, stirring occasionally at first but then, as it thickens, stirring continuously. It will begin to look very like porridge. Go on cooking for 5 more minutes.

Now make the filling. Heat the sugar in the water until it dissolves, then stir in the coconut and let it simmer until all the water has been absorbed into the coconut. Put in a tablespoonful of glutinous rice flour, mix well, and continue cooking for another 2 minutes, stirring all the time.

In another saucepan, boil the thick santen with a pinch of salt. As soon as it is on the point of boiling, this must be stirred continuously for 3 minutes.

At home we make Kue Bugis in banana leaves, but here I use individual small pots or cups without handles. Put about 2 teaspoonfuls of thick santen into each cup, then a tablespoonful of the thick 'porridge'. Smooth this with a spoon and put on top of it a tablespoonful of the filling, then another tablespoonful of the porridge, and top it off with 2 teaspoonfuls of thick santen. Then steam these cups, or pots, for 10–15 minutes.

Kue Bugis can be eaten warm or cold, and are best eaten with a spoon straight from whatever they have been cooked in.

SERIKAYA

This is a lovely steamed cake from Alor. The friend who gave me the recipe complained that she could not find kenari nuts in London and had tried replacing them with ground peanuts; the result, however, had not been very satisfactory. We decided to try almonds instead, and it tasted delicious. Her husband is from Alor; she herself is a Minangkabau from West Sumatra, like me, and when she gave me the recipe she pointed out that it was quite different from the Serikaya we had both been used to at home. In Sumatra we make it with santen and eat it with ketan (see Ketan Serikaya, page 246).

3 large eggs
120 g (4 oz) ground almonds or, in Indonesia, ground kenari nuts
90 g (3 oz) brown sugar (in Indonesia grated gula Jawa, page 240)
1 or 2 pieces of daun pandan about 1 cm long (optional)

Beat the egg until creamy, add the sugar and continue beating for 2 minutes more. Whisk in the ground almond. Mix well. Pour the mixture into a well-oiled 16 cm (6½″) cake tin or soufflé dish—or indeed any suitable tin or dish that will fit into your steamer, remembering that the mixture will rise in cooking just like a cake. Steam for 30 minutes. Serikaya can be cut and served hot, or can be allowed to cool and then served just as if it was an ordinary sponge cake.

The *daun pandan* is used in the same way as a vanilla pod, to give a faint characteristic flavour and aroma to the cake. If you have some of this leaf, put it on the bottom of the cake tin and pour the mix over it. After cooking, throw it away. It will leave a green stain on the underside of the cake, but this does not affect the flavour.

KETAN SERIKAYA

This is a kind of rice cake, with cream made of very thick santen.

500 g (1 lb) beras ketan	*3 small eggs*
(glutinous rice)	*60 g (2 oz) brown sugar (in*
5½ cups thick santen (coconut	*Indonesia gula Jawa, page 240)*
milk)	*large pinch of salt*

Wash the rice and soak it in cold water for 1 hour. Drain, put the rice into a steamer, and steam it for 8 minutes. Pour it into a saucepan, and while it is still hot pour over it 1½ cups of santen. Add a pinch of salt, and stir. Keep on stirring until all the santen has been absorbed into the ketan. Then put it back in the steamer and steam it for another 10 minutes. When this is done, put the ketan into a square, shallow cake tin. Place a piece of greaseproof paper on top of it and pat it firmly down. Take off the greaseproof paper and leave the ketan while you make the serikaya (cream).

Beat the eggs and the sugar until they are thick and fluffy, then add the remaining 4 cups of santen and a pinch of salt. Put the mixture into a pudding basin and steam it in the steamer for 10–15 minutes. The serikaya should be quite thick, something like thick cream.

Take out the ketan from its tin and put it on a serving dish; pour the serikaya over it, or serve separately in a cream jug. The ketan can be cut like a cake. It can be served warm or cold.

GETUK LINDRI

This is something to eat at tea time, the equivalent of a good, plain cake, easy to make and satisfying. It is really a sweet potato purée which we treat very much as a chestnut purée is often treated in Europe: it is put through a ricer (or an old-fashioned mincer) and comes out as long strands. These are then shaped into round or oblong cakes, which are Getuk Lindri.

You can often buy these in Central Java from small cake-shops or from vendors by the roadside. They are sold with freshly grated young coconut sprinkled over them, seasoned with a little salt. The sweet potatoes that we use are called ubi jalar; they have a reddish skin and white flesh, and are not the same as the orange-coloured ones which most English green-grocers call yams. Yams are not much good for Getuk Lindri, because they are too soft.

1 kg (2¼ lb) sweet potatoes
60 g (2 oz) brown sugar (in Indonesia gula Jawa, page 240)
6 tbs thick santen (coconut milk)
60 g (2 oz) freshly grated coconut
salt

Wash the sweet potatoes, cut them into four pieces, and boil them for 15 or 20 minutes in their skins. Treat them as you would ordinary potatoes, and dig a fork or something sharp into them to see if they are done.

While they are still hot, peel off the skin and mash them in a bowl until they are smooth. If you are using gula Jawa, which usually comes in small round blocks, shave them with a knife into a saucepan (they are usually too hard to crumble by hand), add the santen, and heat gently, stirring continuously, until all the sugar is dissolved. Cool the sweetened santen a little, then pour it into the mashed sweet potatoes and mix it in well with a large wooden spoon. Put the mixture through a ricer so that it turns into long, delicate strands. Shape these carefully into small oblongs about 7 cm by 5 cm (3″ by 2″) or into small round buns.

Add a large pinch of salt to the grated coconut, mix them thoroughly with a spoon, and serve in a bowl ready to be sprinkled on top of the Getuk Lindri before eating.

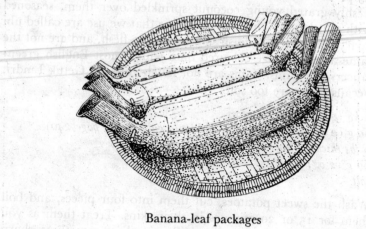

Banana-leaf packages

Banana-leaf container

BIBLIOGRAPHY

This is a highly selective bibliography, containing a few books which I have found interesting or immediately useful, but with no pretensions whatever to completeness or balance.

ALLEN, BETTY MOLESWORTH, *Common Malaysian Fruits*, Longman, Malaysia, 1965.

BURKILL, I. H., *Dictionary of the Economic Products of the Malay Peninsula*, Crown Agents, 1935, reprinted by the Ministry of Agriculture and Co-operatives, 2 vols, Kuala Lumpur, 1966.

CHILD, R., *Coconuts*, 2nd edn, Longman, 1974.

COBLEY, LESLIE S., *An Introduction to the Botany of Tropical Crops*, 2nd edn, extensively revised by W. M. Steele, Longman, 1976.

DAVIDSON, ALAN, *Fish and Fish Dishes of Laos*, Charles E. Tuttle, 1975.

——, *Seafood of South-East Asia*, Federal Publications, Singapore, 1977, and Macmillan, 1978.

DEPARTEMEN PERTANIAN, *Mustika Rasa*, Department of Agriculture, Jakarta, 1967.

Ensiklopedia Indonesia, 3 vols, N. V. Penerbitan W. van Hoeve, Bandung and 's-Gravenhage, 1956.

GEERTZ, CLIFFORD, *The Religion of Java*, The Free Press, 1960, and the University of Chicago Press, Phoenix Edition, 1976.

HERKLOTS, G. A. C., *Vegetables in South-East Asia*, George Allen & Unwin, 1972.

HOWES, F. N., *Nuts*, Faber and Faber, 1948.

LATIEF, NY. TUTY *Resep Masakan Daerah*, PT Bina Ilmu, 1977.

O'NEILL, KEVIN, 'Tempe—a Traditional Food for Tomorrow', in *Indonesia Circle*, no. 21, March, 1980; School of Oriental and African Studies, University of London.

ORTIZ, ELISABETH LAMBERT, *Caribbean Cookery*, André Deutsch, 1975, and Penguin Books, 1977.

PRUTHI, J. S., *Spices and Condiments*, National Book Trust, New Delhi, 1976.

Bibliography

RAFFLES, SIR THOMAS STAMFORD, *History of Java* (2 vols with plates), London, 1817.

SHURTLEFF, WILLIAM and AOYAGI AKIKO, *The Book of Tempeh*, Harper and Row, New York, 1979.

SIMMONDS, N. W., *Bananas*, Longmans, 1959.

STOBART, TOM, *Herbs, Spices and Flavourings*, International Wine and Food Publishing Company, 1970, and Penguin Books, 1977.

ZAINUDDIN-MORO, NY. SITTI NUR, *Nasi dan Sambal-Sambalan*, PT Dian Rakyat, 1977.

INDEX

This index contains the recipe titles in Indonesian and in English, the various Indonesian cooking utensils mentioned and illustrated in the text and the six 'essential ingredients' described in the section of that name. It does not include the Indonesian and English names of spices, fruits and vegetables, as these are arranged alphabetically in the section dealing with them.

Abon ayam 174
Acar campur 205
Acar telur 176
Anchovies, fried dried 124
Anglo 6
Asinan campur 209
Aubergine in soya sauce 188
Aubergine relish 222
Aubergines, fried 188
Ayam bumbu acar 164
Ayam goreng 164
Ayam goreng Jawa 174
Ayam panggang 166
Ayam panggang bumbu besengek 161
Ayam paniké 162
Ayam tauco 165

Babi asam pedas 148
Babi kecap 150
Bakmie godog 236, 237
Bakmie goreng 236
Banana batter pudding 242
Banana heart, sliced 189
Bananas, fried 239
Banana with rice cake 238
Bandeng isi 123
Batter pudding 242
Bean curd, boiled and fried 217
Bean curd, fried 214
Bean curd in soya sauce 214
Bean curd steamed with coconut and chilli 213

Bean curd with savoury stuffing 216
Bean curd with vegetables 215
Bebek bumbu cabé 180, 181
Bebek hijau 183
Bebek tauco 184
Beef, boiled and fried 134
Beef, diced, in coconut sauce 126
Beef, 'hot' fried 130
Beef in a spicy black sauce 131
Beef in chilli and tamarind sauce 133
Beef in grated coconut 135
Beef in soya sauce 132
Beef in tamarind sauce 173
Beef, rolled 128
Beef, sweet and sour 134
Besengek daging 132
Black beans, salted 44, 63
Boiled beef in a spicy sauce 132
Brains in a spicy coconut sauce 157
Buntil 192
Buras 96

Cabbage, quick-fried with egg 187
Cake, steamed 245
Cakes with coconut filling 244
Carrots, stir-fried 186
Chicken and beef in tamarind sauce 173
Chicken, fried with rice 104
Chicken curry, Sumatran 162
Chicken, fried 164
Chicken, Javanese style 174
Chicken, mBok Berek style 166

251

Index

Chicken in aromatic sauce 162
Chicken in candlenut sauce 159
Chicken in coconut sauce 161
Chicken in yellow piquant sauce 164
Chicken, layered and steamed 170
Chicken livers with sago 154
Chicken, shredded and fried 174
Chicken soup 160
Chicken with bamboo shoots 172
Chicken with coconut sauce 161
Chicken with jackfruit 168
Chicken with mushrooms 163
Chicken with soya sauce 166
Chicken with yellow beans 165
Chillis, crushed 224
Cobek 35
Coconut 37; creamed coconut 40; desiccated coconut 39; coconut milk 38; coconut oil 37, 41; coconut water 37
Coconut filled cakes 244
Coconut, grated and roasted 232
Coconut relish 223
Courgette shoots in coconut sauce 190
Crab, spicy hot 112
Cucumber, bitter, in chilli and lime sauce 204
Cuka 44

Dadar gulung 243
Daging asam manis 134
Daging bumbu Bali 133
Daging gulung 128
Dandang 91, 97
Dendeng pedas 130
Dendeng ragi 135
Dried anchovies, fried in batter 228
Duck egg omelette with coconut 179
Duck in green chilli sauce 183
Duck with salted yellow beans 184
Duck, simmered (with coconut) 181

Duck, simmered (without coconut) 180
Duck with white coconut sauce 182

Ebi 44
Eggs in piquant sauce 176
Eggs in tomato sauce 178
Eggs, stuffed 177
Empal 134
Emping 235

Fish baked with coconut 120
Fish cooked with fiddleheads 122
Fish cooked with tamarind 117
Fish curry 121
Fish dish from South Sulawesi 118
Fish in a sour and sweet sauce 116
Fish relish 225
Fried dried anchovies 124
Fried fish with dried shrimps 115
Fruit salad, hot and spicy 240

Gado-gado 196
Gadon tahu 213
Garang asam ikan 124
Getuk lindri 246
Goreng ayam mBok Berek 166
Goreng babat asam pedas 156
Goreng cumi-cumi 113
Goreng ikan dengan udang 115
Goreng teri 124
Goreng terong 188
Grilled fish 119
Gudeg 168
Gulai ayam dengan rebung 172
Gulai nangka 202
Gulai otak 157
Gulai pucuk labu 190
Gulé kambing 140

Ikan asam manis 115
Intip 94

Jackfruit, cooked 202
Javanese boiled noodles 236

Jilabulo 154

Kacang bawang 229
Kacang goreng 228
Kacang tujin 229
Kambing asam manis 139
Kambing bumbu bacem 137
Karamelati 119
Karedok 208
Karé ikan 121
Kécap 42
Kelia ayam 162
Kelia hati 155
Kepiting pedas 112
Kering tempe 218
Keripik tempe dan teri 219
Ketan serikaya 246
Ketupat 95
Kipas 6
Kolak labu 238
Kolak ubi 238
Krupuk udang 237
Kue bugis 244
Kue talam 242
Kue talam pisang 242
Kukuran 35, 36
Kukusan 91, 97

Lamb, boiled spicy 137
Lamb in saté sauce 146
Lamb saté 144
Lamb, spit or oven roasted 138
Lamb stew 140
Lamb, sweet and sour 139
Lapis ayam 170
Lawar jantung pisang 189
Lawar mangga muda 194
Lemang 105
Lemper 98
Liver in spiced sauce 155
Lontong 94

Mango slices in coconut milk 194
Martabak 232
Mie Jawa 236

Minced pork saté 152
Mixed spice relish 226
Mixed vegetables, stir-fried 186

Nagasari 239
Nasi goreng 100
Nasi goreng istimewa 101
Nasi goreng with sardines 101
Nasi goreng with shrimps 102
Nasi kebuli 104
Nasi ketan 97
Nasi kuning 102
Nasi liwet 93
Nasi putih 92
Nasi rames 99
Nasi uduk 94
Noodles, fried, Javanese style 236
Noodle soup 236

Ondé-ondé 241
Opor ayam 175
Opor bebek 182
Orak arik 187
Oseng-oseng campur 186
Oseng-oseng wortel 186

Pais udang 108
Pallu mara ikan 118
Pancakes, savoury, with meat 232
Pancake with coconut filling 243
Pangek 122
Panggang kambing 138
Pangsit goreng 229
Parut 35, 36
Peanut brittle, savoury 227
Peanuts, fried 228, 229
Pelecing peria 204
Pepes ikan 120
Pergedel jagung 231
Pergedel kentang 230
Peria 204
Petola 198
Petola daging 198
Pindang ayam dan daging 173
Pindang ikan 117

Index

Pisang goreng 239
Pork and prawns, crisp-fried 229
Pork and vermicelli 149
Pork in hot and sour sauce 148
Pork in soya sauce 150
Pork saté 151
Potato cakes 230
Prawn and beansprout fritters 110
Prawn crackers 237
Prawn packages 108
Prawns, fried 106
Prawns, fried, with a chilli coating 110
Prawns in rich coconut sauce 107
Prawns, marinated and grilled 109
Prawns, spiced and cooked in tamarind water 112
Pumpkin in coconut syrup 238

Rawon 131
Relish, aubergine 222
Relish, coconut 223
Relish, fish 225
Relish, mixed spice 226
Relish, salted yellow bean 224
Relish, shrimp paste 221
Relish, soya sauce and chilli 222
Relish, vinegar 223
Rempah rempah udang 110
Rempeyek bayem 228
Rempeyek kacang 227
Rempeyek teri 228
Rendang 136
Rice cakes rolled in coconut 241
Rice cake with banana 239
Rice cake with coconut cream 246
Rice, compressed boiled 94
Rice cooked in coconut milk 94
Rice, crust of, on pan bottom 94
Rice, fried 100
Rice, fried, with sardines 101
Rice, fried, with shrimps 102
Rice, glutinous, cooked in bamboo 105

Rice, glutinous or sticky 97
Rice, plain boiled and steamed 92
Rice, plain boiled without steaming 93
Rice, savoury, with chicken 104
Rice, steamed and stuffed 96
Rice steamer 93
Rice, stuffed glutinous 98
Rice, yellow 102
Rijsttafel, miniature 99
Rujak 240
Rujak kangkung 203

Salad, cooked vegetable 205
Salad, fruit and vegetable 209
Salad, mixed vegetable, with peanut sauce 196
Salad, with coconut dressing 206
Salad, with peanut dressing 208
Salted yellow bean relish 224
Sambal bajak 226
Sambal cuka 223
Sambal goreng cumi-cumi 114
Sambal goreng daging 126
Sambal goreng udang 107
Sambal ikan 225
Sambal kecap 222
Sambal kelapa 223
Sambal tauco 224
Sambal terasi 221
Sambal terong 222
Sambal ulek 224
Santen 37
Saté babi 151
Saté godog 146
Saté kambing 144
Saté pentul 152
Savoury meat pancakes 232
Savoury peanut brittle 227
Sayur asam 201
Sayur bayem 185
Sayur kuning 199
Sayur lodeh 200
Semar mendem 99
Semur ayam 171

Semur babi 149
Semur daging 132
Semur lidah 158
Semur tahu 214
Semur terong 188
Serikaya 245
Serundeng 232
Shrimp paste relish 221
Shrimps, dried 44
Silverside, in a spicy sauce 132
Soto ayam 160
Soto daging 129
Sour vegetables 201
Soya sauce 42
Soya sauce and chilli relish 222
Spiced fish steaks 124
Spice relish 226
Spicy meat soup 129
Spicy vegetable stew 200
Spinach, fried in batter 228
Spinach soup 185
Squash shoots in coconut sauce 190
Squid, fried 113
Squid in red chilli sauce 114
Stuffed bottle gourd 198
Stuffed marrow 198
Stuffed milkfish 123
Sweet corn fritters 231
Sweet potatoes in coconut syrup 238
Sweet potato purée cakes 246

Tahu campur 215
Tahu goreng 214
Tahu goreng bacem 217
Tahu isi 216
Taro leaves and spiced coconut filling 192
Tauco 44

Telur bumbu Bali 178
Telur dadar padang 179
Telur isi 177
Tempe, boiled and fried 220
Tempe, crisp-fried 218
Tempe, fried 217
Tempe goreng 217
Tempe goreng bacem 220
Tempe in thick candlenut sauce 218
Tempe, with dried anchovies 219
Terasi 41
Terik ayam 159
Terik tempe 218
Tongue in soya sauce 158
Traditional West Sumatran dish 136
Tripe, hot sour fried 156
Tumis ayam dengan jamur 163
Tumis buncis 191
Turmeric-coloured stew 199

Udang bakar 109
Udang goreng 106
Udang goreng balada 110
Udang pindang tumis 112
Ulek-ulek 35
Urap 206
Urap panggang 195

Vegetables, baked 195
Vegetables, stir-fried 186
Vinegar 44
Vinegar relish 223

Watercress in spicy sauce 203
Water spinach in spicy sauce 203
Wok 32

Yellow beans, salted 44, 63